T0277002

Cinema of Paradox

Cinema of Paradox

French Filmmaking
Under the German Occupation

Evelyn Ehrlich

Columbia University Press   New York   1985

The Andrew W. Mellon Foundation, through a special grant, has assisted the Press in publishing this volume.

Columbia University Press
New York   Guildford, Surrey
Copyright © 1985 Evelyn Ehrlich
All rights reserved

Printed in the United States of America

Library of Congress Cataloging in Publication Data

Ehrlich, Evelyn.
  Cinema of paradox.

  Filmography: p.
  Bibliography: p.
  Includes index.
  1. Moving-pictures—France—History. 2. Moving-picture industry—France—History. 3. Moving-pictures, German—France. 4. World War, 1939–1945—Motion pictures and the war. I. Title.
PN1993.5.F7E38   1985   384'.8'0944   84-28594
ISBN 978-0-231-05926-8

Clothbound editions of Columbia University Press books are Smyth-sewn and printed on permanent and durable acid-free paper.

Contents

vi   Contents

Acknowledgments

There are so many people who helped me to complete this work that I may overlook some of them. To everyone, I would like to express my gratitude.

Among those who cannot be overlooked, I would like first to thank Jay Leyda. His advice and enthusiasm, from the beginning, motivated the work. Along with Professor Leyda, many other members of the New York University faculty have generously contributed their time and support. I would particularly like to thank William G. Simon, William K. Everson, Robert Sklar, and Robert Stam.

My research was aided by many people in many countries; in the United States, Anita Lowry of Columbia University, Charles Silver, Mary Corliss and Eileen Bowser of the Museum of Modern Art, Emily Sieger of the Library of Congress, the staffs of the National Archives and the New York Public Library. I would especially like to thank Robert Daudelin of the Cinémathèque Québécoise in Montreal for making the collection available to me.

In France, my thanks to the staffs of the Bibliothèque de l'Arsénal, Idhec, and the Archives du Film at Bois d'Arcy. Special thanks to Lenny Borger, and to Jacques Ledoux of the Cinémathèque Royale de Belgique.

Many people shared their knowledge and memories with me. It was both a pleasure and a help to talk to Louis-Emile Galey, the late Louis Daquin, Roger Régent, Paul Leglise, and Armand Panigel. One of the delights of this project was the opportunity to spend the morning with Pierre Prévert at the Café de Flore.

Numerous friends have aided me in substantial ways: Susan Clare found me the means to conduct my research, Marsha Witten and Leslie Clark helped edit the manuscript, and Elaine Mancini and Michael Cudney gave me invaluable research assistance. To all my friends, I would like to express my thanks for their patient support and encouragement.

Most of all, I would like to thank two people who gave me support, encouragement and a great deal more. For five months, they spent hours every day translating faded microfilmed documents. Their work was both tedious and painful, but without their help this book would never have been written. For all that they've done, I would like to dedicate this book to my parents.

Introduction

On August 13, 1940, France was in chaos. The country was divided in two. In the Southern sector, the flood of refugees from the occupied zone had swollen cities to three times their normal size. In the North, English bombs were falling on the seacoasts of France and the army of occupation was erecting road signs in German in anticipation of the thousand-year Reich.

On that August 13, two months after the fall of France, Marcel Pagnol entered his Marseille studio to direct the first French film of the new era. Despite the new and terrifying conditions of life, France did not stop making films. Almost as soon as studios in Marseille and Nice could be reconstructed, and actors and technicians located in the many corners of Southern France to which they had fled, cameras began to roll. They would continue to roll—from Pagnol's *La Fille du Puisatier* (The Well-Digger's Daughter) on that August 13, to Pierre Billon's *Mademoiselle X* on May 23, 1944—under conditions of war and occupation never before encountered by filmmakers in France.

France during the occupation was a country torn geographically and ideologically. It suffered economic exploitation and religious persecution. A foreign power dictated how the French were to live their lives, in matters ranging from the number of cigarettes they could smoke to how many hostages would be shot in reprisal for some resistance attack. The occupation was a time of starvation, fear, and danger, a time when the cinema would hardly seem to matter.

But to those who endured the occupation, the cinema was of great importance. Movie theaters provided refuge from the uncertainty and hardship of everyday life. The French public flocked to the darkened theaters to see a world they had lost or one that existed only in their dreams. They went to the movies because it was the only outlet they had, and they went in greater number than ever before in history.

For those who made the movies, it was a crucial matter that the French film industry continue to function. France had always been one of the world's most important film-producing nations; it was essential that France continue making films whatever the hardships and compromises. For filmmakers, the issue was not merely economic survival. Rather, they believed they had a responsibility to entertain and lift the spirits of the public, and to sustain what they could of French cultural life. Amidst the despair of military defeat, the French cinema needed to prove to itself and to the world that France was not dead. To go on making movies of substance and stature was to affirm that the French spirit had survived.

During the four years of German occupation, the French produced more than 200 feature films. Many were enduring works of art that continue to be viewed and discussed today. Robert Bresson made his first two films during the occupation, as did Henri-Georges Clouzot. Major figures of the theater turned their talents to the cinema, enriching it with new ideas; among them were playwrights Jean Giraudoux, Jean Anouilh, and Jean Cocteau, and actors Jean-Louis Barrault and Jean Marais. The film that is perhaps the most highly regarded French film of all time was made during the occupation—*Children of Paradise*.

That a cultural blossoming should occur during a time of subjugation is a paradox. And it is this paradox that the following chapters seek to explain. To do so, some basic questions are posed. What were the conditions under which filmmakers worked? What political, economic, and cultural currents buffeted the cinema of these years? Only by understanding the historical context of filmmaking during the period can one arrive at an answer to the central question: how was it possible for a relatively independent, aesthetically important cinema to survive the destruction of a nation?

In the years before the war, France had developed a cinema of worldwide importance. Even though the French film industry was relatively weak economically, out of the small number of films produced between 1937 and 1939, there emerged an extraordinary number of internationally admired classics, among them: *La Grande Illusion, Carnet de bal, Pépé le Moko, Quai des brumes, Entrée des artistes, La Femme du boulanger, La Bête humaine* and *L'Hôtel du Nord*. In the summer of 1939, only months before the war broke out, two of the cinema's greatest masterpieces were released in France: *Le Jour se lève* and *La Règle du jeu*.

And then came disaster. With the defeat and occupation in June 1940, it seemed inevitable that the history of French cinema would end with the destruction of France. The months of war between September 1939 and May 1940 had disrupted normal production; the defeat and occupation threatened to destroy it. During the first year of occupation, the Germans prohibited filmmaking in the occupied zone, and in the South there was neither money nor material for production. Many of France's most celebrated figures left the country; other filmmakers were in prisoner of war camps or in hiding.

When France was liberated, four years later, the film industry felt it had reason to boast. Not only had France produced some 220 feature films in the four years of misery, but many of these films were laudable achievements. None of them provided any direct support for the Germans. Most of them maintained the French standards of craftsmanship that had given the industry its international reputation. And some of these films would mark a beginning of a new style in French filmmaking, one that would be the standard until the 1960s.

There has been much debate on the aesthetic value of the style that emerged during the occupation, and film history has not been kind to the developments of French cinema in the 1940s and 1950s. One of the ironies of the period is that, despite its heroic efforts to save itself from destruction, the French cinema emerged from its four-year chrysalis to discover that international film culture had passed it by. It would take another fifteen years for the French to reestablish their international reputation.

It has not been my concern to defend the styles of film-making that developed during the occupation; in fact, there is little emphasis in the pages that follow on critical analyses of individual films. Rather, the purpose of this work has been to set the debate within historical terms; to ask not whether these films have value but rather why a new current of filmmaking should arise during this period.

Similarly, this work attempts to recast another much debated question—that of the political values of the films made during the occupation. There has been little written about the cinema of the occupation outside of France, and for the French the period remains an emotional one. Yet the intensity aroused by the question of whether the cinema of the occupation was collaborationist has often obscured more fundamental issues.

The polemics have centered on the meaning of the films themselves and of the responsibility of individual filmmakers. But examining the films and the intentions of those who made them does not clarify the political issues. In fact, many of the films can be read as having both resistance and collaborationist sentiments. Rather than focusing solely on the intentions and actions of the filmmakers, it is more revealing to approach the cinema of the occupation in terms of the multiple forces that shaped it. By examining documents originating in the period, it is possible to gain an insight into the complex motives and behaviors of four distinctive groups: filmmakers, producers, the Vichy government, and the Germans.

For the most part, French writers have ignored these other forces. Yet, particularly in the case of the Germans, it is crucial to understand their perspective, because it profoundly affects the question of French collaboration and resistance. Most writers about the period have accepted a one-dimensional stereotype of the German occupiers. They have assumed, largely because of some misleading entries in Goebbels' diaries, that Nazi policy was to destroy the French cinema. But reports issued by the German film office in France indicate that German policy was, in fact, to encourage the French to continue producing films of high technical quality and commercial appeal. The nationalist, even resistance sentiments that the French sometimes attempted to express in their films were of little importance to the Germans. Rather than concerning themselves with content, the Germans were far more interested in sustaining the French cinema's overall reputation for quality, for they regarded the international prestige of the French cinema as an opportunity for themselves. The Germans intended to release French films throughout occupied Europe and the neutral countries as products of the "New Europe." In this way, they could exploit the popularity of the French cinema both as a propaganda tool and, more importantly, as an economic wedge in their efforts to dominate international film markets. By encouraging the French to make the best films they could, the Germans were hoping to build up a European film industry that could successfully compete with Hollywood.

That the French cinema survived largely because the Germans wanted it to survive is only one of the period's many paradoxes. It was not a simple era and the political questions cannot be resolved without an understanding of the complex political, economic, and social forces that influenced the cinema.

The temporal context of the cinema of the occupation is another area that has been oversimplified by polemics. For example, many writers who argue that the cinema of 1940–1944 was a collaborationist cinema have collapsed the films of these four years into one rubric, "Vichy Cinema." But such a label is misleading, for there were many changes during the period and Vichy was not an important factor in the cinema after 1941.

In order to understand the conditions of filmmaking, one must follow the internal and external changes as they affected France as a whole. One of the key changes was the progress of the war itself. One obvious, but often forgotten point must be made at the outset: when the occupation began in 1940, no one knew it would only last four years. In fact, in 1940 it appeared likely that Germany would soon win the war and that France would be, indefinitely, an adjunct of the Third Reich.

During the first year of occupation, the major concern of

the French film industry was survival. If some of the choices made at that time, such as acceptance of Vichy's economic support, are suspect now, they must also be evaluated within the context of conditions and expectations at that time. As both internal and external conditions stabilized, there were different choices and different responses. The middle period of the occupation—from June 1941 to early 1943—is, in many ways, more revealing of how the French cinema adapted to an entirely new set of conditions and values. These months of consolidation, when the ultimate outcome of the war was in doubt and the French tried to reestablish as normal a life as possible, are the focus of much of what follows.

It was only after 1943, when the tide of war turned against the Germans, that most of the French began to look beyond the immediate situation and consider the long-term consequences of the choices they were making. As Liberation neared, the French began accusing one another of complicity with the occupiers. While the choices were, in some areas of French life, quite clear-cut, in the cinema they were not as obvious. Since the French did not recognize that the Germans were supporting the same goals as the French themselves, the debate over moral responsibility tended to focus on particular cases. The accusations continue to this day.

It seemed to be a time of absolutes, of good and evil, of cowardice and courage. Yet, there are few heroes in this account—and few villains. The moral issues are not yet resolved. But before one can ask whether the choices made were justifiable, one must first ask why they were made. Judgment cannot precede historical understanding.

Cinema of Paradox

Chapter 1

War and Defeat

Between September 1938 and March 1939, France mobilized its troops twice: in response to Hitler's annexation of the Sudetenland and the subsequent invasion of Czechoslovakia. In response to the signing of the German-Soviet nonaggression pact on August 24, 1939, the French government mobilized its troops for the third time in a year. There was one difference this time. Ten days later, on September 3, 1939, France was at war.

Mobilization created havoc in all but war-related industries. The film industry was not spared. Twenty films, in various stages of production, were shut down as actors, technicians, and production staff were called up to their units. Exhibition of films was curtailed when Parisian theaters were forced to close for an 8 P.M. curfew, mandated in anticipation of German bombing attacks. But the attacks never came.

The period between the beginning of the war on September 3, 1939, and May 10, 1940, came to be known as the "drôle de guerre" (the phony war), because the opposing armies, camped on opposite sides of the border, neither moved nor engaged in battle. The German armies were preoccupied in the East. The French soldiers, living in trenches and unheated barracks, grew tired of waiting for a German offensive that did not materialize. Demoralization among the troops set in from boredom, the cold, and the inefficiency of their commanders. By October, the French government, recognizing the need to entertain the troops and the civilian population, allowed certain film productions to begin once more.

The government had other reasons for encouraging renewed production. Learning a lesson from the mistakes of World War I when most French feature production had been halted, French leaders did not want to see the French film product eliminated from the international market. They felt French film must continue for the prestige of France. Another reason the government had for renewing production was the effectiveness of the enemy's propaganda campaign. German newsreels and documentary features were distributed in neutral countries and proclaimed the invincibility of the German army. The intent of these films was to terrify their audiences so that they would not resist German advances.[1] France needed to counteract the Nazi message with propaganda of its own.

Thus, for the first time in French history, the government took direct control of certain aspects of the film industry. Under the general offices of the Commissariat de l'Information, directed by playwright Jean Giraudoux, the government centralized its film activities through a Service du Cinéma. It commissioned both fictional and documentary films, produced newsreels through the Service Cinématographique de l'Armée, and specified for private producers what sorts of films could or could not be made. Direct government supervision of the French film industry did not begin with the Vichy dictatorship but, out of the necessities of war, under the democratic Third Republic.

One of the first actions taken by the government concerned the censorship and banning of certain types of prewar films. On October 13, 1939, La Cinématographie Française published a directive issued by Suzanne Borel, assistant director of the Service du Cinéma. There were three categories of films which would no longer be permitted: 1) any film about war which tended to be demoralizing to the troops (films affected included such pacifist films as All Quiet on the Western Front and Kameradschaft); 2) films which were "depressing, morbid, immoral, or distressing to children" (Quai des brumes, L'Hôtel du Nord, La Bête humaine, among many others); and 3) all films which ridiculed the armed forces, including the many popular military farces. The order continued: "Concerning censorship of films for export, especially to those countries where we have many friends [i.e., the neutral countries], we must particularly avoid . . . representing our country, our traditions and our race through a lens that is distorted, lying or deformed by the prism of an artistic individuality which may be original, but is not always healthy."

Even before these directives had been issued, producers had been warned to make "healthy and optimistic films" (La Cinématographie Française, September 2, 1939). In view of the cinema's importance to the war effort, two of France's biggest stars, Jean Gabin and Pierre Fresnay, were demobilized in October, to complete their respective films Remorques and Le Duel (which Fresnay also directed). Other films interrupted by the mobilization order which were permitted to resume filming included several films by noted directors, including Max Ophuls' De Mayerling à Sarajevo, Abel Gance's Paradis Perdu, and Jacques Feyder's La Loi du Nord (released in 1942 as La Piste du Nord). But not all directors were able to gather their cast and crew together, despite the government's new policy. The first cinematographic casualty of the war was René Clair's L'Air pur, which was to have been the first French production since 1934 for France's most famous director.

Production of new films also began in October. Many of these films were encouraged or commissioned by the government for propaganda purposes. Among the more overt propaganda efforts were two feature length "pseudo-documentaries" which used newsreels and staged footage to show the evil designs of Hitler (Alexandre Ryder's Après Mein Kampf, mes crimes) and the Hitler-Stalin pact (Georges Rony's De Lenine à Hitler).

Only a handful of commercial productions were made and released during the "drôle de guerre." Many of the films made independently of the government also had war-related plots, but these tended to be comedies and musicals which were meant to entertain the troops and civilian audiences. The titles alone indicate the general escapism of such films as Chantons quand même

(Let's Sing Anyway), directed by Pierre Caron, and Fausse Alerte (False Alarm) directed by Jacques de Baroncelli, with Josephine Baker.

The most noteworthy fictional film produced for the war effort was Julien Duvivier's Untel père et fils, begun on December 22, 1939. It told the story of three generations of peaceful Frenchmen forced to take arms against their barbarous German neighbors. It had an all-star cast led by Louis Jouvet, Raimu, and Michèle Morgan. Editing was completed in June 1940, and Duvivier took the film with him when he fled to the United States after the Armistice. It was released in the United States as Hearts of France, and presumably served a propaganda purpose—although not the one originally intended. It was not released in France until 1945.

The only other major production begun during the "drôle de guerre" was Maurice Tourneur's Volpone, with Harry Baur and Louis Jouvet, begun on March 23, 1940. Although production was completed before the Armistice, the film was not released until May 10, 1941.

Some of France's best known filmmakers were asked to serve the French cause in other ways. The government, hoping to cement Franco-Italian relations and to prevent Italy from joining the war on the Axis side, organized a number of good-will efforts. These included sending Jean Renoir to Rome, where he began production of La Tosca for the Italian production company, Scalera, in February 1940 (later completed by Carl Koch). In March, Marcel l'Herbier began filming La Comédie de bonheur, also for Scalera. Michel Simon, one of France's biggest stars (who was, however, a Swiss citizen) went along and starred in both films.[2]

These Franco-Italian co-productions aroused some controversy in the trade—La Cinématographie Française was outraged by the loss of France's much needed filmmaking talent.[3] Nonetheless, in the spring of 1940 there were announcements that other French directors, including Julien Duvivier and Abel Gance, would work in Rome. These plans did not materialize, and despite these friendly gestures, Italy declared war on France on June 10, 1940.

In addition to its activities in the areas of censorship, encouragement of production for propaganda, morale, and good-will, the government also produced films itself. Le Service Cinématographique de l'Armée (S.C.A.), which had been organized in 1925, found its activities expanded. During the war the S.C.A. had three primary functions: the production of educational films for the troops; a Cinémathèque for the storage and preservation of filmic documents; and a foreign propaganda section, charged with the production of films that would serve the French cause abroad. Because the neutral countries would not accept the films of France's private newsreel services (Eclair-Journal, France Actualités, Fox-Movietone, Paramount News, and Pathé-Journal), the S.C.A. began production of its own "Journal de Guerre," which was distributed for showing in French embassies abroad.[4]

The Real War Begins

On May 10, 1940, bypassing the "invincible" Maginot line, German tanks and bombers poured across the Belgian and Dutch borders, finally opening the war in the West. French and Allied armies, caught unprepared, poorly commanded and under-equipped, were no match for the armored troops of the Wehrmacht or the daily poundings of the Luftwaffe. Within fifteen days, the armies found themselves trapped at Dunkirk, where the British rapidly evacuated, but hundreds of thousands of mostly French prisoners were taken. By June 14, the German army had taken Paris and the French government, moving from Tours to Bordeaux to Clermont-Ferrand, reconstituted itself under the leadership of an eighty-four-year old World War I hero. On June 16, the new government of Maréchal Philippe Pétain instituted the first measures that would lead to an Armistice, which was signed on June 25. Soon thereafter, the Third Republic dissolved itself and a new government was formed at the spa of Vichy.

On the first day of the "real" war, May 10, Une Robe blanche dans la nuit, directed by Maurice Cloche, went into production. (It was never finished.) On May 20, the last two films of the Third Republic were begun: Pierre Caron's Ils Etaient 5 permissionnaires and Marcel Pagnol's La Fille du puisatier. The former was not finished until 1945; the latter would become the first production under the new Vichy regime.

Filmmakers, like the rest of their countrymen, found themselves caught in the mad exodus that preceded the oncoming German troops. Most of the important filmmakers who were in the armed forces were well behind front lines at desk jobs, but not all were so fortunate. The greatest loss of the war for the French film industry was the death at the front of composer Maurice Jaubert, shortly before the Armistice.

Even for those behind French lines, however, the French Army's rout led to confusion and panic. Marcel Carné describes how

> the order was given to flee—there is no other word for it—as others had before us.
>
> I will say about the voyage only that everyone gave orders but no one was in command.
>
> In effect, all high-ranking officers had disappeared, and we were left to our own devices.
>
> Trains, trucks, buses succeeded one another, it seemed to us by improvisation, and we did not move straight forward, but in perpetual zig zags, coming and going.
>
> And each time we looked out the window of our train compartment or of the bus, we saw the same heart-rending spectacle of an entire people marching toward an unknown destiny.[5]

Almost three-fourths of the population of Paris had fled the city when the German armies marched in on June 14. Some parts of the countryside lost even greater portions of their population. These hordes of civilians, carrying their possessions with them, swarmed into small southern cities, swelling their population to three times normal. With no government in charge, the civilian population had to fend for itself in finding food and shelter.

Most of these refugees were not motivated by politics, but simply by fear of the unknown consequences of German occupation. As the Germans established their civilian authority, and as it became clear that the German armies were not looting or threatening the civilian population, citizens began drifting back to their homes and jobs, a voyage complicated by the new boundary that now cut France in two.

Some of the refugees had good reason to fear the Germans, however. Jews from other parts of Europe, who had sought sanctuary in prewar France, found themselves fleeing the Nazis once more. Many in the film community were among the refugees. Major Jewish emigré producers—Gregor Rabinovitch, Jacques Haik, the Hakim brothers—congregated on the Côte d'Azur and began planning new productions for unoccupied France.[6] The United States was, however, the ultimate goal for most of these foreign and French-born Jews. Getting exit visas from Vichy entailed enormous difficulties, and the circuitous route to safety often led through Spain, Switzerland, North Africa, or Portugal. Among those who followed these paths were directors Robert Siodmak, Léonide Moguy, and Max Ophuls, the last of whom spent a year in Switzerland before being able to continue his journey to the United States; cinematographer Boris Kaufman, and actors Marcel Dalio and Jean-Pierre Aumont. Aumont, after spending a year in unoccupied France, fortuitously made the acquaintance of the Honduran consul to Vichy and got a visa for Honduras. From there he made his way to the United States where he made propaganda films in favor of the Free French and later joined de Gaulle's forces.[7]

Others feared Nazi persecution for political reasons. Jean Renoir, whose La Grande Illusion had been denounced in Berlin, moved South with friends, finding shelter in La Creuse, where "the villagers welcomed us with open arms, proud to have 'their' refugees. Our presence lent them prestige and aroused the jealousy of the neighboring villages."[8]

After the Armistice, Renoir sent word of his whereabouts to Paris and received in reply

> a letter from America—from my friend Robert Flaherty . . . urging me to go to the American consulate in Nice, where a visa for the United States awaited me. He had guessed that I was in danger because of my anti-Hitler attitude. Films such as Le Crime de M. Lange, La Marseillaise and La Vie est à Nous, together with numerous news-

paper articles, if they had not moved the masses had at
least caused a lot of ink to flow. I had to wait some
months before the French authorities let me have an
exit visa . . .

What had persuaded me to accept the American offer were the visits of two Frenchmen representing
Nazi cultural institutions. They wanted me to work within
the framework of the New France, saying that I would
be given all possible assistance in making any films I
chose.[9]

Renoir was not the only major director to leave France.
Julien Duvivier and René Clair both accepted standing offers from
Hollywood. The Vichy government was so angered by Clair's
"treason" that they included him in a group of twenty-three peo-
ple who had "forfeited their French nationality" for having left
French territory "under certain circumstances."[10]

Actress Françoise Rosay, faced with the choice of working for the German-owned film company in Paris or not being
permitted to work at all, opted to leave France with her husband,
Jacques Feyder.[11] They accepted an invitation to make Une Femme
disparaît (1941) in Switzerland.[12] Rosay eventually made her way to
London, where she broadcast resistance messages for the B.B.C.

Other important exiles included France's biggest female
star, Michèle Morgan. Citing a previously signed contract with RKO
to make one film, Morgan promised to return immediately to
France. Le Film resented her leaving at all and complained that
she should not have been given an exit visa (November 15, 1940).
Their fears were justified, for she did indeed remain in Hollywood, making such anti-Nazi films as Joan of Paris and Passage to
Marseilles. On February 15, 1941, Le Film announced "another highly
regrettable departure," that of Jean Gabin, then in Portugal on his
way to Hollywood. He, too, would remain in exile throughout the
occupation.

For those who stayed, the most pressing problems were
financial. Some filmmakers, like Marcel Carné, simply could not
get hold of their funds in northern banks, because of the difficul-

ties in crossing the demarcation line. Those without reserves were near bankruptcy after three months of unemployment. No one yet knew where or when film production would begin again. Most people expected activity to resume in the South, despite the scarcity of capital, material, and studio space in the unoccupied zone.

Others, like director Louis Daquin, "believed that we must return to Paris, that things would happen there. I returned very soon. So did [Jean] Grémillon. And others, like [Charles] Spaak, [Jacques] Becker, [Georges] Lacombe. It was a very difficult time because one didn't know what to do or what would happen."[13]

Many actors and directors living in the South began working on plays and even nightclub acts. Many movie theaters had been turned into music halls, for lack of film product.[14]

Pierre Brasseur, Pierre Prévert, Maurice Baquet, and Odette Joyeux, finding themselves without funds, organized a touring company of Marcel Achard's play Domino, which traveled through the unoccupied zone and Vichy-controlled North Africa. The tour ended when Brasseur's drunken behavior caused local authorities to give the group twenty-four hours to leave the territory.[15]

Louis Jouvet took his company to Switzerland in January 1941 to make a film of their production of l'Ecole des Femmes. The film's director, Max Ophuls, offended the star by having an affair with his mistress, Madeleine Ozeray.[16] Jouvet left Switzerland with the film uncompleted. He and his company had previously contracted for a South American tour and, once there, found they could not return. Thus, France's greatest actor spent the rest of the war on the other side of the Atlantic Ocean.

The Occupied Zone

While the major portion of the French film industry gathered on the Côte d'Azur, the Germans were losing no time in organizing their own film activity. As early as June 28, the Militär-befehlshaber in Frankreich (military authority in France) had established a Propaganda Staffel (propaganda section) for the Paris region, to oversee the reopening of theaters and the distribution of German newsreels, as well as to assure the confiscation of anti-German and pro-Allied films.

Fearing that such confiscations were imminent, some French filmmakers had taken precautions. The negatives of films which had been completed, but unreleased, such as Grémillon's *Remorques* and Duvivier's *Untel père et fils*, were transported by their directors on their exodus to the South. Christian-Jaque's uncompleted *Tourelle 3* was lost in the confusion, as undoubtedly were others. Henri Langlois, fearful that the Germans might destroy the collection of rare films held by his Cinémathèque Française, hid some of his cache in the cellars and attics of friends' houses.

The Germans were quick to begin their confiscation. Even before issuing their first official ordinance concerning the cinema on September 9, 1940, which mandated the submission of all films to the German authorities, they had begun confiscating films belonging to American and Jewish-owned production companies, laboratories, and theater circuits. They were particularly interested in finding and destroying all anti-Fascist films, including André Malraux's recently completed film about the Spanish Civil War, *Sierra de Teruel*. Malraux, after his escape from a German prisoner of war camp, managed to save one copy of the film and, after many months of secret negotiations with the Library of Congress, it was finally smuggled to Washington.[17] Some of the confiscated films were destroyed outright; those that might prove useful were sent to archives in Germany. Sometimes the Germans had bizarre reasons for wanting the films—it was reported, for example, that the Germans studied confiscated French newsreels in order to find doubles for the French officials depicted.[18]

German Exhibition Policy

Of the 2,800,000 people who had constituted Paris' pre-war population, only 700,000 remained when the German armies swarmed through the open city on June 14.[19] With neither staff nor audiences, Parisian movie theaters had all shut down. But normal life soon began to return and twenty first-run theaters reopened on June 19, along with two "Soldatenkinos," reserved for

German military personnel. By August 1, 200 theaters (of 310) were operating in Paris.[20] The German authorities were eager to have theaters open, in order to begin distribution of their own films. Since all films had to be cleared by the German authorities before they could be exhibited, the Germans had no difficulty in ridding the market of the most popular films. Even though the United States and Germany were not yet at war, American films were immediately banned from the occupied sector. British films were, naturally, prohibited as well. Some prewar French films were cleared for exhibition.[21] But the bulk of film product was provided by the first distributor to reopen, l'Alliance Cinématographique Européenne (A.C.E.), the German-owned distributor for the Ufa and Tobis production companies in France.

No German films had been shown in France since September 1939, and German imports had been insignificant after 1935.[22] Therefore, the French market represented a valuable source of profits for German film companies. In the first summer of the occupation, audiences flocked to prewar German comedies and melodramas, such as Veit Harlan's *Le Sonate à Kreutzer* (*Die Kreutzersonate*, 1937) and Willi Forst's *Bel Ami* (1939). Not only were these German films the only new films available, but French audiences were curious to see the German product, and came to like such German stars as Zarah Leander and Marika Rökk. German feature films were furthermore allowed free access to theaters in the unoccupied zone, although they were forced to compete there with those American films held by distributors at the time of the Armistice.[23] In the first season of the occupation (1940–41), audiences throughout France made hits of Willi Forst's *Operette* (1940) and Gustav Ucicky's *Le Maître de Poste* (*Der Postmeister*, 1940). Veit Harlan's infamous *Jud Süss* of 1940 (released in France as *Le Juif Süss*) was one of the biggest hits of the season, breaking box office records in Lyon, Toulouse, and Vichy (*Le Film*, May 24, 1941). This prestigious production was a pet project of Propaganda Minister Joseph Goebbels. It detailed the career of a nefarious eighteenth-century Jew and was "applauded frenetically" in Marseille and Lyon (*Le Film*, May 10, 1941).

But these audiences were probably less interested in the

film's ideological message than in its lavish production. The other big hit in Marseille at the same time was Warner Brothers' *The Private Lives of Elizabeth and Essex*. French audiences wanted to see films, and without new French production, they would take what they could get. As French production began slowly to start up again, these German films would lose their popularity.

Conclusion

As had occurred in September 1939, film production in France simply stopped in June 1940. After eight months of fighting a phony war and six weeks of losing a real one, the French public needed the diversion of the movies more than ever before. But the problems facing filmmakers in the summer of 1940 seemed nearly insurmountable. The bulk of the French territory was occupied by the enemy, which had no reason to want to see French production resume as competition for its own industry. If audiences were content with German films, the German propaganda office was only too happy to supply them.

The new Vichy government was in no position to help the film industry. Although most of the 60,000 people who ordinarily made their living in the cinema were now unemployed, Vichy had more pressing matters to attend to.[24] Moreover, even if Vichy had wanted to help, the French film industry's personnel was scattered throughout the world—in German prisoner of war camps, on the "wrong" side of the demarcation line, in hamlets and towns throughout the unoccupied zone, or making their way to America. The debacle of June 1940 had abruptly ended nine months of increasingly difficult conditions for the film industry. Now with factories destroyed, communications paralyzed, and chaos permeating the country, filmmaking was unimaginable. Except to filmmakers.

Chapter 2

Filmmaking in Vichy

The first producer to begin work after June 1940 was fortunate. He had sufficient capital to finance the film himself and he owned a production studio safely situated in the unoccupied zone. His screenplay had only to be slightly altered to take account of the political changes that had occurred since the film first went into production before the fall of France. Although he lost one of his stars, Betty Daussmond, to the general chaos of that first summer after the defeat, his director was at hand.[1] Writer-director-producer Marcel Pagnol did not need to wait for conditions to normalize before beginning the first film of the new Vichy era, La Fille du puisatier.

Most filmmakers in Vichy would be forced to wait however. There were too many problems to overcome before large-scale production could commence in the South. Studio space, raw materials, and capital were all in short supply. Uncertainties about new laws affecting the film industry in both Vichy and the occupied zone made producers uneasy about starting work. In order to resolve these problems, the film industry needed structure and organization. It was, however, neither the filmmakers nor the Vichy government that would initiate such an organization. Paradoxically, the impetus for the formation of an organization to aid and supervise the French film industry would come from the Germans.

In July 1940, the propaganda office of the German Military Command in France had begun to organize a series of "corporative groups" (groupements corporatifs) for each branch of the film industry. The Germans needed to have some organized representation within the French film industry in order to provide a bureaucratic means of handling routine requests to German officials for such matters as the reopening of theaters and the establishment of uniform ticket prices. Although the functions of these groups were to be purely administrative, the effect of their formation under German auspices would have been to give the Germans control over the French film industry.

Feature filmmaking was not a pressing priority to the Pétain government, but keeping French information services out of German hands was. Therefore Vichy quickly reorganized its own bureaucracy in charge of the cinema, using the same organization plan as had existed during the war, and with much of the same staff. In August 1940, a new director was appointed head of the Service du Cinéma. Guy de Carmoy had been an inspector of finances under the Third Republic, and in that capacity had reported on the needs and problems of the French film industry. De Carmoy's political beliefs were anti-collaborationist. The Germans would later arrest him for resistance activity and deport him to a German prison camp. But in August 1940, de Carmoy agreed to take over Vichy's Film Office because he knew that if Vichy didn't take the initiative in organizing the French film industry, the Germans would.

Whether or not filmmakers supported Vichy as the legitimate government of France, they were in agreement with Vichy that the film industry had to be kept out of German control. Both the filmmakers and the government also agreed, for different reasons, that the French film industry needed a centralized organization that would be responsible for planning, allocation of resources, and all administrative matters concerning the industry as a whole. For Vichy, such an organization was concordant with its overall economic objectives in establishing the "National Revolution"; for filmmakers, centralized organization was a way of bringing rational economic policy to an industry that had been on the verge of financial collapse throughout the 1930s.

Vichy Economic Policy

Although the film industry was not high on Vichy's list of priorities, the government was concerned with the French economy in general, and in particular wished to introduce planning and centralized control to French industry. Vichy's economic theory, corporatism, was similar to that developed in Mussolini's Italy. Among its fundamental precepts was the encouragement of industrial oligarchy and a determination to eliminate labor as a force in determining economic policy.[2]

Vichy's corporatist philosophy and the importance of businessmen both in official Vichy circles and in supporting the regime was not solely responsible for the shaping of Vichy's economic policy. External economic circumstances would have impelled Vichy toward a planned economy dominated by large industrial concerns in any case. The scarcity of raw materials and fuel, the heavy occupation costs dictated by the Germans, and, later in the war, the German demands for manufactured goods for the war effort, made it imperative for the government to intervene in the allocation of resources and the setting of production goals. Rather than do so directly, however, the Vichy government organized a series of "comités d'organisation" (CO) (organization committees) for various industries, which were placed under the supervision of appropriate government ministries.

On August 16, 1940, the law concerning the formation of these CO's was enacted. Its initial purpose was to "encourage the return of employers to their posts and to permit the resumption of production at the earliest possible moment."[3] The CO's replaced all former associations of labor and management in each industry. Their long range goals included providing statistical information (which had been almost totally lacking in most industries before the war), organizing the purchase and distribution of raw materials, and fixing prices.

The establishment of CO's was initially intended to serve only thirty industries: primarily those concerned with manufacture of industrial materials and other essential goods. By war's end, however, 234 *comités d'organisation* had been established.[4] The effect of their establishment was to concentrate power in the hands of the biggest members of any particular industry, and to create a corporatist structure characterized by the close integration of government bureaucracy and these economic oligarchies. The benefits of Vichy economic policy to French industrialists were numerous. Among them were the elimination of labor demands, direct government subsidies for key industries, and government measures aimed at concentration of capital.

The COIC

The restructuring of industrial control under Vichy was a boon to large industrial concerns in most areas. In the film industry, such a reorganization was a necessity, long recognized by both the government and the film industry. As early as 1936, Guy de Carmoy had presented a report to the Conseil National Economique, calling for major changes in the organization and financing of the film industry. At that time, it was estimated, the film industry was losing 100 million francs a year, and every year saw the bankruptcy of fifty to sixty production firms. Unlike the situation in most important film producing countries, the French film industry was not dominated by several large companies, but rather was an amalgam of several hundred smaller firms, mostly under-capitalized.[5] By the mid-1930s, the two giants of the post-World War I film industry were both facing disaster. Gaumont was in receivership to the Banque Nationale de Crédit, and Pathé-Cinéma was the object of legal action for fraud which resulted in the imprisonment of its administrator, Bernard Natan, in 1938. "L'affaire Natan," which had scandalized the film industry and implicated high government officials, had involved the establishment of phantom corporations, which succeeded in stealing 900 million francs from stockholders and banks over a period of six years. This scandal was often presented as justification for "cleansing a profession and an industry which, before the war, saw bankruptcies multiplying and credit gravely compromised."[6]

The film industry recognized that some form of control was needed. Their need meshed with Vichy's general policy of industrial consolidation under government auspices. All that was lacking was a final push toward reorganization, and the Germans provided it with the formation of their corporative groups.

In October 1940, the Secretary General for Information, Jean Tixier-Vignancour, wrote to Guy de Carmoy, headquartered in Paris, informing him that the German corporative groups were illegal and that he must stop their activities. "The duty of these French representatives is to fall in line behind my department, which has been duly and exclusively mandated by the government to reorganize and direct the French film industry."[7]

By this time, feature film production had already begun in the unoccupied zone, but there was still no official body to control production activities. Given the urgency of assuming control, the enabling legislation for the creation of a *comité d'organisation de l'industrie cinématographique* (COIC) was enacted on November 2, 1940, and took effect on December 4, 1940, making the COIC one of the earliest CO's formed.

The COIC represented the first peacetime initiative in French history toward direct government control over the feature film industry. The members of the COIC were appointed by the government. Producer Raoul Ploquin, who had been in charge of French productions at Ufa's Berlin studio in the 1930s, was chosen as the director because he had excellent contacts in the German film industry. There were twenty (later twenty-five) members on the committee which was divided into five subcommittees representing each branch of the industry: 1) technical industries (film and equipment manufacturers, studios, laboratories); 2) creative collaborators (authors, actors, directors, technicians); 3) producers; 4) distributors and exporters (exporters were later moved to the producer's subcommittee); and 5) theater owners.[8]

The Law of December 2 (its date of publication in the *Journal Officiel*) specified the following functions for the COIC;

> to direct the totality of the cinematographic industry and its personnel, and to take all measures which it deems indispensable concerning technical, economic and social matters; and in particular, the recruitment, employment, training and allotment of personnel to assure their maximum utilization.

The COIC was further charged with:

> the representation of the profession in its dealing with all organisms, public or private, French or foreign. It may further effectively assume the direction of all communal organisms, whether technical or commercial, in order to improve the quality and economy of production.[9]

The last clause assured that the COIC would replace all previous trade associations and trade unions within the industry.

It must be understood that the COIC was not a government agency, although its authority was derived from government decree. As a quasi-official organization, the COIC had to serve two constituencies: the film industry and the State. The COIC was a private trade organization, financed by taxes on its members. Its governing board was made up of professionals actively engaged in filmmaking, who saw themselves as representing the interests of the film industry, rather than those of the government. The COIC's headquarters were in Paris, not Vichy, allowing a certain independence from the state.

On the other hand, the directeur général of Vichy's Service du Cinéma had veto power over the COIC's decisions and the government could replace the COIC's director or any of its members as it saw fit. In practice, the Service du Cinéma never vetoed COIC decisions, but this was largely because the two incumbents—Guy de Carmoy and, after October 1941, Louis-Emile Galey—supported film industry concerns and were by no means Vichy ideologues.[10] The government did change the administrative makeup of the COIC's governing board on two occasions. In May 1942, a new law replaced Ploquin's sole directorship with a committee of three (made up of producer Roger Richebé, writer Marcel Achard, and manufacturer André Debrie). In October 1943, the directeur général du cinéma (Galey) became functional head of the COIC, and the directorship of the organization was again reduced to one (Richebé).

It is not altogether clear whether these reorganizations were due to bureaucratic needs or policy differences between the COIC and the government. The official announcement of the first reorganization cited Ploquin's desire to return to work as a producer (he subsequently produced *Le Ciel est à vous* and *Les Dames du Bois de Boulogne*). However, in a letter written to Jacques Siclier, Ploquin gave a different version of events.

> Continental Films [the German-owned production company established in October 1940] was incorporated as a French company; therefore, I expected it to submit to COIC directives. Our claim appeared unwarranted to [the firm's director] Alfred Greven who informed me several times, and with increasing annoyance, of his intention to ignore the laws in effect . . . With the support of Louis-Emile Galey . . . I refused to modify my position. In the end, one of us had to give way. Pierre Laval [Vichy's Prime Minister] sent me a letter on May 25, 1942, in which, among the flatteries, he announced his intention to "modify the structures of the COIC."[11]

Very likely, a combination of factors was involved in the reorganizations. Whatever the specific reasons, it appears that Vichy did not wish the COIC to become too independent and that the COIC had autonomy only to the extent that it did not deviate too far from official Vichy policy.

The film industry supported the COIC because it served a crucial function. As Raoul Ploquin pointed out in an address delivered to the COIC on September 10, 1941, conditions facing the industry before the COIC's formation were critical:

> The studios were deserted and laboratories without work; producers contemplated their balance sheets with de-

spair and could only watch hopelessly as enormous sums were lost because of the interdiction of their films. Unemployment was rampant. Horrible cases of individual suffering came to our attention, about which we could do nothing. Even in those areas where work was permitted by the occupation authorities [i.e., exhibition, distribution], the lack of films caused a rapid decline in activity.[12]

The COIC's most pressing task was to gain permission to resume production in the North, which was finally accomplished in June 1941 (see chapter 3). Aside from production, the COIC engaged in a range of activities issuing twenty directives in 1941 on such diverse matters as:

No. 1—Concerning the fixing of prices for prints
No. 8—Concerning foreign travel for artists
No. 17—Concerning the packaging of negatives
No. 20—Concerning charity showings.

Ploquin, in his speech, outlined three major areas (besides production) that had concerned the COIC during the year:

1) The expedition of present affairs: Publication of relevant laws to instruct the industry on present obligations and restrictions; finding coal to heat theaters; interceding in fiscal matters; mediating disagreements between organizations; organizing trade shows; mediating between owners and employees; finding positions for workers; providing consultative services.
2) Cleansing the market: The former practice of presenting a double bill to the public and the practice of distributors' selling films to exhibitors outright has prevented a normal amortization of French production. From now on, a good film will benefit the producer, as well as the distributor and exhibitor.
3) Cleansing the profession.[13]

The term "cleansing" (assainissement) is one of the most loaded terms in the vocabulary of the period. Although COIC officials would insist, after the Liberation, that the term referred only to ridding the industry of those who had been involved in the financial scandals of the thirties, it is clear that during the occupation, the primary targets of the industry's "housecleaning" were Jews.

Even before the COIC was established, Vichy had already instituted a law in October 1940 aimed directly at the cinema, which mandated that all film industry personnel be cleared for work.

> As to the regulation of the French cinema:
> Article 1: No enterprise belonging to any branch of the film industry may carry out its activities unless it has obtained an authorization from the Ministry of Information, on the advice of the organization committee for the profession . . .
> Article 2: The principal collaborators of film enterprises, and film artists, must possess a professional identity card issued by the organization committee for the profession . . .[14]

Ploquin, in his speech, described the law as providing

> a means of eliminating phantom societies and the men who created them. The periodic scandals which we have witnessed will no longer occur. We now have the means to prevent an individual from repeating a regrettable incident. I have decided to forbid the practice of the profession to anyone who has failed in his financial duties.[15]

Notwithstanding Ploquin's disingenuousness, it is obvious that the primary objective of the October 26 law was to eliminate Jews from the film industry. This goal was stated explicitly in the COIC's decision No. 4, which specified the conditions for receiving an identity card:

> 1) that the requestor not be a Jew
> 2) that he must never have been convicted of a crime

3) that he must have a recognized professional and commercial probity
4) that he be able to justify his professional competence.[16]

The issue of Jews and the French film industry is discussed in chapter 4. It is mentioned here only as a corrective to the impression that the COIC was nothing less than beneficial to the film industry. While it is true that the COIC was basically concerned with promoting film practice in France during a period of extreme uncertainty, its benefits were felt only by those who already had control over the industry, and by those who conformed to Vichy ideology and prejudice. The self-congratulatory tone of those connected with the COIC (and of later observers like Léglise) must be put in perspective: without the COIC, the French film industry would have produced fewer films, of lesser quality, during the occupation. Nonetheless, the COIC was a creature of Vichy, subscribing to many of its policies and goals. The credit for the COIC's successes must be balanced by a recognition of its responsibility in perpetuating the most obnoxious aspects of that regime.

Other Film Industry Concerns
For some producers in the South, the refusal of the Germans to allow production to resume in the occupied zone was a boon. With no activity in the fourteen major studios centered in Paris, all new French feature films would have to come from the unoccupied zone. Filmmaking talent was plentiful, because the majority of the industry's directors, actors, and technicians had fled the capital in June 1940. Features could be produced cheaply, yet seemingly be assured of a large profit, since audiences were starved for new French productions. There were, however, three major problems preventing the rapid resumption of wide-scale production: the shortage of studio space, the scarcity of production capital, and, most seriously, the lack of raw film stock.
Aside from Pagnol's small studio in Marseille (with two

sound stages), there were only two studios equipped for production of sound films in the South. The Victorine studio in Nice was the largest, with seven sound stages. It had been held in receivership by the Banque Nationale de Crédit since the liquidation of Franco-Film Aubert in 1930. The property was leased to producer André Paulvé, for the Société d'Exploitation des Studios de la Côte d'Azur (SESCA) in late 1940. The other studio, also in Nice, was the St. Laurent du Var. It had three stages and was controlled by Nicaea Films.[17]

Despite this small number of facilities, the film industry had grandiose plans for turning Nice into the "French Hollywood." In an article in L'Eclaireur on July 28, 1940, Pierre Rocher called for "more than a simple resumption of film activity on the Côte d'Azur. We must see a vast amount of construction, which looks to the future. France will soon see a Renaissance; its cinematographic brilliance will be unparalleled. We must create, on the Mediterranean coast, an artistic and industrial center which will serve not only for our national production, but for all of Europe."[18]

For Abel Gance, the resumption of film activity in the South was a pressing priority, in order to "carry abroad the message of France, the message of a spirit which cannot be vanquished." Gance, however, called for production to take place, not in the studios, but in "the fresh grass, the moving horizons of the seas and hills."[19]

Although Gance's vision of predominantly location shooting was not to become a reality, many Vichy productions were shot on location, in whole or in part, for lack of studio space. Michel Dulud's La Troisième Dalle, for example, begun on August 25, 1940, was shot entirely in a chateau in Haut-les-Cagnes. André Berthomieu's production of the following year, La Neige sur les pas, was filmed completely in the Alps. In fact, even after the Parisian studios reopened in June 1941, studio space in France remained scarce. The screenplays for many productions, both major and minor, emphasized regional geography to allow for location shooting.[20]

The second problem facing producers in the unoccupied zone—shortage of capital—was due to a number of factors. German confiscation of American- and Jewish-owned businesses had eliminated a major source of production capital. Even for those unaffected by these confiscations, liquidity was a problem with capital located in the northern sector. Given the uncertainty of circumstances, and later the indication by the Germans that productions from the South would not be permitted exhibition in the occupied zone, banks were reluctant to advance funds for so risky a venture.

The problem was resolved in several ways. Some producers continued to receive financing from Jewish- and American-owned companies via third parties, although such financing was suspected by German officials. When these officials began permitting exhibition of films made in the South after May 1942, they demanded that producers indicate the source of their capital.[21]

Many producers sought and received financing from Italian firms. André Paulvé's firm, Discina, for example, entered into an arrangement with Cinecittà in 1942, to form La Société Cinématographique Méditerranéenne d'Exploitation (CIMEX), 60 percent of which was owned by the Italians. The firm produced such major films of the period as Grémillon's Lumière d'été, Jean Delannoy's L'Eternel Retour, and Marcel Carné's Les Visiteurs du soir.[22] The company was also the producer of Les Enfants du Paradis, but its funds were cut off in mid-production and the film was completed with funds from Pathé.

Cinecittà also provided 50 percent of the capital for La Société Méditerranéenne de Production (CIMEP), which produced four films in early 1943, including Les Petites du Quai aux Fleurs, which was produced in both French and Italian versions. Italian interests in several prewar French production companies were maintained, and Zenith (99.9 percent Italian participation), Francinex (25 percent), Scalera (20 percent), and Lux (42 percent) together produced six films.[23] Among the films were Louis Daquin's Le Voyageur de la Toussaint, Marcel l'Herbier's La Vie de Bohème, and Abel Gance's Capitaine Fracasse. Cinecittà also shared interests in the two studios in Nice and owned two theaters there outright.

The Vichy government encouraged Franco-Italian cooperation as a buffer against German domination. Attempts were made to sign a far-reaching coproduction agreement. German film officials, however, opposed these moves, and attempted to arrest Lous-Emile Galey, the head of Vichy's film office, for traveling to Italy without authorization in 1941.[24]

Although several Franco-Italian coproductions were finished (including two language versions of Robert Vernay's Le Comte de Monte Cristo, shot in France, and Christian-Jaque's major production of Carmen, shot in Rome), the Germans blocked any formal agreement on the governmental level.

The third measure taken to provide production capital was initiated by the COIC in 1941. One of the measures that had been enacted to assure the "health" of the French film industry was a proviso that producers must have the capital to cover the costs of the film before a production visa would be granted. The producer could provide such assurances in two ways: either he could provide the entire production capital himself and place it in escrow, or he could apply to the COIC for co-financing through the Crédit National (a nationally owned financing agency).

The Crédit National was authorized to finance up to 65 percent of a film's production, provided the producer had liquid assets amounting to 35 percent of the budget, and that the COIC considered the project worthy of aid. If the project was approved, the producer had to freeze 50 percent of his share (i.e., 17.5 percent of the total budget) to be used for pre-production. With the completion of pre-production, the producer was to submit a budget, along with the shooting script, continuity, work table, contracts, and drawings of sets. He was also to provide a 10 percent guaranty against going over budget.

A formula was devised whereby the producer recouped his costs in advance of the Crédit National. All profits after expenses reverted to the producer. Interest on the Crédit National's advance was a modest 5.25 percent.[25]

Certainly, one of the primary reasons Vichy initiated the practice of government financing was to maintain control over the content and personnel of films produced. But the Direction Générale du Cinéma and the COIC were not solely interested in promoting Vichy ideology, unless the more fundamental propaganda value of financing films which would glorify French culture and artistry is considered. The films which were aided by the Crédit National included not only blatant Vichy apologias, but also such respected efforts as *Nous les gosses, La Nuit fantastique, Lumière d'été, Le Baron Fantôme, Le Ciel est à vous,* and *Les Anges du péché.*[26]

The third area preventing a rapid resumption of production in Vichy was the scarcity of raw materials, film stock in particular. Before the war, France had imported most of its negative film. Only one large firm, Kodak-Pathé (jointly owned by Eastman Kodak and Pathé), produced film stock in large quantity. The firm had provided about 20 percent of negative stock and about 75 percent of France's positive film.[27]

With the occupation of France, the Germans confiscated Kodak-Pathé and appointed a provisional administrator. The Chemical Group of the German military authority took control of the firm's operation and granted it a temporary permit to sell film stock in March 1941, to the German army only (R141/F380). With the appointment of the administrator, the firm was induced to export 70 percent of its total production to Germany, at discounted prices. In exchange, a small amount of Agfa film was imported to France.[28]

What stock was available was of very poor quality. Kodak-Pathé, when finally permitted to sell to French companies, was short of silver oxide and consequently the film it produced required a lot of light for adequate exposure. Unfortunately, there was insufficient electricity to run the lights in the studios. Undoubtedly, this problem also contributed to the reliance on exterior shooting.

In the unoccupied zone, only the small Lumière factory produced any film stock at all, and the factory was forced to close in February 1942, when its coal supply was cut off.[29] The Germans further maintained total control over film manufacture by banning any further production of 9.5mm and 17.5mm film. These reduced sizes were the norm for a large number of theaters in the smaller towns and countryside, as well as in the schools. Most amateur equipment was also in these sizes. The occupiers gave a monopoly over the new standard for reduced size prints—16mm—

to the German-owned companies Tobis and ACE. They thus not only assured immense profits for these companies, but effectively prevented the production of clandestine films.

By squeezing all film manufacturers out of the market, the Germans hoped to maintain complete control over the number of films produced. The German film office established a contingent for each year, and the COIC arranged distribution of the film stock. In 1942, for example, French firms were permitted to make seventy-two films, none longer than 2,800 meters, with the number of copies restricted to between twenty-five and thirty. In 1943, the total amount of film stock provided per film was 16,000m negative and sound, and 25,000m positive.[30]

Not all films produced in France managed to stay within these limits. There was an active black market in film stock; Le Film frequently reported on missing shipments of film, which presumably landed in the hands of black marketers. Trading on the black market even reached the official level—both Louis-Emile Galey and Roger Richebé (of the COIC) reported that they provided black market film stock for such lengthy productions as Les Visiteurs du soir and Les Enfants du Paradis.[31] Some of the film stock was also smuggled in from Switzerland and other neutral countries.

Perhaps the most imaginative way of securing needed production supplies was devised by Marc Allégret. For his production of L'Arlésienne in the South, his crew hijacked a sound truck and brought it clandestinely across the demarcation line. When production was finished, they sold it to the Germans on the black market.[32]

In addition to the material factors restricting production in the unoccupied zone, political factors hampered new production in the South. Foremost among these factors was the German refusal to allow Vichy-made films to cross the demarcation line. This refusal was primarily meant to assure a German monopoly over the French exhibition market, and would undoubtedly have remained in force if box-office receipts had not plummeted in spring 1941. On April 21, 1941, the Germans permitted La Fille du *puisatier* to open in Paris (after it had already run several months in the South and in Switzerland). The film was enthusiastically received by Parisian audiences starved for new French films. It had a 21-week first run in Paris; Le *Film* proclaimed it one of the greatest successes ever (November 8, 1941). Perhaps because of this great success, most of the other films from the unoccupied zone were not permitted Parisian openings until an agreement centering all production in Paris had been reached in May 1942.

For producers in Vichy, this ban effectively prevented their films from making a profit. Although the population of the unoccupied zone had increased following the Armistice, the bulk of France's population still resided in the occupied sector. Moreover, the German authorities also attempted to block export to neutral countries. Therefore, the market for Vichy-made films was largely limited to the southern two-fifths of France and French North Africa. In these areas, however, the French product was still competing with prewar American films, which retained their popularity until they were finally banned in October 1942.[33]

Social Policy in Vichy

Despite these obstacles, producers in Vichy attempted to make films. In order to do so, however, they had to limit themselves to the areas circumscribed by Vichy's ideology. Government censorship of films was not new in France. The Third Republic had banned such films as L'*Age d'or* and *Zéro de conduite* for attacking the authority of the State and its institutions. But to this political censorship, Vichy added censorship on moral grounds, lest films undermine the fundamental goals of government social policy.

Vichy ideologues saw the primary purpose of the National Revolution as the moral uplift of the French people. The ideology was largely a reaction to what Vichy viewed to be the decadence of the Third Republic. There was a strong tendency toward puritanism in Vichy thinking, which led to stricter laws against, for example, drunkenness, obscenity, and prostitution. The Church, which had long been officially powerless, was restored to a position of moral authority.

For Vichy dogmatists, the family was sacrosanct. Pétain proclaimed the family "the cell of French life." [34] In support of this philosophy, divorce laws were tightened, large families were subsidized, and childless men were officially discriminated against in job selection. Youth, the bearer of France's future, was glorified. Children were to be indoctrinated in the Vichy spirit from the earliest age in school and in official youth programs.

To further insure France's regeneration, Vichy encouraged a "return to the soil," a mass exodus from the unhealthy cities, which had been breeding grounds for degradation and leftist ideas. Instead, France's youth was to return to the land, where the values of eternal France reposed.

Vichy's official motto was "travail, famille, patrie" (work, family, country), and patriotism was fanned in inverse proportion to France's actual status in the world. Despite the fact that Vichy existed only on German sufferance, Vichy paraded its generals and its armies before an admiring citizenry, and made a demi-god out of its increasingly senile leader. As in Mussolini's Italy, France was glorified by looking backward to the imperial past: Louis XIV and Napoleon were its Caesars, Molière and Racine its cultural archetypes. The years from 1940 to 1942 may have been France's darkest, but for Vichy, the past was glorious and the future assured.

Censorship

In order to assure that French filmmakers would uphold the spirit of "travail, famille, patrie," Vichy not only censored completed films but instituted a policy of pre-censorship as well. The official censorship board, the Commission de Contrôle, was attached to the Ministry of Information, as it had been since July 1939. The head of this commission was the Secretary General for Information and Propaganda. Three members of the commission were appointed directly by the head of the government. In addition, there was representation from the offices of the Secretary of

State for Foreign Affairs, the Secretary of State for the Interior, the Ministry of National Defense, the Secretary of State for National Education and Youth, the General Commissioner of the Family, the Légion Française des Combattants (the Veterans organization), and the COIC.

The purpose of this Commission was defined in a decree issued by Vichy's premier, Admiral Darlan, on December 20, 1941: "In order to perform the advisory function which it has been called upon to render . . . the most important matter which the consultative commission must take into account is the defense of public morals and respect for national traditions." (R142/F449).

Vichy's moralism weighed heavily on filmmakers in the South. The lack of a uniform production code often led to arbitrary decisions on what was permitted. Suzanne Borel, then the Foreign Ministry's representative to the commission, described the meetings as highly contentious, with each ministry objecting to various aspects of an individual scenario or film.

At one meeting in 1940, after the Germans had demanded the withdrawal of all French war-time propaganda films, the commission proceeded, on its own initiative, to demand that offending passages be cut from British and American films as well. In *Goodbye Mr. Chips*, for example, the board removed the scene in which Chips remembers his former students killed in World War I, on the grounds that "one must not remind the French people that young Englishmen had died defending their land."

An unnamed American film was objectionable to the commission because divorce was a major plot element, "which is not in accord with the Maréchal's thoughts." Borel managed to get the film passed by pointing out that the Maréchal was himself married to a divorcée. The commission was so stunned that the subject had been mentioned that the film was allowed.[35]

In terms of French production, the censorship board not only passed on completed films, but on film projects as well. The Parisian press snidely attributed the refusal of production permits to "a senile band of old maiden men who attempt in vain to impose from Vichy a hypocritical facade of pseudo-virtue that is the antithesis of our national character."[36]

On June 23, 1941, Robert André wrote in *Le Petit Parisien*:
"Vichy censorship is Draconian, and one can cite as an example
the interdiction of *Petrus*, by Marcel Achard, which Marc Allégret
was to direct, because it contained a few gunshots."

The most outspoken critic of Vichy's censorship policies
was Nino Frank, who wrote in the collaborationist weekly *Les Nouveaux Temps*. He claimed that a screenplay based on Alphonse
Daudet's *Lettres de Mon Moulin* had been banned "because in one
of the letters, country priests are mocked," and that *Le Journal Tombe
à 5 Heures* (a northern production) was having difficulty getting past
Vichy censorship "because it shows, in a picturesque manner, the
life of a newspaper; and to the dignitaries of that torture chamber
in Vichy, this life appears too gay, scarcely suitable to our time of
National Revolution" (August 30, 1941).

Frank's last caustic comment on Vichy was published on
July 1, 1942. He noted that a film about Molière had been turned
down "because it would also have shown Molière as a histrionic,
a cuckold, truculent and misanthropic, instead of guarding the
image of Molière enstatued in the Petit Larousse." Soon thereafter, Frank was dismissed from his post, at German insistence,
for being too independent.

Screenwriter Charles Spaak found himself running afoul
of Vichy censorship on at least three occasions. In the case of his
screenplay for *Le Collier de la Reine*, based on Dumas's historical
melodrama filmed several times before, the project was refused
and he was advised by Pétain's representative on the commission
that one should "retain from the history of France all that is edi-
fying and exalting, and leave in silence the embarrassing incidents which might discredit the kings and queens who did so much
for the country." Another member of the commission objected to
showing a Cardinal as the queen's lover and a third objected to
the glorification of Robespierre and the Revolution.[37]

In the case of *Le Lit à colonnes*, based on a novel by Louise
de Vilmorin, critic Roger Régent accused the Vichy censorship
commission of ruining the film by forcing Spaak and director Roland Tual to change the ending. In the book, the escaped inmate
kills the prison director who had taken credit for the convict's

musical compositions. Such attacks on authority were unthinkable, so that in the film, the prison director's death becomes an "indirect, accidental suicide."[38]

Still another Spaak screenplay, for L'Escalier sans fin, led to a dispute between the censorship commission and the film's star. The commission did not want the main character to be identified as a social worker because she was immoral and would throw a bad light on social workers.[39] Madeleine Renaud, who played the character, objected to the proposed change of identification to a "dame visiteuse" (presumably a "visiting lady" had no governmental connection). The dispute was finally resolved by the head of the State film office, who substituted the following dialogue: "And you are a nurse?" "Yes, something like that."[40]

The absurdities of Vichy censorship are nearly endless. The popular play by Sarment, "Mamouret," which had run for years under that title, was renamed Le Briseur de chaînes (The Chain-Breaker, an odd title for a comedy), because the title character was a 106-year old woman who was not in possession of all her faculties. The censorship office maintained that "at that age, one should show an example of good sense worthy of a young spirit, as for example, the Maréchal." In Jean Anouilh's Le Voyageur sans bagage, a scene was cut in which "a dog obeys the call of nature against an obelisk erected to the glory of the family."

Fortunately for French filmmakers, not all the members of the censorship board were Mrs. Grundys. The more clear-sighted members of the commission overcame one member's objections to Grémillon's Lumière d'été, which he would have banned in its entirety on the grounds that "when one shows the type of characters that you show in the film, people will ask themselves on whom they can rely to effect the National Revolution."

Vichy-Sponsored Films

One way Vichy found to insure that its message would be heard was to commission films through its various ministries. The Légion Française des·Combattants subsidized several films whose intent was moral uplift.

From the description of *Port d'Attache* in *Le Film* (February 20, 1943), one imagines a kind of right-wing *Our Daily Bread*. A demobilized sailor encounters an old farmer whose children have abandoned the family homestead. The sailor organizes a group of unemployed Parisians who move out to the farm and help the farmer to work his land.

Another Légion-sponsored film, *Jeannou*, shot on location in Périgord, details the conflict between a traditionalist father and his rebellious daughter. The conflict is resolved when the daughter sees the wisdom of her father's refusal to allow a mine to operate on his land, "out of respect for the past and because he preferred agriculture to industry" (*Le Film*, November 20, 1943).

A variation on the return to the land theme was provided by *Cap au large*. Writing in 1948, Roger Régent commented:

> In place of the peasant returning to the land, there is a sailor returning to the sea. Fishing replaces the harvest, waves replace the furrows. One can see the risks of placing these symbols in inept hands. If those in charge had succeeded in multiplying these *Caps au Large*, nothing would have remained on our screens but naive dabblings, like illustrations for bank calendars. (p. 89)

Another government agency eager to promote the policies of the National Revolution was the Ministry for the Family. It commissioned *Le Bal des passants*, an anti-abortion tract, which Régent dismissed as imbecilic: "The characters in *Le Bal des Passants* behave like sinister idiots and one realizes again how little French officials understood about the cinema's possibilities as a medium of propaganda" (p. 251).

La Loi du printemps, another pro-family propaganda effort, is about the adjustment of children to their new step-families when their widowed parents remarry. Régent remarked that "the scenario was composed in such a way that instead of celebrating the joys of family life, the film showed us an aspect of the family that was perfectly detestable, and likely to turn one forever from domestic bliss" (p. 64).

Vichy "Inspired" Films

Not every film that celebrated Vichyist values was commissioned by the State. There were many filmmakers agreeable to glorifying the National Revolution, although it is not clear whether they did so because they believed it to be profitable, or to curry favor, or from true conviction. One of the first of these films was *La Nuit merveilleuse*, begun on December 2, 1940, which retold the Nativity story in a modern setting. The couple who could find no shelter were refugees from the June 1940 exodus, taken in by a peasant and given work on the land. "If one works the land, it will not refuse one nourishment," concludes the modern Joseph. The film was dedicated to Maréchal Pétain, and it had its premiere in Vichy, in time for Christmas.

The glorification of the Maréchal as France's redeemer was implicit in this film. Marcel Pagnol also made reference to Pétain in *La Fille du puisatier*. The story is typical of Pagnol: a young woman bears an illegitimate child to a rich young man who is separated from her by the war. The conflict is resolved with Pétain's June 17 broadcast calling for a halt to the fighting. With war's end, the couple is reconciled and bring their warring families to peace as well. With the exception of this reference, the film is really no more "pétainist" than any of Pagnol's other films, which similarly glorify the peasantry and the "petits métiers." Postwar prints of the film do not contain the Pétain reference, and its excision does nothing to change the film's message.[41]

The return to the land was a favorite subject for Vichy filmmakers, whether they were directly encouraged by the government or simply influenced by prevailing sentiments. *Après l'orage* tells the story of a farmer who leaves his devoted fiancée and his land to go to Paris, where he gets mixed up with an actress and an unscrupulous producer. "Luckily," war comes along, and after the defeat he returns to his land and his faithful fiancée (*Le Film*, February 20, 1943).

The return to the land could even be a subject for comedy. André Zwoboda, a former assistant to Jean Renoir, made *Une Etoile au soleil*, a light-hearted film about a Parisian nightclub singer who gives up the high life for his true love in the country.

Reputedly, the best of these return-to-the-land films was *Monsieur des Lourdines*, based on a turn-of-the-century novel by Alphonse de Châteaubriant, who was editor of the collaborationist paper *La Gerbe* during the occupation. The film was directed by a newcomer, Pierre de Hérain, whose career no doubt profited by his connections—he was Pétain's stepson. The film is a prodigal child story, concerning the son of a wealthy landowner who squanders the family fortune on gambling and women, but who in the end renounces Paris and returns to the ancestral estate.

Other Vichy Films

The vogue for glorification of the National Revolution was concentrated during the 1941–42 period, when Vichy was still an essentially autonomous state and popular support for the regime was at its height. Almost all of the films made by companies in the unoccupied zone were influenced by Vichy ideology. The subjects ranged from the sacrifice of a few for the good of mankind in *Les Hommes sans peur* (Yvan Noé), a film about doctors who accepted the risk of fatal illness in order to study the effects of radiation; to the inevitability of punishment for immoral behavior. In Marc Allégret's *Félicie Nanteuil*, based on Anatole France's *L'Histoire comique*, Micheline Presle rejects the earnest actor (Claude Dauphin) who has helped her to become a great actress because she has become the mistress of a wealthy nobleman (Louis Jourdan). The actor, insane with jealousy, kills himself on her doorstep and haunts her throughout her life.

Some films managed to discreetly promote Vichy's nationalistic impulse. *L'Appel du bled* (Maurice Gleize) concerns the sacrifices of colonial officers' wives, while *Mermoz* (Louis Cuny) is a reconstruction of the life of France's most famous aviator, who pioneered night flying. *Mermoz* is a curious blend of Riefenstahl-like cloud and mountain formations with stage-bound conversational sequences that emphasize the wooden performance of the star, Robert-Hugues Lambert, an amateur who was selected for his resemblance to the original Mermoz.

The bulk of production in the unoccupied zone was considered mediocre by critics of the time, and when released in Paris suffered in comparison to the slick and expensive productions later made in the North. The shortage of material for sets and costumes led filmmakers to rely largely on easy-to-film scenarios set in vaguely contemporary times, such as burlesque comedies (*Un Chapeau de paille d'Italie* and *Une Vie de chien*, both with Fernandel), boulevard comedies (*Le Valet maître*), or else classic stage plays with assured audience recognition (*L'Arlésienne*, *Les Deux Timides*). Unfortunately, the quality of sound reproduction was often so poor that the dialogue of these stage adaptations was nearly indecipherable.

Although most of the films were hampered by material shortages in the South, some directors found these shortages a challenge. Roger Régent notes that André Berthomieu's *Promesse à l'inconnue*, an original drama about a literary *monstre sacré*, accommodated itself to the lack of material for fancy sets by employing no sets at all. Instead, the film was shot largely in extreme closeup. Although the story was weak, the first-rate cast (Charles Vanel, Claude Dauphin, Pierre Brasseur, and Madeleine Robinson) capitalized on the method of shooting to turn in exemplary performances (Régent, pp. 83–84).

Other oddities of the period included Abel Gance's *La Vénus aveugle*, with Viviane Romance playing a Camille going blind, and *Feu sacré* (Maurice Gleize), with a screenplay by Viviane Romance, purportedly based on her own autobiography. With the exception of *La Fille du puisatier*, only two films made in the unoccupied zone generated critical enthusiasm: Pierre Billon's comedy *Le Soleil a toujours raison*, with a screenplay by Jacques Prévert, and Marc Allégret's *Félicie Nanteuil*, which was not released until after the Liberation because its star, Claude Dauphin, had escaped to London shortly after production was completed. His broadcasts over the BBC so infuriated the Germans that they banned all of his films.

Conclusion

Between August 1940 and May 1942, approximately thirty-five feature films were produced by companies in the unoccupied zone. Few of these films were important either artistically or commercially. Some filmmakers chose to remain in the South rather than work under German supervision but, paradoxically, the German censors proved to be far less exacting than their Vichy counterparts. Once production began in the North in June 1941, most filmmakers preferred the well-appointed facilities and bigger budgets available to them in Paris. By the time the German film office succeeded in centralizing all production in Paris in May 1942, few filmmakers were left in the South except for the apologists for Vichy propaganda.

With the German occupation of the South in November 1942, the Vichy government became a figurehead, no longer able to carry out its programs. Government interest in feature-film production abated, and the films produced in southern studios were essentially Parisian productions, brought to the South for the sunshine and picturesque views. The dream of Hollywood on the Côte d'Azur was never to be realized.

Despite the failure of the government and the film industry to turn southern France into a new production center, Vichy's accomplishments were not negligible. The formation of the COIC not only provided a badly needed structure for the film industry, but it also served to counterbalance the demands of the German film offices. The COIC protected the autonomy of the French film industry, assuring that once filmmaking began in the North it would not be dominated by German interests but rather by the interests of the French film industry itself. If the Vichy government accomplished nothing else, it set in motion a force that assured the continued survival of a strong and independent film industry.

Chapter 3

German Initiatives, 1940–1941, and Continental Films

G iven the necessity of defending its film industry from extinction, the Vichy govern-
ment succeeded in creating a single organization to supervise all
matters pertaining to the industry. The COIC, directed by France's
film community, had the unified support of the film industry in
its dealings with both Vichy and the occupiers.

The occupiers did not have the advantage of unity. Unlike the French, German film interests in France were neither consolidated nor single-minded. At least three agencies were officially charged with handling German film matters in France, and
each had its own interests to serve. Furthermore, groups outside
the official hierarchy had a major impact on policy-making decisions. The complex and often overlapping interests of all these
groups led to a German film policy that was changeable and often
contradictory.

The first German authority charged with supervision of
film activities in France was the Propaganda Staffel (Propaganda
Section), established in June 1940, by the military command. On
July 18, a second propaganda department was formed, the Propaganda Abteilung (Propaganda Department), which was administratively directed by the Wehrmacht in France, but in fact con-

trolled by Goebbels' Ministry of Propaganda in Berlin. By the winter of 1941, jurisdictional disputes between the two organizations led to the Propaganda Abteilung's assumption of authority over the Propaganda Staffel, and eventually to the dissolution of the Propaganda Staffel in November 1942.[1]

In addition, a third propaganda office was established under the authority of the German Embassy, and was thus linked to the Foreign Ministry in Berlin. After a number of jurisdictional disputes, an agreement was reached in July 1942, relegating all matters concerning production of films for propaganda purposes to the Embassy. The Propaganda Abteilung retained control of matters pertaining to the French film industry—censorship, liaison, allocation of resources, etc. The key German organization concerned with the French film industry was thus the Propaganda Abteilung.

The Propaganda Abteilung was directed by a Major Schmidtke of the Wehrmacht, who relegated film matters to "Sonderführer" (special leader) Dr. Diedrich, reputedly a tyrant, who "hated France and all Frenchmen," but who was essentially a figurehead.[2] Under their direction was the Filmprüfstelle (Film Control Board), created on July 31, 1940.[3] This agency supervised French film activities, and was directed first by a Major Koegl, and then by Oberleutnant (first lieutenant) Dr. Derichsweiler, whom Galey characterized as "a bureaucrat—not a Nazi. He created no difficulties for us."

Although the personnel of the Filmprüfstelle were under the authority of the military command, they maintained direct contact with the Propaganda Ministry in Berlin through frequent visits to and from the German capital and weekly activity reports.[4] The authority of the Filmprüfstelle extended throughout occupied France (and after November 1942, in the southern zone as well), except for the two northernmost departments which were administratively attached to the Propaganda Abteilung in Belgium, and Alsace-Lorraine, which had been annexed to Germany. Regional film censorship offices attached to the various military commands in France were accountable to the Filmprüfstelle in Paris.

Initial Film Policy

The first measures enacted by the Filmprüfstelle were primarily reflections of overall German policy in France—consolidation of economic interests and the elimination of Jews from public life (see chapter 4). The Filmprüfstelle's first goal was the creation of a market for German films in France. To this end, they immediately began confiscation of films held by French distributors and exhibitors, and began issuing permits for selected members of these groups to resume activities. Exhibition was very quickly reestablished and by August 1940 nearly two-thirds of Paris's movie theaters were open. Distribution was held back, however, until a dominant market position could be established for l'Alliance Cinématographique Européenne (ACE), the Ufa-controlled German distribution arm in France.

In addition to distributing German feature films in France, ACE was granted a monopoly on the distribution of newsreels in the occupied zone. This French edition of the Deutsche Wochenschau, titled "Actualités Mondiales" (world news) was compulsory showing for all theaters in the North.[5]

It appears likely that the Filmprüfstelle's initial policy of economic monopolization was formulated in Berlin, since this policy was not altogether in the interests of the film office in Paris. As an arm of the military authority, the Filmprüfstelle was concerned with the pacification of France. In order to assure French cooperation with the German command, a certain measure of normalcy in economic matters was essential. Large-scale unemployment could only lead to increasing disaffection with the occupying regime, which in turn would necessitate a larger military commitment to France. To free German armies for the active fronts, it was essential that at least some French interests be served.

One of the ways of pacifying the civilian population was to assure a supply of entertainment. Theaters, night clubs, and music halls were rapidly reopened in Paris, because these diversions were not in competition with German products. As long as French audiences were satisfied with new German films and revivals of old French films however, there was no immediate need to resume French feature production.

But discontent was growing within the film industry itself. Even before the COIC was established, film industry representatives were clamoring for permission to produce. Le Film complained in its first issue of October 12, 1940, that the only activity going on in the studios was the dubbing of French sound tracks for German films. Caught between two contradictory policies—monopoly and pacification—the Filmprüfstelle delayed granting new production visas until it became apparent that such a policy was counterproductive to both of its goals. By February 1941, box office receipts had declined to such an extent that all exhibitors and distributors were in danger of bankruptcy.

Despite their limited choice of entertainment, Parisian audiences had evidently not taken to German films in the way the occupiers had hoped. The initial curiosity of French audiences soon gave way to indifference, and movie attendance dropped accordingly. Although the decline in movie attendance had begun during the unsettled "drôle de guerre" period, only a rise in ticket prices had prevented a real loss in cinema receipts in the first six months of the occupation. Attendance figures showed a real drop— in the first quarter of 1941, attendance reached only 84 percent of what it had been the previous year, and represented only 56 percent of comparable totals for the base year of 1938.[6] Evidently, without new French production, movie theaters would soon be bankrupt and audiences would simply lose the habit of going to the movies.

The decline and subsequent rise in gross receipts (appendix table 3.1) indicate the nature of the occupier's dilemma. Declining receipts during the war period had not been reversed by the appearance of new German films on the market. Only with the reappearance of French films in late 1941 did audiences return to movie theaters. Once full French production had begun, however, receipts rose rapidly. Despite the cold, the boredom, and the fear, the public would not leave their homes merely to see German actors in German films. However, once moviegoing became habitual again, the spillover would undoubtedly benefit German films as well.[7]

The Other Power—Continental Films

If the Filmprüfstelle had no choice but to allow French production to begin in the spring of 1941, it is not altogether clear whether their initial policy of obstruction was intended to be temporary or permanent. It is certain, however, that one major reason for the delay in allowing new French production was the desire of one man to see his own interests in France served.

In the previous discussion of the German film hierarchy in France, one major figure has been omitted. Although he had no official position in either the German government or the military command, Alfred Greven had considerable power over German film policy in France.

On October 1, 1940, a company named Continental Film Société à Responsabilité Limitée was formed.[8] Although funded entirely by German capital, and thus a German company, Continental occupies a central position in the history of the French film industry during the occupation.

Financially and administratively, the firm was entirely controlled by Germans. Its head—Alfred Greven—had previously been a producer for Terra Filmkunst and Ufa AG.[9] Greven ruled Continental like an autocrat, personally overseeing all levels of the company's activities. Greven had been appointed by Max Winkler, director of the Cautio trust, which had financed Continental and had bought control in all of the major German film companies before the war.[10] Winkler, in turn, reported directly to Propaganda Minister Joseph Goebbels. In January 1942, all of the various branches of the German film industry including Continental were consolidated in one company, known as Ufa-Film GmbH or Ufi. Thus, Continental was directly controlled by Winkler and Goebbels.

Jürgen Spiker, in his thorough study of the Nazi film industry, *Film und Kapital*, maintains that although Greven officially owned 99 percent of Continental Films, his dependence on Winkler's directives was contractually established (p. 193). Nonetheless, Greven exercised considerable autonomy, not only over the affairs of Continental, but over the Filmprüfstelle as well. For, in addition to his relationship with Goebbels, Greven was a close personal friend of Reichsmarschall Hermann Goering, with whom he had served in the German air force during World War I.[11] Given the notorious infighting among Nazi ministries, Greven, with a foot in two camps, could afford a larger degree of independence than a man less well-connected. He used his position both to assure Continental's preeminence in film production in France, and to see that German film policy in France suited his purposes.

Continental Films did indeed have a privileged position among production companies in France. While French producers, especially in the South, were severely undercapitalized, Continental's initial capital investment was 10 million Reichsmarks or 200 million francs (the average cost of a film in 1941 was 3.4 million francs).[12] In addition to its production branch, Continental also controlled the Paris-Cinéma and Neuilly studios and the C.T.M. labs. Most importantly, it controlled the biggest theater chain in France. Derived in large part from the confiscation of the Siritsky and Haik chains, la Société de Gestion et d'Exploitation de Cinéma (SOGEC) employed French "front men" to run 39 theaters in France, 4 in Belgium, and an additional 10 under its control.[13]

Continental not only had more money than French production companies, it also had first call on all raw materials, including film stock, material for set construction, and the increasingly scarce electricity. Continental's production contingent was not part of the general French production quota established yearly by the Filmprüfstelle. Instead, the firm received a special contingent that was from two to three times higher than any French firm. Over the course of the occupation, Continental produced 30 of the approximately 220 films (16 percent) made in both zones, more than any other company in France.

The German film office in France considered Continental to be a branch of Ufa. (Early Filmprüfstelle reports refer to Continental's productions as Ufa productions.) Greven and Continental operated independently of the film office, and reported directly to Berlin. Because of his connections, Greven was in a position to influence the Filmprüfstelle to arrange matters for the benefit of his company. "A false and authoritarian person, who used power acquired through others to its limit,"[14] Greven was not above using his influence for personal ends. He ordered the Filmprüfstelle to withdraw critic Nino Frank's credentials, for having written an unflattering article, and prevented André Paulvé from producing Marcel Carné's *Juliette ou la clef des songes* out of pique for Carné's refusal to work for Continental.[15] Basically, however, "Greven was a businessman, whose primary interest was in making as much money as possible for his firm and for himself."[16]

It is likely that the Filmprüfstelle's initial policy of preventing all production in the occupied zone was initiated by Greven, who hoped to establish a preeminent market position for Continental. Two facts bear out this hypothesis: first, French firms were prevented from resuming production in the North until March 1941. By that time, Continental already had its first two films in production, and twelve more in pre-production, assuring that the company would be the first to release any new French features. Second, with no other firms producing films, Continental was the only company in Paris where filmmakers could find work. Greven thus succeeded in putting many of France's most famous actors, directors, and screenwriters under exclusive contract.

Financial concerns were undoubtedly behind the decision of these French personnel to work for a German company. They signed their contracts reluctantly, and only after considerable negotiation. Georges Lacombe, Christian-Jaque, and Marcel Carné described these negotiations in a television interview with Armand Panigel in 1975:

> We were summoned by the head of Continental, Alfred Greven//and told to choose—either the French cinema would resume or it would not//I was told, if you don't sign, the French cinema will not be revived//We met with Greven and we asked him questions. It was understood that there was no question of our making propaganda films//I insisted that the films had to be shot in France, and that we would decide on projects by mutual agreement. In other words, that no one could force me to work in Germany or to make a film with any sort of propagandistic content.[17]

Carné, in his memoirs, gives a more colorful account of Greven's ingenious methods of signing French directors. Carné claims he was called in by Greven and told that Lacombe, Henri Decoin, Christian-Jaque, and others had already signed contracts. After putting forward a number of conditions, which were accepted, Carné felt he no longer had any excuse not to sign. It was only afterward that he learned from the others that they had not yet signed, and only did so after being assured by Greven that Carné was under contract.[18]

By whatever means, Greven had managed to put some of France's most important directors under contract, along with such other notables as screenwriter Charles Spaak, and actors Pierre Fresnay, Danielle Darrieux, Albert Préjean, Fernand Ledoux, and Jean-Louis Barrault. The reasons for his success were obvious: Continental had the most money, the best technicians and facilities, and perhaps most importantly, its films were not subject to review by Vichy censors. Therefore, filmmakers at Continental were not constrained by the moralistic tone and bland content imposed by Vichy censors on most French productions. Paradoxically, the greatest artistic liberty in occupied France was to be had under the aegis of the German production company.[19]

Continental's Production

The fears of French filmmakers that they might be coerced into making propaganda films for Continental were unfounded. Greven was not interested in making solemn thesis films for the glorification of the Reich. What he wanted were films that would be popular with audiences and so make money for his company. But Greven undoubtedly had his own ideas about the kind of films these would be:

> For the Germans, Paris meant pretty women, high living . . . They expected us to make films at the Casino de Paris, full of dancers and nude women. I think they were surprised that the subjects we proposed to them had nothing to do with their idea of "gay Paree."[20]

Certainly Continental did produce some trifling films which exemplified German notions of the French style. *Défense d'aimer* (Richard Pottier, 1942), was a German-style operetta set in that mythical "gay Paree" of German imagination. Its tale recounted the romance of a manicurist and the son of the hotel owner who employed her. Production values were high (sets included a luxury Parisian hotel, an operetta-style mythical country complete with grand casino and elegant spa), but the film's style is thoroughly Teutonic in its incongruous amalgamation of songs and narrative. Short snippets of melody are interspersed throughout the film: the manicurists' ode to "the true Parisienne—pretty, flirtatious, resourceful and honest"; a record the son sends his father refusing to marry a rich Latin American movie star ("non, Papa"); a film within the film of the star's latest gaucho musical. This bizarre film is far closer in spirit to German operettas than to the French music hall tradition or a René Clair type of fantasy. It is doubtful that French audiences would have been drawn back into movie theaters had this type of film been their sole fare.

Audiences did flock to see Continental's production, however—with French stars and high production values, its films were among the most popular of the period. Although individual box office figures were not published, one can estimate the most popular films by notices in *Le Film* of the success of individual productions.[21] Of the twenty-seven French films mentioned as hugely successful or breaking all box office records, fourteen (fifty-two percent) were films produced by Continental.

Typical of Continental's successful production was *Annette et la dame blonde* (Jean Dréville, 1942). Based on a comedy by Georges Simenon, the film represented a tendency toward

the American formula of fast-paced comedies, which drew their substance from their gags and visual imagery, and not from a story, an atmosphere or from an unusual character. It is amusing to note that those most determined to follow this path, those who were most obsessed with Hollywood and its mechanisms, were the producers at Continental Films. *Premier Rendez-Vous, Ca-*

prices, Annette and others were the purest specimens of this American mania which permeated the company.[22]

Continental strove to fill the gap left by the banned American product with comedies and mysteries in the American style. To the American formula of fast paced dialogue and lots of action, it added a slightly French touch of illicit sex and "joie de vivre." The company emerged with such successful comedies as Henri Decoin's *Premier Rendez-Vous*, with Danielle Darrieux, Fernand Ledoux, and Louis Jourdan (in his first major role), Léo Joannon's *Caprices*, in which Darrieux again played the French Irene Dunne, this time with Albert Préjean, and Richard Pottier's *La Ferme aux loups*, a comedy/mystery set in a newspaper milieu which introduced another newcomer, Martine Carole.

Two adaptations of comedy/mysteries by S. A. Steeman were undoubtedly designed to copy the light-hearted style and sophisticated banter of *The Thin Man* series. With Pierre Fresnay as the suave Inspector Wens and Suzy Delair as his screwball girlfriend, Mila-Malou, Continental struck gold with *Le Dernier des six* (Georges Lacombe) and its sequel, *L'Assassin habite au 21* (Henri-Georges Clouzot's directorial debut).

In both films, the complicated murder plot is secondary to the sparring relationship between the couple. Henri-Georges Clouzot's dialogue for both films maintains an acerbically comic tone throughout. One exchange, in *Le Dernier des six*, between Fresnay and a nightclub owner played by André Luguet is typical:

Sir, my name is Wenceslas Vorobeietchik.
That's not my fault.
And I am also the commissioner of police.
Then naturally you are dismayed.
And I am the lover of Mlle. Mila-Malou.
Then I will give you some advice: get a new name, a
   new job, and a new mistress.

Not content with a snappy comedy/mystery à la Dashiell Hammett, Continental decided to throw a dash of Busby Berkeley into *Le Dernier des six*. Since the film took place in a music-hall milieu, it felt no compunction about adding an elaborate production number, with overhead shots of chorus girls forming flowers, stop action to produce naked chorus girls on a winding staircase, double exposures of the chorus on top of a jet of water, a woman in a glass of champagne, and a through-the-legs tracking shot of cancan dancers. Director Lacombe felt the sequence ruined the film, however, and refused to shoot it. Continental fired Lacombe and the sequence was shot by Jean Dréville.[23]

Other formula films of an American type included the Simenon adaptation *Picpus* (Richard Pottier) and *Cécile est morte* (Maurice Tourneur), both starring Albert Préjean as inspector Maigret.

Not all of Continental's films were American in concept—certain popular French styles were cultivated as well. No doubt the Germans were puzzled by the French mania for Fernandel, but his success in France was assured and they starred him in three films: *Le Club des Soupirants* (Maurice Gleize), *Simplet*, and *Adrien* (both directed by Fernandel). The popular singer, Tino Rossi, was another acquired taste. In Richard Pottier's *Mon Amour est près de toi*, Rossi played a singer who loses his memory while dressed in the costume of a bum, and finds love and a pastoral idyll as he leads the romantic life of the open road. The film was one of the biggest hits of fall 1943.

Nor did Continental ignore the classics of French literature. André Cayatte's *Au Bonheur des Dames*, based on Zola, was a careful recreation of Second Empire Paris, which showed the death struggle between tradition and progress, represented by small shopkeepers versus modern merchandizers. Whether the enormous success of the film was due to the painstaking recreation of period detail (a department store circa 1850, an outdoor divertissement with hundreds of dress extras, period acrobats, etc.) or to the reappearance of Michel Simon after three years in Italy, the film was certainly one of the best of the historical reconstructions which would become especially popular in France during the occupation.

Cayatte, who made his directorial debut at Continental in 1942 with the highly popular *La Fausse Maîtresse*, with Darrieux and adapted from Balzac, was less successful with his adaptation of De Maupassant's *Pierre et Jean*, whose action was updated to 1910 and the contemporary era. But Maurice Tourneur's *Mam'zelle Bonaparte*, another costume drama, starring Edwige Feuillère, became one of the two biggest hits in France in the spring of 1942.[24]

A reasonable analogy can be proposed to suggest that Continental was the MGM of French studios during the occupation. Its product was star-studded and "tasteful," similar in type to such films as *Naughty Marietta*, *Dinner at Eight*, or *David Copperfield*. For the most part, the company eschewed controversy, preferring subjects that were politically innocuous and assuredly popular.

Not all of Continental's films managed to avoid political controversy, however. Of the thirty films it produced, three were bitterly attacked by the Resistance press, and banned after the Liberation.[25] These three films, *La Vie de plaisir*, *Les Inconnus dans la Maison*, and *Le Corbeau*, were offered as evidence by the clandestine paper *L'Ecran Français* that Continental intended to subvert the French public by offering anti-French propaganda. Of Albert Valentin's *La Vie de plaisir*, written by Charles Spaak, *L'Ecran Français* wrote:

> For those who are still in doubt, who refused to see in *Les Inconnus dans la maison*, *Le Corbeau* and other Continental productions, a systematic desire to degrade and diminish France, *La Vie de plaisir* brings us striking proof. In seeing this film one might believe that this time, having been unmasked by us, Continental decided to unveil themselves openly. The film, which is an outrageous attack on the nobility and the clergy has no other goal than to serve as propaganda in exploiting the so-called bad taste of the public, and in presenting certain clichés which, in the Nazi spirit, might have found a warm welcome from the masses. (June 1944)

This odd attack by the left-wing press on a film intended as a satire on aristocratic manners was joined by the clergy, who objected to such scenes as a bishop blessing a pack of dogs before the hunt and counselling his nephew to arrange an abortion for his mistress. Yet the film was one of the few overtly anti-bourgeois films made during the occupation, and one wonders whether it would not have been applauded by the same press if it had been produced by a French company.

The story, told in flashbacks, concerns a "man of the people" (Albert Préjean) married to an aristocrat. Beginning with their divorce proceedings, the scenes of their married life are commented on, in voice-over, by the opposing attorneys. The film's notoriety might have made it successful at the box office, had it not been released on May 16, 1944, shortly before Parisian theaters closed until after the Liberation.

Henri Decoin's Les Inconnus dans la Maison, with a script by Clouzot, was a big success at the box office in 1942, and roused L'Ecran Français's ire for showing France as "a weakened nation, a republic of Apaches." The paper also claimed, erroneously, that the film was shown in Germany as Die Französische Jugend (Youth of France).[26]

This comparatively mild charge against the film is surprising, for Les Inconnus is the only French feature film of the period that can legitimately be charged with an anti-Semitic bias. The story, from a Simenon novel, concerns a provincial lawyer, Loursat (Raimu), who had withdrawn from society and become an alcoholic when his wife left him twenty years before. Unknown to the self-pitying Loursat, his daughter Nicole had become involved with a crowd of juvenile delinquents, who turned casually to crime. When a body is discovered in Loursat's house, Nicole's boyfriend is accused of the murder, and Loursat, intrigued, agrees to defend him.

The first two-thirds of the film are typically Simenonian views of the haute bourgeoisie of the provinces—Loursat's sister, an indolent and overprotective mother of the leader of the gang; the town notables more concerned with protecting their reputation than seeing that justice is done. In the climactic courtroom scene, Loursat gives an impassioned speech, condemning the town and the parents for their failure to take charge of their children.[27]

Finally, through a series of brilliant cross-examinations, the real murderer confesses—the accused's friend, Ephraim Louska, an evident "foreigner" and outsider.

Unlike the novel, which is pointedly anti-Semitic (Louska has an unpleasant smell), the murderer in the film is never overtly identified as a Jew, although few in the audience would have failed to make that assumption (he was played by an Arab actor, Marcel Mouloudji). To reinforce the point, the film was shown with an anti-Semitic propaganda short, Les Corrupteurs, on its initial release.

In the film's defense, it must be pointed out that Louska is a minor character in the film, which was undoubtedly intended as a condemnation of the selfishness and irresponsibility of bourgeois parents. Like La Vie de plaisir and Le Corbeau, these films took advantage of Continental's freedom from Vichy's censorship restrictions to blast the sacrosanct icons of Vichy ideology (Church, family, youth), only to be accused of anti-French propaganda. Since Le Corbeau is the best-known of these films, these charges will be discussed in a long analysis of the film in chapter 8.

It is doubtful that Greven in any way encouraged his staff to make "anti-French" films. Greven's major concern was to make money, and "épater le bourgeois" was good box office especially in a period when most films hewed to the most inoffensive conventionality.

A few filmmakers working at Continental took advantage of the relative freedom from censorship constraints provided by Continental to insert veiled messages of nationalism and even resistance in their films. If Continental had been concerned with the political positions of the films made under its sponsorship, at least three of them would have caused it some discomfort.

Maurice Tourneur's La Main du Diable, with a script by Jean-Paul le Chanois, based on Gérard de Nerval's La Main enchantée, was an atmospheric variation on the Faust myth, whose style recalled the German Expressionist classics of the 1920s. With Pierre Fresnay as a talentless painter who sells his soul for the magical hand of the devil, the film was regarded by many people in France as a political allegory, condemning collaboration with the devil's emissaries. The painter dies in his struggle with the devil, but his soul is saved. The French audiences who flocked to see the film in June 1943 could scarcely have overlooked the meaning of the ending, which had already been expressed in a similar way in the popular Les Visiteurs du soir.

Nor did it take much imagination for French audiences to understand the ending of L'Assassinat du Père Noël, Continental's first production, directed by Christian-Jaque with a screenplay by Charles Spaak. Based on a novel by Pierre Véry, the film was a poetic fantasy set in the French Alps (filmed in Chamonix), with Harry Baur as a Santa Claus figure named Père Cornus. The fairy-tale story, filmed by Christian-Jaque in the vertiginous moving camera style that was his trademark, resolved itself happily with Père Cornus' Sleeping Beauty-like daughter married to the hand-some Prince Charming. It may have been this context which blinded Continental's producers to the real meaning of the film's final dialogue, in which the visuals coyly tracked from Cornus, the globe-maker, and one of his child admirers, through the pine trees to the happy couple.

> Boy: Where is China?
> Cornus, pointing to the globe: Here.
> Boy: And the little Chinese children, do they also have a Father Christmas.
> Cornus: Yes, a Father Christmas and a Father Cornus, all that they need to be happy.
> Boy: And what stories do they tell to these little Chinese children?
> Cornus: They tell of France, and of little French chil-dren, and also of a certain beautiful princess who fell asleep in her chair. And she has been asleep a long time. One might have thought she was dead. And there are those who would have thought so, but they are wrong. She was very much alive and in her sleep she had a dream, a marvelous dream, always the same one. She dreamt of a Prince Charming who would one day come and awaken her and bring her happiness.[28]

The expectation or hope of eventual liberation was a rarely expressed sentiment in 1941. Far more common was an incipient reappearance of French nationalism, which was discreetly encouraged by Vichy. Vichy-inspired films were, not surprisingly, filled with homilies about the glories of the French past and the eternity of the French spirit, but it is surprising that the most nationalistic film made during the occupation was made for Continental.

Christian-Jaque's *La Symphonie Fantastique*, with Jean-Louis Barrault as Hector Berlioz, inspired Joseph Goebbels to remark: "The film is of excellent quality and amounts to a first-class national fanfare. I shall unfortunately not be able to release it for public showing." [29]

The film was released, however, on April 1, 1942, and had a very successful commercial run. The script, by Jean-Pierre Feydeau and H. A. Legrand, emphasized the rebellious roots of Berlioz' romanticism, and his association with the "Jeune France" of Victor Hugo, Prosper Mérimée, Alexandre Dumas, Eugène Delacroix, and the other heroes of the French Romantic movement in such dialogue as:

> Hugo: Long live "Young France."
> Mérimée: We will be friends in glory as well as in sadness.
> Berlioz: Long live "Young France." A fine name, gentlemen.
> Hugo: It will be yours as well. France is all that is brilliant. Youth, everything that shines . . .

The producer spared no expense on this excessively Romantic production. For a short sequence depicting the triumphant reception of Berlioz' *Symphonie Funèbre et Triomphale* in St. Petersburg, Christian-Jaque and his conductor, Paul Guillot, amassed 500 musicians, five conductors, and both a men's and women's choir. [30] The finale, of the *Requiem*, was shot in the chapel of Les Invalides, and ends with the image of Berlioz superimposed over the cathedral and Hugo's epitaph, "he was a martyr to his era."

Conclusion

In May 1944, there were rumors that Continental's assets were to be bought by MGM. [31] But the sale never materialized. After the Liberation, the French government seized Continental's property and other assets. A distribution company was formed to handle Continental's films, many of which were then released abroad as examples of French film artistry. The French were ambivalent about Continental—economically, they regarded it as one of the many attempts by the occupier to colonize the French film industry; yet, culturally, the French insisted on regarding Continental's production as representative of the indomitable French spirit.

If, as the reparations commission claimed, "economically, the occupier sought to make the French cinema a kind of subsidiary of the German cinema,"[32] it was not entirely successful. The German film office in France succeeded neither in preventing French production nor in imposing German-made films on French audiences. The success of Continental Films, while redounding financially to German interests, depended on the idiosyncracies of French artists, who maintained a stubborn intransigence toward their employers.

The difficulties presented by Continental Films are not limited to determining whether the films it produced were French or German. Far more troubling are the political and moral issues arising from the very existence of a German-owned film company in occupied France. These issues are addressed in a discussion of German aims toward the French cinema in chapter 7. It will only be pointed out here that Continental occupies a paradoxical place in the history of the French cinema of the occupation. Because Continental was owned by the Germans, some filmmakers who worked for the company were accused by their countrymen of collaboration with the enemy. Yet, by virtue of its being German, Continental provided filmmakers with more economic and political freedom than did any other production company in France. The ultimate paradox of Continental Films is that, by establishing their own presence within the French film industry, the Germans helped assure the survival of the French cinema.

Chapter 4

The Film Industry
and the Jews

L ike many areas of French cultural and intel-
lectual life before the war, the French film in-
dustry benefited from the influx of Jews and other refugees. France's
historic status as an asylum for those persecuted in other parts
of the world had encouraged many emigré writers, directors, producers, and technicians to work for the French cinema. For example, among the important directors who worked in France in
the thirties were Fritz Lang, Anatole Litvak, Max Ophuls, and Billy
Wilder.

For many of the emigrés, France was merely a stopover
on the way to Hollywood. Yet, the refugees were responsible for
some of the greatest films produced during the "golden age" of
the thirties. They left a permanent mark on the French cinema.

After the fall of France, the degree to which the French
cinema had been influenced by these refugees, particularly the Jews,
became a major issue—not only to the Germans, but to Vichy as
well. Although their reasons were different, both Vichy and the
Germans were determined to rid the film industry of any taint of
Jewish influence.

The first two German ordinances concerning the film industry went into effect on September 9, 1940. Both were in-

tended, in large part, to assure the "Aryanization" of the industry. The first, "Concerning the Operation of Cinema Theaters and Film Rental Offices," mandated that all exhibitors and distributors receive permission to operate from the Military Command. This law was enacted to assure that only non-Jews could own exhibition and distribution firms.

The second law, "Concerning the Admission of Films for Public Presentation," required all films to be passed by the German authorities before they could be shown, and served a double function. It both limited the number of films available on the market, and more importantly, it assured that no films made by Jewish personnel would be exhibited.

The prewar films banned during the occupation were not primarily those whose political content might be suspect (although films made during the "drôle de guerre" were banned on October 17, 1940), but rather those films in which personnel who were "non-Aryan" or "enemies of the Reich" had been involved. Thus, while Duvivier's Popular Front-inspired *La Belle Equipe* and Renoir's *Le Crime de* M. *Lange* (which was re-released in 1943) were permitted, films starring such Jewish actors as Jean-Pierre Aumont and Marcel Dalio, or made by emigré directors like Robert Siodmak, were banned.

In September 1941, the Filmprüfstelle compiled two lists, for internal use, of Jewish and non-Jewish proscribed personnel (R141/F1025-1029). The first was a list of "non-Jewish filmworkers" whose films were not to be allowed exhibition. Among these non-Jewish personnel were German emigrés Lilian Harvey, Marlene Dietrich, and Conrad Veidt, French emigrés Michèle Morgan, Charles Boyer, and Simone Simon, directors of "hate films" (i.e., anti-Nazi films) Joris Ivens and Pierre Billon, as well as figures peripheral to the film industry such as Thomas Mann.[1]

The second list was of French Jews in the film industry, and oddly overlapped the first list. Director Germaine Dulac was on both lists, identified as a Jew and a Communist. She managed to prove to the Germans' satisfaction that she was neither, and worked on newsreels in the unoccupied zone until her death in 1942. Certainly the most curious name on these lists was that of

Fred Astaire, the only American identified by name. Since all American films and film stars were automatically banned, the Filmprüfstelle stated that there was no need to identify them individually. Yet Astaire is listed as "American, enemy of Germany, Jew," although for what reason is not known.

Those producers who hoped to re-release films with forbidden personnel had the option of removing the offending names from the credits, or in the case of actors, to cut the scenes in question or to reshoot them with actors acceptable to the Germans. Some actors refused to refilm another actor's role, despite pressures to conform. Roger Blin nearly lost his professional card, and with it the right to work, for refusing to reshoot his scenes with the actor who substituted for Dalio in Marc Allégret's *Entrée des artistes*.[2] Other filmmakers were less sensitive, and reluctantly accepted German demands. Director Jean Delannoy, for example, had finished shooting *Macao* by June 1940, but it had not yet been released. The film was highly praised at clandestine screenings and the director was eager for the critical recognition the film would bring him. However, the film starred a particular *bête noire* to the Germans—Erich von Stroheim. Delannoy reshot Stroheim's part with Pierre Renoir in the lead, and this version was released in 1941 as *L'Enfer du jeu*.

First Legal Measures Against Jews

Ridding the movie screens of France of Jewish and other undesirable images was only a small portion of the Filmprüfstelle's concerns. In line with overall German policy, measures had to be taken to assure that all Jews be isolated from economic and social activities, as a first step toward the "final solution."

In the occupied zone, the first general law concerning Jews was issued on September 27, 1940. It forbade the return of Jews who had fled the occupied zone, and mandated a registry of all remaining Jews. The second German law, of October 18, 1940, mandated the assignment of Aryan administrators to all Jewish property. (Confiscation of property belonging to Jews who had left the occupied zone had already begun.) On April 26, 1941, Jews were

banned from all professions "involving public contact or authority over Aryan employees."

Of the laws directly affecting film industry personnel, the
first was issued by the Propaganda Abteilung on November 26,
1940, and directed all members of the film profession to be cleared
for work by the Military Command. Although this directive effectively eliminated Jews from the film profession, it was not until
June 5, 1942, that a decree specifically banning Jews from the film
industry was passed. By then, deportations to concentration camps
had already begun.

Despite later protests by Vichy officials that anti-Jewish
measures were forced on them by the Germans, many of Vichy's
anti-Jewish laws actually antedate those in the occupied zone. The
first such law, of October 3, 1940, enumerated the professions
henceforth banned to all Jews. Article 5 specified:

> Under no circumstances may Jews occupy the following
> professions . . . directors, administrators, managers of
> enterprises whose object is the manufacture, produc-
> tion, distribution or presentation of cinematographic film;
> film directors or chief cameramen; administrators or
> managers of theaters; entrepreneurs of entertainment
> shows.[3]

The same law also empowered the government to order the internment of all non-French Jews.

It is well-established that Vichy's anti-Semitic policy was
not merely a result of German pressure, but was rather a natural
outgrowth of decades of anti-Semitism among right-wing political
groups.[4] One of the major concerns of these groups had been the
dominance of Jews in certain professions, among them the film
industry. As early as 1935, Bardèche and Brasillach could remark:
"Rug sellers, Rumanians, Arabs or Poles, adventurers of all kinds,
who made themselves masters of a portion of the cinema, wors-
ened its economic situation through procedures that would have
been menacing to the future of any industry, and which naturally

drew all production, and French production in particular, toward a definitive mediocritv."[5]

Critic and novelist Lucien Rebatet, who wrote under the pseudonym of François Vinneuil, published a flagrantly anti-Semitic tract in 1941, titled *Les Tribus du cinéma et du théâtre* (The Tribes of the Cinema and Theatre), which blamed every misfortune of the French cinema for the previous ten years on "those most depraved Jews, the most pernicious, those convicted of the worst crimes, those with the most disquieting political pasts, spongers on the stock exchange, pillagers, provocateurs, agitators, pimps, sellers of young boys, whores and drugs."[6] Such posturings were not altogether Nazi-inspired. Vinneuil had been a well-known anti-Semite in the 1930s whose ideas had merely come into fashion at last.

The degree of anti-Semitic propaganda in prewar France may be gauged by the fact that the government of the Third Republic passed a law in April 1939, outlawing anti-Semitic articles and remarks in the press. One of Vichy's first measures was to rescind that law. Other laws—the internment of foreign Jews, officially sanctioned job and housing discrimination against all Jews—soon followed. Vichy's policy was not, however, aimed at the extermination of the Jews. Vichy's goal was to isolate Jews economically and prevent them from practicing professions with influence (medicine, law, etc.). Compared to the Nazis, Vichy anti-Semitic policy was lenient, and those Jews who could do so fled occupied France for the relative safety of the unoccupied zone.

Most of the prominent Jews in the film industry had left Paris before the Germans entered, and many eventually settled on the Côte d'Azur. Despite Vichy's measures to eliminate all Jewish influence from the film industry, the collaborationist newspapers in Paris accused the "Jewish cabal" of plotting to take over the film industry in the South. While such charges were absurd, it is likely that a few early productions in the unoccupied zone were financed, via third parties, by Jewish producers.[7] By June 1941, however, the Filmprüfstelle could boast that "the entire French film industry is completely without Jews" (R141/F652).

Economic Measures Against the Jews

For both Vichy and the Germans, professional isolation of Jews was insufficient to guarantee France's purity. Economic measures had to be taken to assure that no Jew benefited from the new order. These economic measures were profitable as well, both to the regimes and to their supporters.

In the occupied zone, the Propaganda Abteilung confiscated the most desirable Jewish-owned film businesses for German interests and then assigned provisional administrators to the rest.[8] Vichy instituted a similar system of provisional administrators in July 1941. The administrators in both zones were generally French. They received salaries from the proceeds of the concerns they ran, as well as a percentage of the profit if the business was liquidated or sold.[9]

The total number of Jewish businesses seized was approximately 40,000 in the occupied zone, and 1,900 in the South.[10] It is therefore apparent that finding administrators and buyers for these businesses was not difficult, at least in the early years of the occupation. That this practice was not universally approved, however, is evident from a notice published in Le Tout Cinéma in 1942.

> A large number of cinemas, formerly Jewish, have been Aryanized. It does not seem to us useful to publish a list of theaters in the hands of a provisional administrator. The publication of such a list could cause prejudice to the present proprietors, who have purchased these establishments in good faith and according to the law. (p. 105)

The provisional administrators were not the only members of the film community to benefit from these confiscations.[11] Many firms were liquidated outright or acquired at bargain rates by businessmen who already had substantial holdings in the film industry, thus reducing competition. Thus, the anti-Jewish measures accentuated the trend toward oligopoly which had been an outgrowth of Vichy's overall economic policy. According to figures compiled by the Filmprüfstelle in April 1942, the number of producers had been reduced from 410 in 1939 to 42 in 1942. Distributors declined from 419 to 52 in the same period (R142/F612). For those who remained, the economic advantages were obvious.

Some businessmen took advantage of the anti-Jewish laws in other ways. A communiqué issued by the COIC in 1942 noted that "in order to avoid paying their debts, some debtors have been demanding proof that the debt-holder is not Jewish" (Le Film, March 14, 1942). Certainly, it was not only the Nazis who reaped financial benefits from the persecution of the Jews.

The Germans were, of course, the most dedicated persecutors. The Filmprüfstelle noted in its reports on March 5 and 13, 1941, that Minerva Films would not receive a production permit because 10 percent of its stock was in Jewish hands; that the Propaganda Abteilung had appointed new heads for Gaumont to replace their Jewish directors, and that Pathé's board was to meet soon to "secure the complete Aryanization of its personnel and capital."

Anti-Jewish Propaganda

Vichy's primary interest in Jewish matters was economic. The Germans' propaganda machine was directed, however, toward making the unthinkable acceptable. Before Jews could be rounded up and shipped out of France, public opinion had to be oriented toward the acceptance of extreme measures.

The occupiers employed all their resources in disseminating anti-Jewish propaganda. The Parisian press, which was controlled by the Propaganda Abteilung, was particularly useful in creating an atmosphere that encouraged even nonpolitical writers to engage in casual anti-Semitism. Thus Le Film, in an otherwise straightforward obituary for Henri Chomette (René Clair's brother) added that his career had been destroyed by Jewish producers because he had founded a society in 1933 that was opposed to Jewish interests in film (August 30, 1941). Critic (later screenwriter) Nino Frank, an iconoclast who later ran afoul of German censorship, could offhandedly denounce Jewish control over the prewar industry in the course of an attack against the moralism of

Vichy censors in *Les Nouveaux Temps* (September 13, 1941). Radio programs also kept up the anti-Jewish barrage. Radio-Paris had a weekly program devoted to the "Jewish question" and at least one well-known actor, Robert le Vigan, lent his voice to the attack.

On September 4, 1941, a major exposition opened at the Palais Berlitz, called "Le Juif et la France." It was sponsored by L'Institut d'Étude des Questions Juives (Institute for the Study of Jewish questions), with funds from the German Embassy. Among the halls devoted to the "Jewish problem" was an entire room given over to "The Jew and the Cinema," where pictures of Jewish actors, technicians, and producers lined the walls. The catalogue for this exhibition noted of Jewish producers:

> All of their productions, whether they are noteworthy, or valueless, or luxurious, reflect their attraction for depravity. Whether they are American or French, criminals are their heroes. The noxious effects of these unhealthy subjects instill us with the venom of vice.[12]

To combat the "pro-Jewish propaganda" of these productions, the Germans provided films which showed the "truth" about the Jews. The feature film *Jud Süss* was one of the hits of the 1941 season throughout France, but not all the German propaganda films achieved this popularity. *Le Péril Juif*, a French version of *Der Ewige Jude* (1940) released in 1941, was a reconstructed documentary feature purporting to show the baseness of Jewish customs and beliefs. It was distributed without charge to any theater that would take it, and failing to get sufficient response was shown privately to meetings of youth and right-wing organizations (R142/F123).

Only one anti-Semitic film is known to have been made in France by French personnel. *Les Corrupteurs* (1942) was directed by ex-screenwriter Pierre Ramelot for German-controlled Nova-Films. This fifty-minute film was shown on the same bill as *Les Inconnus dans la Maison*, thus achieving wide distribution. It showed the evil influence of the Jews through three short narratives. In the first, a young man "influenced by the Judeo-American gangster films, becomes a depraved criminal. The second shows a young girl who wants to become a movie actress, but is turned into a prostitute by Jewish producers. The third shows the ruin of small investors, fleeced by Jewish bankers" (Le Film, September 12, 1942). The Filmprüfstelle, in its report of November 28, 1942, noted that the film had a mixed reception—at some theaters it was applauded, while in others audiences hissed. German newsreels, which were shown in every theater, also kept up a barrage of anti-Semitic propaganda. These newsreels were so detested by audiences, however, that they probably generated more sympathy than ill will for the Jews.[13]

Extermination of the Jews

The goal of this propaganda was to encourage a tacit acceptance of the measures to come. In May 1942, Jews in the occupied zone were required to wear a yellow star—a measure the French public found repellent, and which was opposed by Vichy in the unoccupied zone. Two months later, arrest of non-French Jews began in both zones. In the Paris area alone, nearly 13,000 people were arrested between July 16 and 19, and held at the Vélodrome d'Hiver, before being shipped first to the prison at Drancy and then to Auschwitz.[14] Although some 9,000 foreign Jews were handed over to the Germans for deportation in the summer of 1942 by the Vichy police, officials in the unoccupied zone firmly refused to arrest French citizens. Those who could fled the occupied zone for the South, but their refuge was temporary. On November 11, 1942, German armies occupied the entire French territory, and the Jewish population of France was rounded up and sent to death camps. Of the estimated 75,000 Jews deported, less than 3,000 returned.[15]

Most of the Jews in the film industry were among the fortunate group with money and connections. Many left for the United States or other neutral countries at the beginning of the occupation. Others lived in hiding, protected by friends. Because many of the Jews in the film industry congregated in Nice, they were protected until September 1943, by the relative benevolence of the Italian occupation of that city. Luigi Freddi, head of the Italian State Film Office and Cinecittà, claimed in his memoirs that he employed scriptwriter Curt Alexander on the film *Les Petites du Quai aux Fleurs* during this period. But following the Badoglio armistice, the Germans occupied this territory as well, and Alexander died in the camps.[16]

There is no record of other film-related personalities who were deported, although there were undoubtedly film industry personnel among the French victims in the death camps. With one exception, the most famous of the Jews in the film community went into hiding or exile, protecting themselves against the ultimate horror of the Nazi occupation.

The most famous member of France's film community to suffer the full measure of Nazi persecution was actor Harry Baur. Baur had been one of the most popular stars of the thirties, appearing in such important films as *Poil de Carotte*, *Crime et Châtiment*, *Un Carnet de Bal*, and *Volpone*. After film production resumed in the occupied zone in February 1941, Baur appeared in the first production of the German-owned company, Continental Films—Christian-Jaque's *L'Assassinat du Père Noel*. He later starred in Maurice Tourneur's *Péchés de jeunesse*, also made for Continental.

On September 27, 1941, *Le Film* announced that Baur had left for Berlin to make a film for Tobis. The film was Hans Bertram's *Symphonie eines Lebens*, and was released in Germany in 1943. Baur did not live to see the film's release. The Filmprüfstelle report in May 1943 noted simply that "the famous actor, Harry Baur, died on April 8, 1943" (R141/F1100). No obituary appeared in the trade or popular press.

The mystery of Harry Baur's death remains unsolved. David Hull, in his *Film in the Third Reich*, maintains that Baur was a Jew who had managed to conceal the fact from the Germans, but was discovered and died in a concentration camp.[17] The anonymous author of an article in *Les Dossiers du Clan* claims that Baur's crime was having a Jewish wife, and that although he was released from imprisonment, he died of the wounds and illness that followed his detention.[18] As to why a man wishing to conceal his religious background would risk working in Germany, Sacha Guitry maintained that "his trouble was greed for money. He was rich, but he had to have more. He obtained forged papers to show that he was not a Jew, was paid 6 million francs to star in a big film in Berlin, was detected and died in a French prison." [19]

A more heroic account of Harry Baur's "crime" and death is provided by Robert Aron, citing an account published just after the Liberation by the newspaper *Résistance*.[20] According to this version, Baur was released from the French prison of Cherche-Midi on September 19, 1942:

> This great actor was unrecognizable. He had lost 37 kilos. His body was one great sore. For four months, he had been forced to wear the same suit and shirt.
>
> Held in secret, he was forbidden to receive packages, linen, food or medicine. He was deprived of the iodine medication he had been taking for years. Among the cruelties he had been forced to endure by his accusers must be added the progressive breakdown of his health.
>
> As he had arrived on death's doorstep, the Nazis sent him home, with the proviso that he not leave his apartment.

Aron continues that the principal accusation against Baur was

> that each time Baur traveled to Germany, he used the opportunity to effect the escape of several prisoners. He was also accused of being Jewish . . .
>
> From the beginning of the occupation, he had shown an anti-German attitude and had financed the beginnings of a resistance movement. When his son, Cécil Gran, announced to him on June 18, 1940, that he was leaving for London, Baur answered "I regret not being able to follow you." But he helped numerous young people to reach England.

Sacha Guitry, who was imprisoned after the Liberation for his collaborationist activities, self-servingly prefers to see Baur as a victim of his own weaknesses, rather than as an example of the horrors collaboration led to. The account in *Résistance* is no less self-serving in creating a Resistance hero out of Baur. Both accounts disengage the authors from any responsibility for the fate of Baur and other French Jews (if he was indeed a Jew). If Baur's tragedy was brought on by his own actions, then those who stood by without protesting, without helping, were not implicated in his fate. In the immediate post-Liberation period, it is easy to understand why few recognized their own culpability in allowing the Nazis to apply the final solution in France.

The Underground Jews

Public protest would have been suicidal, but there were some who risked their lives to save Jewish comrades. Such was the case of the Prévert brothers, who shielded their friends, composer Joseph Kosma and designer Alexandre Trauner, hidden throughout the occupation in small towns in Provence. It is now well-known that Kosma and Trauner were responsible for the music and sets of the two Jacques Prévert–Marcel Carné collaborations of the period: *Les Visiteurs du soir* and *Les Enfants du Paradis*. What is less well-known is the number of people who were actively or tacitly involved in the deception.

Carné recounts in his memoirs that by 1942 both Trauner and Kosma were penniless, but too proud to accept handouts. He and Prévert therefore hired them to work on *Les Visiteurs*. Carné was to serve as the go-between with the two men who had agreed to serve as "fronts." Trauner suggested that Carné speak to Georges Wakhevitch, "who didn't hesitate to accept" (p. 193). Wakhevitch did insist that Trauner not show his designs to anyone but Carné and himself, and that they be executed in Wakhevitch's own atelier.

To find a front for Kosma was somewhat more difficult. The director of production suggested Maurice Thiriet, who at first declined, out of fear, but was finally persuaded to accept.

The participation of these outlawed men was an open secret in the industry. Producer André Paulvé was one of the more courageous producers, and was himself later threatened by the

Germans for employing members of the Resistance, among other charges. Even Louis-Emile Galey, director of Vichy's Cinema Section, was in on the secret.[21]

Other cases of Jewish participation in film production included Joseph Kosma's score for *Adieu, Léonard* (Pierre Prévert), and Jean Wiéner's scores for Autant-Lara's *Le Mariage de Chiffon*, Robert Vernay's *Le Père Goriot*, and Louis Daquin's *Le Voyageur de la Toussaint* and *Madame et le mort* (all officially credited to Roger Desormière). In his memoirs, Wiéner described the cloak and dagger procedure by which his participation was arranged:

> Daquin phoned me to tell me I should go to a café in front of the studio at 9 o'clock the next morning. I was to wait there until I saw a short woman carrying cans of film. I was then to follow this woman [whom he described]. "You understand, we no longer know each other. I only know Roger Desormière. Be careful."[22]

That the Germans did not discover these deceptions must be considered something of a miracle, for they overlooked no accusation or rumor. Among the important (and thoroughly Gentile) figures who were investigated by the Propaganda Abteilung were Viviane Romance, Abel Gance, and Sacha Guitry.

Notwithstanding the Propaganda Abteilung's diligence in investigating the origins of France's film colony, one of its failures is truly astounding. On the Filmprüfstelle's list of Jews in the profession compiled in September 1941, the name J.-P. Dreyfuss appears. Jean-Paul Dreyfuss had been an assistant to Renoir during the thirties, and had directed documentaries for the left-wing Ciné-Liberté group. With the advent of the occupation, Dreyfuss chose to abandon his father's name and instead used his mother's maiden name of le Chanois. With this pseudonym, he claims he was given a "certificate of not belonging to the Jewish race," and could thus work.[23]

What is astounding about le Chanois's case is that he worked for Continental Films, the German owned and operated production company in Paris. As a scriptwriter for Continental, he wrote the screenplays for two Simenon adaptations, *Picpus* and *Cécile est morte*, as well as the original scenario for Maurice Tourneur's *La Main du Diable*.

According to Roger Richebé (then director of the COIC), the head of Continental, Alfred Greven, knew that le Chanois was Dreyfuss. One day, in the course of a conversation, Greven remarked that "in the cinema, Jews are the best." When Richebé did not respond to this remark, Greven added, "I have a Jew working for me, but he doesn't know that I know."[24] Richebé thought Greven was joking, and only later found out that le Chanois was not only Dreyfuss, but was called Bayard in his resistance cell. For not only did Greven have a half-Jew in his employ, but one of the leaders of the Comité de Libération du Cinéma Français.

After the Liberation, le Chanois released his film *Au Coeur de l'orage*, which included footage shot clandestinely among the maquis of Vercors. He went on to have a successful career as a film director.

Conclusion

Within the context of the fate of Europe's Jews as a whole, the Jewish individuals prominent in France's film industry were relatively privileged. Most of them survived the occupation and returned to their activities in the film industry after the war.

Yet within the context of the history of French filmmaking during the occupation, the fate of these Jews becomes a touchstone against which the industry's accomplishments must be measured. If the French film industry managed to save itself, it did so by shutting its eyes to those individuals who lost their homes, their livelihoods, and sometimes their lives. The leaders of the French film industry felt a justifiable pride in having assured the survival of a relatively independent cinema in the face of pressure from both Vichy and the Germans. But in the matter of the Jews, the industry gave way to the pressure and what they sacrificed was not the prestige of the French cinema but human lives. The final accounting of the French film industry during the occupation must not overlook their failure.

Chapter 5

"An Industry Made of Gold": Production 1941–1942

B y June 1941, the "new France" was in place. With their political presence ratified, and a new economic and "Aryan" order established, the Germans turned their attention eastward to the Soviet Union. For French society as a whole, having accommodated itself as well as possible to the new order, the middle years of the occupation were years of relative stability. For the French film industry, June 1941 marked the beginning of its rebirth.[1]

One month after Continental began production of its first two films, L'*Assassinat du Père Noël* and Le *Dernier des six*, the Filmprüfstelle finally instructed the COIC to begin submitting film projects for consideration. After more than a year of inactivity, Parisian film studios reopened to French production on June 3, 1941, with the start of Pathé's *Romance de Paris* and Roger Richebé's *Madame Sans-Gêne*.

This victory for French film interests was not made without accommodation to the new political order. At the ceremony celebrating the reopening of Pathé's studio, Raoul Ploquin of the COIC spoke, congratulating the board of directors for taking Pathé out of "unworthy hands," as Dr. Diedrich and Major Schmidtke of the Propaganda Abteilung looked on.[2]

France was becoming Germanized and the film industry reflected the change. Sometimes, the presence of the Germans caused unexpected problems. Roger Richebé recounts in his memoirs an incident that occurred while shooting *Madame Sans-Gêne*. The story, based on a Sardou play, was set in the Napoleonic era, necessitating the use of an authentic chateau dating from that time. The site selected was the château de Grosbois, located outside of Paris. The house was occupied, however, by the commander of the Luftwaffe in France.

> By the hierarchical route [i.e., through the COIC], I sought authorization . . . which was accorded with one condition. I had to specify the day and hour of the shooting for the general. Although I tried to explain that shooting exteriors depended less on my desires than on those of that God who makes rain and clear weather, he would have none of it. Thus I set a precise moment for the arrival of the imperial coach before the terrace of Grosbois. Alas, the good Lord was in a bad mood that day and hid the sun behind enormous black clouds.

When Richebé reapplied for permission to shoot, it was turned down because the general, "who was undoubtedly bored between bombing sorties, had organized a reception with an impressive buffet where his guests were to have been greeted with the spectacle of a heroic but roguish Napoleon in the arms of the impulsive and ravishing Arletty." Annoyed at being stood up, the general refused further contact with the group.

Unable to accomplish anything through official channels, Richebé arranged, through contacts, for the shooting to be carried on secretly. The matter was handled by a young German officer who spoke excellent French, "with a slight British accent."[3]

This young officer, whom Arletty refers to in her memoirs as Hans S., was to become her lover and the cause of her imprisonment for a year and a half after the Liberation. In her version of the events, the weather was perfect the day before the filming was to begin when, by some caprice of the general's, permission to shoot was cancelled. Richebé, furious, fulminated against the officer in charge, a certain S. Arletty, who had met this young German of the "Conrad Veidt type," decided to "play Boule de Suif"; "S. agreed to overlook the breaking of protocol which by now had become a diplomatic incident, on the condition that I appear at exactly 8 a.m. in front of the château de Grosbois—he would be there to open the gate . . . And thus it began."[4]

The whims of the occupiers were only one of the new conditions faced by French producers in 1941. A far more basic change had occurred within the structure of the film industry itself. The anarchic free market of the prewar French film industry had given way to a planned and hierarchical structure along German lines. The COIC served as the focal point, mediating between producers and both the Vichy and German regimes. No longer could a producer simply rent a studio, hire a crew, and make a film. There would be no more opportunities for experiments in cooperative filmmaking, like those that had characterized the Ciné-Liberté group of the 1930s. Instead there were forms and channels, and a bureaucratic set of rules. These new rules caused a fundamental change in the way the French film industry conducted its activity.

The steps needed to make a film were set out in a communiqué issued by the COIC in October 1941:

> In order to receive authorization to produce a film from the COIC, all scenarios, synopses or other material must be presented to the COIC by the producer who is going to make the film, and he must be in possession of a general authorization to operate and a professional card . . .
> He must then submit to the COIC:
> 1) Ten copies of a synopsis of approximately ten pages, in French, and one German summary, written on his letterhead and indicating the genre of the film
> 2) A provisional estimate of costs
> 3) The option on the subject or play
> 4) The name of the proposed director
> 5) A list of the proposed actors
> 6) The proposed process of financing the film.

Before production can begin, the producer must be in possession of five authorizations:
1) From the occupation authorities (submitted through the COIC), subject to the following conditions:

a) The film must be shot in a studio in the occupied zone which has been authorized by the military command. Exteriors may only be shot in the occupied zone.

b) All post-production must be done in the occupied zone, in establishments authorized by the military command.

c) All film stock must be bought from enterprises in the occupied zone.

d) All publicity material must be made in the occupied zone.

e) All personnel must receive separate authorizations from the military command.

f) Any film for export must receive express permission from the Propaganda Abteilung.

g) Special authorization must be obtained from the Propaganda Abteilung to shoot any exteriors.
2) Authorization of the French Pre-Censorship Commission (through the COIC) . . .
3) Provisional authorization of the COIC . . .
4) Authorization of the French Censorship Commission . . .
5) Definitive authorization from the COIC . . .[5]

Under the Third Republic, producers had been forced to submit their completed films to a censorship board. During the occupation, films had to pass five separate reviews before production could even begin. The completed film was then examined again by both German and Vichy censors.[6]

Still another problem faced producers in the spring of 1941. Even with all their permissions in hand, their financing assured, and their crew cleared for work, major obstacles remained.

Typical of the problems were those facing Pathé's production of Nous les gosses, shot at the Joinville studio in July 1941.

Since the fire [the studio had been bombed in 1940]
the studios of Joinville have been closed, the [techni-
cal] teams dispersed, from which some will return and
others are still missing—prisoners; the workshops are
covered with dust and the machines asleep.

To construct the city set, ingenuity was required—*ersatz* wood and iron; gas and oil procured on
the black market. By the third week of construction,
builders had exhausted their supply of modelling plaster and wood, so heavy plaster was used and special
staff teams were assigned to scour around for reusable
wood.[7]

Material shortages would worsen over the course of the
occupation. These shortages necessitated ingenuity and sometimes considerable expense to rectify. An elaborate production,
such as Marcel Carné's *Les Visiteurs du soir*, was particularly vulner-
able to the problems of scarcity, as Carné recounts in his memoirs.

[The script] contained nothing but banquets, hunts and
tourneys, ending with the destruction of a chateau.

How could I manage, during a time of such
scarcity and poverty, such extravagances as the script
entailed? (p. 194)

Carné's question was addressed to issues of practicality,
not morality. If the money could be found, Carné and other filmmakers did not feel the need to justify the expense of making films
during a time of general starvation and misery; on the contrary,
they saw it as their duty to offer the French public a respite from
its misery.

And the money was found. Producer André Paulvé, whose
production company, Discina, was partially bankrolled by Italian
interests, gave Carné *carte blanche* to make the film. Nevertheless,
the material difficulties the production encountered were daunt-
ing.

One of the first "extravagances" were the costumes—

velvet, satin, and brocade were not easily procured. Carné managed to locate a shop that could supply enough of the materials for the principals' costumes, but the shopkeeper, who had no previous experience with theatrical costuming, insisted that he be allowed to make the costumes himself. The exorbitant price of these costumes precluded their use for extras, so *ersatz* materials like rayon had to be used.

Materials for costumes were not the only items in short supply. The script called for a hunt scene with large numbers of horses and hounds. The horses proved to be no problem—they were borrowed from the Garde Républicaine—but dog breeders no longer had large packs because they had become too expensive to feed. The assistant director did, however, finally locate a pack of scrawny, starving beasts.

The director of production did not manage as well with the snakes needed for the scene in which Jules Berry breaks a vase and huge, terrifying snakes pour out:

> Where I had imagined enormous serpents, he brought me tiny creatures, hardly bigger than worms. Seemingly, he could find nothing better. One would have thought the Germans had also requisitioned all the snakes in France. As public gossip put it, "they" decidedly took everything from us.[8]

The production of Les Visiteurs du soir typifies the problems faced by all filmmakers during the occupation. One of the most severe problems was the rapidly escalating cost of production, which was often due to factors beyond the filmmakers' control. In this case, the production of Les Visiteurs began in April 1942 with exterior shooting near the Côte d'Azur. Rain delayed filming for twenty-one days, tying up production past the date on which the studio had been rented in Paris for interior shooting. Studio space was so scarce that it was impossible to delay, and the exteriors were abandoned in the interim. When the company returned south to complete shooting, they found that an abnormally hot summer had completely altered the landscape: "I had left a countryside green with high grass and young spring sprouts.

I returned to a devastated scene, burnt by the sun to yellowish-red, with not a single blade of grass" (p. 208). Carné's solution was an expensive one. He had grass sod and other necessary vegetation brought from nearby Grasse and replanted at the location.

Nor was interior shooting without its problems. Because the substance ordinarily applied to plaster to prevent moisture was unavailable, circles of humidity formed on the walls as soon as the lights were turned on. After every take, the walls had to be repainted. The paint caused problems as well—it dissolved under the heat of the lights so that when an actor walked across the painted floor, he left his footprints in the paint. The solution to this problem was found when a wardrober invented a substance that was applied to the actors' shoes.

There were times when material scarcity created moral dilemmas as well. Although Carné managed to keep some extras on the payroll after they had completed their scenes (including Simone Signoret and Alain Resnais), feeding the large company was difficult. The extras were so hungry that Carné feared for the provisions for the banquet scene, which had been procured with great difficulty. "No sooner had the pewter server filled with a pyramid of fruit been placed on the table than the pieces of fruit disappeared" (p. 206). Despite the vigil of production assistants, the small supply of food continued to disappear. In desperation, Carné had the fruit injected with a poison, carbolic acid.

New times demanded new responses. If one were to complete a film during the occupation, the one thing that could no longer be afforded was sentiment.

"Normalcy"

Neither bureaucracy, material shortages, nor the whims of the conquerors could deter French producers. After more than a year of inactivity, filmmaking rebounded in June 1941 to levels that nearly equaled prewar production. From June 1940 to June 1941, new film starts (all in the unoccupied zone) had averaged less than three per month. After permission was finally granted for production to resume in the North, this level tripled—between the beginning of June and the end of September 1941, thirty-five new films were begun in the two zones.[9] During the winter months that followed, production levels declined once more, due to the cost of heating studios and the shortage of coal. But the 1941–42 season was without question the high point of the occupation period in levels of production. From June 1941 to September 1942, a total of 114 films went into production, more than 50 percent of total production for the occupation period.

That this sixteen-month period (of a total fifty months of occupation) should see the greatest film activity is not surprising, since the period corresponds with the months of greatest relative "normalcy" in the society in general. In June 1941, the war in the West turned quiescent, as the Germans launched their invasion of Russia. Although the French later paid heavily for the costs of the Russian campaign, its initial effects were at least temporarily beneficial to the French. Concentrating their efforts and forces in the East, the Germans wanted stability in France. They left the French with a good deal of latitude, providing they met German production quotas and didn't cause trouble. Although the invasion of the Soviet Union turned the French Communist Party to the opposition, their outlaw status swelling the ranks of the incipient resistance, the Pétain regime still had a broad base of popular support in France, and resistance activities tended to be localized and limited to small groups. The Germans had not yet found it necessary to resort to mass deportations of Communists and other resisters, nor to take hostages on a large scale in retaliation for underground sabotage. Nor had they yet instituted their final solution to the Jewish problem. Having identified and excluded Jews from most professions, the Germans would wait until mid-1942 before beginning mass deportations.

Economically, conditions were neither better nor worse than could be expected under the circumstances. Rationing of food and other consumer goods increased steadily, as industrial and agricultural goods became scarcer due primarily to the Armistice costs. However, many factories badly damaged during the spring 1940 campaign had been made operational and employment levels were rising in most industries. Communication and passage between the two zones, while still difficult, had improved. The mass of refugees had mostly returned to their homes in the occupied sector. The issue of French prisoners of war, still uppermost in many French minds, had, through negotiations, resulted in at least a trickling of returning prisoners of war.

Externally, most Frenchmen no longer expected a quick German victory in the war, as they had in June 1940. By mid-1941, it began to become clear that the war would be a long one. While the Germans still appeared likely to win, their failure to conquer England put the ultimate outcome of the war in doubt. The sensible policy for most of the French public seemed to be that taken by their leaders: "attentisme"—or "wait and see."

By June 1941 then, France had largely adjusted to the new political and social order. With the exception of a small number of people on the political extremes—collaborators or resisters—most Frenchmen chose to ignore contemporary realities as far as possible, and go on with their day-to-day business. For the film industry, business as usual meant making films.

Profits and Losses

The major problem that had faced film producers in Vichy—a shortage of capital—was no longer an issue. The initial difficulty in finding producers willing to finance production had been reversed: too many producers were now clamoring to make films. In September 1941, the COIC complained that they had received nearly 150 proposed projects, far more than the market could bear. Therefore, they added, they were compelled to limit the number of films to approximately fifty for the 1941–42 season, and to grant visas only to firms which were "well-equipped technically and financially." [10]

This sudden influx of capital into the film industry contradicts the claim made by many producers at the time that film-making was an unprofitable activity. There were two reasons given for making this claim: that production costs were skyrocketing and that the percentage of profits returned to producers was low.

Both of these complaints were undoubtedly justified. Between 1938 and 1941, the average cost of making a film had risen from 2.9 million francs to 3.4 million (17 percent).[11] These costs would continue rising throughout the occupation period, and by 1944 the average cost of a film would reach more than 13 million francs, a nearly 400 percent increase over 1938.

The second complaint—low return on investment—centered around two factors: high taxation and the low percentage of gross receipts returned to producers. A variety of taxes were collected on box office receipts, amounting to over 26 percent of the gross in 1941 and 1942, and slightly higher thereafter. After-tax receipts were divided among exhibitor, distributor, newsreel, short and feature, with the feature receiving a share of approximately 17 percent of the gross. From this amount, the costs of prints, publicity, overhead, contribution to the COIC (1½ percent), and various additional taxes were then deducted, leaving the producer with a net share of approximately 13 percent of gross receipts.[12]

Although producers complained that profits were too low to make investment attractive, they continued making films. The reason was obvious—gross receipts rose at a far more rapid pace than expenses (see appendix table 5.2). Box office receipts in 1941 were double those of 1938, and by 1943 they had tripled.[13]

Although the average return on investment is not known, the eagerness shown by producers to make films can be taken as evidence that filmmaking was indeed a highly profitable activity during the period. Several factors must be taken into account to explain why this was so.

The first factor to be considered is the elimination of American films from the French market. Before the war, approximately 35 percent of domestic rentals had gone to American producers.[14] This foreign share of the market was not replaced to the same extent by German films. The number of German and, later, Italian films on the French market was relatively high—approximately 44 percent of the films shown in France in 1941 and 1942, and 35 percent in 1943 and 1944 were non-French. These films did not, however, find the audience acceptance that American films had received. Most observers maintain that no more than 20 percent of box office receipts went to these foreign productions.[15]

While it is true that during the occupation France lost a portion of its export market, this market had only accounted for 30 percent of total receipts before the war.[16] The most important prewar markets, Belgium and Switzerland, continued to import some French films. In any case, the increased size of the domestic market for French films more than made up for any export losses. France's economic isolation during the occupation, while disastrous for industries relying heavily on export, was extremely beneficial for French film producers.

A second factor explaining increased profits was the banning of double features in October 1940. Previously, receipts had been divided between two feature films, which mainly benefited American producers, who had already amortized the costs of their films. After 1940, the producers' share of net receipts was divided 85.3 percent for the single feature and 14.7 percent for the short and the newsreel.[17] Even with the rise in taxes, the percentage of receipts returned to producers was far greater than before the war.

A third reason producers found filmmaking profitable can be traced to Vichy's labor policy. During the occupation, Vichy helped employers keep salaries at artificially low levels by banning strikes and unions. In the film industry, this policy served to prevent personnel costs from rising at the same rate as other costs. Between 1941 and 1944, non-salary production costs rose by 320 percent; costs for salaries rose by only 240 percent over the same period.[18] Thus, the profitability of the period benefited those who financed the films, at the expense of the people who made them.

Another aspect of Vichy policy which promoted higher profits was the encouragement of industrial oligopolies. The COIC promoted this policy by denying production visas to any firm that had not previously produced films, thus preventing new producers from entering the market. Since production visas were also denied to any Jewish producers, and many prewar companies had dropped out of the market, the total number of production companies showed a dramatic decline. According to Filmprüfstelle figures, there had been 410 producers in 1939. By 1942, there were only forty-two (R142/F612).

The producers who remained consequently had a larger share of the market. Continental was the major beneficiary of this situation, accounting for 14 percent of the total number of films made during the occupation. But French producers also benefited, especially those with ties to the COIC. Six companies—Pathé, SNEG (Gaumont), Regina, Richebé, Synops, and CCFC—were directed by members of the COIC, and together made forty-nine films, or 22 percent of all films during the period. Vichy's policy of corporatism was no doubt of great benefit if one were a ranking member of the corporation.

All of these factors would have been meaningless, of course, had audiences not gone to see the films these producers made. The primary reason for the period's profitability was that audiences were starved for entertainment. As Louis-Emile Galey pointed out:

> There was no gas for the few private cars that still existed, and in any event there was no place to go, since the beaches were off-limits [for military reasons] and the borders closed. In the cafés, only *ersatz* liquor was served, and most restaurants had closed for lack of provisions. Cigarettes were rationed. There was not enough heat or electricity. There was only one diversion. Everyone went to the movies, and everyone who made movies made money.[19]

Raymond Borde, recalling the period thirty years later, wrote:

> Of the cinema of the Vichy period, what comes first to mind is the memory of the crowds, of the interminable lines in front of the cashiers, of people pressed together like sardines, of scrambling for seats in the human flood at the opening of the doors. Never had the indications of attendance been higher, never had the French cinema been more fashionable. Movie theaters

were always packed and, as in all periods of crisis, the entertainment industry was made of gold.[20]

These memories are confirmed by attendance statistics. In 1938, the annual number of spectators was 220 million. By 1943, this figure had risen by 35 percent to 304.5 million. This increase in attendance is more remarkable when the countervailing forces are taken into account. The population which constituted the French market was considerably smaller during the occupation than before the war, due to the loss of the northeastern departments and Alsace-Lorraine, not to mention the two million French prisoners of war. The number of theaters was also diminished, Allied bombing having destroyed many on the northern coast and others having been requisitioned as Soldatenkinos. Furthermore, audiences were getting less for their money—the limited number of new features and the elimination of double features gave audiences a smaller choice of films. And the cost of moviegoing increased as well—average ticket prices escalated by 108 percent from 6 francs in 1938 to 12.50 in 1943.[21]

Because of the increase in ticket prices, annual gross receipts rose at an even faster rate than attendance: from 1.3 billion francs in 1938 to 3.8 billion in 1943, an increase of nearly 200 percent. (See appendix table 5.2) For producers, at least, the occupation was indeed the golden age of the French cinema.

"Average" Production, 1941–42
During the period of "normalcy" from June 1941 to September 1942, ninety films went into production in the occupied zone.[22] Most of these films were unremarkable works, created for immediate consumption and quickly forgotten. No more than fifteen films from this sixteen-month period can be considered works of lasting value. These and other "prestige" productions made later in the occupation are discussed in the next chapter. The following remarks are confined to the seventy-five films that can be considered typical of average production during this period of normalcy.

What is most remarkable about these "average" productions is how much they resemble their counterparts of the prewar period. Unlike those nations involved in active combat, whose overall production is marked by a shift to overt propagandizing for the war effort, France during the occupation was locked in a time capsule. To judge by most of the films made in France, the war, the occupation, had never happened.

The sense of atemporality is evident both in the lack of references to everyday life under the occupation and in the marked similarity between the films of the thirties and those of the occupation. The first factor is perhaps not surprising—like American films of the Depression, the French cinema chose to show its miserable, starving audience the antithesis of its everyday life. The world portrayed in the films of the occupation is one of plenty, where Frenchmen gather in cafés with tobacco in their pipes, drinking Pernod. In the French towns and cities where these films take place German is never spoken and air raid sirens never blare. It is the rare Northern production that even mentions some contemporary event in passing; the reality of occupied France is reflected in none of them.[23]

Given conditions at the time, however, it is surprising that the films of the occupation do not show evidence of the difficulties of production. Notwithstanding the vigilant eye of German and Vichy censors, the material shortages, the disappearance of experienced production personnel to exile, banishment, prisoner of war camps, the unaccustomed bureaucracy, and the demoralization of a nation split in two, there is little to distinguish the average occupation-era film in style or production values from that of the 1930s.[24]

One reason for the continuity of style is that at the level of average production, personnel had not changed greatly from the 1930s. While it is true that the top level of talent was no longer in France, it should not be forgotten that most of the films made in the 1930s were not signed by Clair, Renoir, Duvivier, or Feyder, nor did they star Jean Gabin, Louis Jouvet, or Michèle Morgan. It is the work of these major talents which served to characterize the French cinema outside of France, and this work is what is best remembered of the thirties period today. But the characterization of an era of film history must include both the exceptional and the ordinary—and among the ordinary, the names change only slightly.

Georges Sadoul, in *French Film*, argued that the average film of the thirties had no lasting value:

> If, by their talent, Renoir, Feyder, Marcel Carné and René Clair had dominated the French cinema of the years 1930 to 1940, they were by no means the only filmmakers of that period. Exponents of the old silent films were kept very busy with the new medium, but of all their works nothing worth remembering remains.

And, Sadoul continued, "the record of those who joined the industry after 1930 and seemed at the time to offer new hope for the French cinema was no more successful."[25] Whether one agrees or not with Sadoul's assessment of their work in the 1930s, most of the names he cites would reappear in the 1940s: in the first group, Abel Gance, Marcel l'Herbier, Jacques de Baroncelli, and Léon Poirier; among the second, Marc Allégret, Sacha Guitry, Marcel Pagnol, and Georges Lacombe.

Some of these men (e.g., l'Herbier) would surpass their thirties' work, and others, cited by Sadoul as minor directors in the thirties would emerge as major talents in the forties, notably Jean Grémillon, Claude Autant-Lara, and Christian-Jaque. With the exception of the Jews and political refugees, however, there was a continuity of directorial personnel at the level of "average" production. To Sadoul's list of prolific, if minor, directors who spanned both periods, such names may be added as Jean Boyer, André Berthomieu, Henri Decoin, Jean Dréville, Edmond Gréville, Maurice Gleize, André Hugon, Léo Joannon, and Yves Mirande.

Continuity in the directorial ranks insured a stylistic continuity between the two periods. So did the continuity among screenwriters. In this field, loss of talent, even in the front ranks, was minimal. The fame of the prewar French cinema had rested nearly as much on the poetic dialogue and acerbic wit of its screenplays as on its directors, and this tradition was sustained by the works of Charles Spaak, Jacques Prévert, and a certain Monsieur Privey. This last writer was Henri Jeanson, whose prewar credits had included *Pépé le Moko*, *Entrée des Artistes*, *L'Hôtel du Nord*, and many others. His pseudonym was a pun, based on the fact that the Germans had deprived him ("privé") of the right to work.

Although French production in the early 1940s cannot solely be credited to veteran filmmakers, there was sufficient continuity in most areas of production to insure that prewar standards of craftsmanship would be sustained. Among art directors, for example, the French cinema lost two of its most noted talents: Eugène Lourié emigrated to the United States and Alexandre Trauner went into hiding (although he did work on Carné's two productions of the period). Lourié's place was taken, however, by his assistant on *La Règle du jeu*, Max Douy, who would become one of the French cinema's leading set designers. Other celebrated names in French art direction who worked during the occupation included veterans Lucien Aguettand, André Andrejew, Jacques Krauss, and Georges Wakhevitch.

Among cinematographers, noteworthy talents who spanned both decades included Philippe Agostini, Jean Bachelet, Roger Hubert, and Christian Matras. In the field of music, veteran film composer Georges van Parys scored several productions during the period, as did figures from the renowned Groupe des Six: Georges Auric, Arthur Honegger, and Francis Poulenc.

While any four-year period of film history can expect to see a certain turnover in filmmaking talent, the conditions of the occupation do not appear to have disrupted the continuity of the French cinema to any major degree. In terms of production values, the French film industry continued to produce films that were of a high degree of craftsmanship. The technical limitations experienced by filmmakers in the unoccupied zone were overcome by larger capital investments and the greater resources available in Paris. Considering the disruption caused by the conditions of occupation, one would expect far more discontinuity than, in fact, occurred.

What discontinuity existed occurred at the level of subject matter, and even here, the changes were more of degree than of kind. Given Vichy's moralism and the watchful eye of the Propaganda Abteilung, one expects that certain subjects would be avoided. Some popular genres of the thirties did disappear—military and sex farces, for example—but other popular genres simply became more numerous. Other types of comedies, such as burlesques and screwball comedies, proliferated; mysteries, musicals, adaptations of stage plays and novels were the standard subjects in both eras.

Although some recent French critics have seen Vichyist values in the bulk of occupation-era production, most filmmakers working in the North were isolated from the social currents of the regime. In fact, the general attitude of Parisian artists and intellectuals, even on the Right, was to regard Vichy and its social goals with contempt.[26] Most filmmakers avoided subjects with political overtones of any kind. The goal of filmmakers was to make films which would make money. In order to do so, they relied on formulas that had proved popular in the past.

A Sampling of Films

To get a sense of what "average" production was like during the occupation, it is useful to consider a particular group of films. The twelve films that opened in Paris in the three-month period from late December 1941 to late March 1942 typify many of the characteristics of this production and have been selected largely because Régent, from whom the list is drawn, maintains that there are no "masterpieces" among them.

The first two films to open were both based on stage plays and directed by veteran filmmakers. Le Briseur de chaînes (J. D. Norman) was adapted by the playwright, Jean Sarment, from his long running hit "Mamouret." The subject is a Pagnol-like character study of a small provincial town which is celebrating the feast day of Mamouret, the oldest woman in France. Although the direction makes the film static and talky, emphasizing its theatrical origin, the characters are convincingly drawn by an exceptional cast. The principals, Pierre Fresnay and Blanchette Brunoy, are overshadowed by the colorful performances of the character actors—always among the strengths of the French cinema. Particularly notable are Charles Dullin as the aged son of the venerable Mamouret; she is played with both humor and sympathy by Marcelle Géniat.

Marcel l'Herbier's *Histoire de rire* was a well-received adaptation of Armand Salacrou's play, also adapted by the author. The cast included veteran actors, such as Fernand Gravey and Pierre Renoir, as well as two newcomers who would soon become important stars—Marie Déa and Micheline Presle.

Comedies dominated this three-month period, as they did throughout the occupation. Léo Joannon's *Caprices*, made for Continental, was based on an original screenplay by Joannon and André Cayatte.[27] Régent says of this screwball comedy that "the plot didn't really make any sense, but it was propelled by the many gags strewn throughout its 2,500 meters" (p. 51). Starring two of the most popular actors of the 1930s, Danielle Darrieux and Albert Préjean, the film was one of the biggest hits of the occupation period.

Pension Jonas (Pierre Caron) was adapted by novelist Pierre Véry but he later had his name removed from the credits. According to Régent, the film suffered the singular fate of being banned for "imbecility."[28] There are other critics who maintain, however, that this farce had some amusing burlesque scenes that recalled the Marx Brothers.[29]

The film establishes a potentially amusing situation: an animal-loving tramp (Pierre Larquey), who lives in the belly of a whale in the museum of natural history, takes charge of the well-being of the animals in a nearby zoo and of the people who come there. Much of the film was shot on location at the Zoo de Vincennes, and it offers glimpses of real Parisians on holiday. But the comic situations are insufficiently developed: when a hippopotamus escapes, the director resorts to a brief montage of crowds scurrying and close-ups of women screaming, rather than developing a series of gags. If the film recalls the Marx Brothers at all, it is in the intrusive presence of the juvenile lead whose songs insistently interrupt the comic action.

Pathé's *Boléro* (Jean Boyer) was another comedy that failed to develop its comic premise. The milieu of the film is the haut monde, and the film's interest lies more in its sets and costumes than in its script or direction. One of the main characters is a couturière, and the film opens with an elaborate fashion show. The lavish costumes were given a full-page spread in *Le Film* which commented that "despite these difficult times, the prestige of French haute couture remains high" (March 28, 1942).

Although expensively produced, the film suffers from an unengaging script and a miscast Arletty in a farce about mistaken identities and the noisy playing of Ravel's "Bolero." One noteworthy point about the film is a walk-on by an unbilled but recognizable Simone Signoret, in her second film appearance. At that time, she was being groomed by Pathé, who hoped to make her into a star. Her career was stymied, however, because she lacked an identity card, which was denied her because she was half-Jewish.[30]

Annette et la dame blonde (Jean Dréville), produced by Continental, was similar in type to its *Caprices*, although this comedy was based on a story by Georges Simenon. Another Simenon adaptation released during this three-month period was *La Maison des sept jeunes filles*, scripted by Charles Spaak and directed by Albert Valentin, a former scenarist who had directed his first film in 1939. Although both of these films were comedy/mysteries, straight mysteries were also very popular during the occupation. Of all authors, Simenon was the most often adapted. Between 1941 and 1944, eight films were made based on Simenon stories and novels.

Mam'zelle Bonaparte, directed by Maurice Tourneur, belonged to a genre that became enormously popular in France during the occupation—the costume drama. The nineteenth century was the favored setting for such films. This biography of an adventuress was set in the Second Empire and featured a sword fight between its two female stars, Edwige Feuillère and Monique Joyce. It was one of the most popular films of the occupation.

Another big box-office success was Jean Delannoy's *Fièvres*, which of all the films in this sampling is closest in spirit to Vichy's National Revolution. This melodrama starred popular singer

Tino Rossi as an operatic star who is seduced from the side of his dying wife and eventually enters a monastery to atone for his sins. These uplifting tearjerkers were quite common during the period, but the film is mainly noteworthy for providing a small role to the actress about to become France's top female star: Madeleine Sologne.

The film that made Sologne a star, *L'Eternel Retour*, was released in 1943. Her co-star in that film would also vault to number one at the box office. But Jean Marais's first major role was in a film released in December 1941: *Le Pavillon brûle* (Jacques de Baroncelli). This adventure story was shot in a working copper mine in Caen, one of many films of the period shot on location. During a time of severe travel restrictions and no private transport, many scenarios nonetheless concentrated on picturesque areas of the French countryside. This paradox is not due simply to the filmmakers' desire to vary the scenery—with studio space in high demand, shooting on location offered an alternative to expensive set construction and many days of studio rental.

The last two films represent still another popular genre, the musical. *Cartacalha* (Léon Mathot) was a musical about Gypsy life (shot in the Camargue region) and starred Viviane Romance and Georges Flamant.[31] *Opéra-Musette* was another musical, directed by a *débutant*, actor René Lefèvre (the star of *Le Crime de M. Lange*). This film was among the first for a young technician who would later become one of France's leading cinematographers, Claude Renoir. Lefèvre claims he engaged Jean Renoir's nephew to be his assistant primarily because he wanted to use the Renoir apartment in Montmartre as a location.[32]

There is little in the film's direction or cinematography to distinguish it, the two newcomers having relied on standard continuity cutting and functional camera placement. They did, however, manage to conceal their low budget, by shooting the apartment from every possible vantage point and relying a great deal on exteriors. (There are only two interior sets.) The story, also written by Lefèvre, concerns a street singer (Lefèvre) who is mistaken for a great classical composer and fêted by a would-be composer (Saturnin Fabre) in a small provincial town. It is not known how the film fared at the box office, but today it offers a charming view of French life at the time, in a manner reminiscent of the more realistic comedies of the thirties.

Despite the diversity of subjects, the quality common to all these films was a high degree of craftsmanship and a resolute evasion of serious themes. In comparing these films to their equivalents of the 1930s, one finds no diminution in standards of production or of performance. Nor, unsurprisingly, does one find any greater determination to explore subjects with uncertain commercial appeal. While political conditions caused a slight alteration in the acceptance of certain genres—more "uplifting" melodrama and historical romance, less emphasis on sex—formularization of subject matter was the norm in both eras. The majority of French filmmakers continued making the films they had always made, neither better nor worse. If the bulk of the occupation-era films did not rise above the pedestrian, neither did the period see any loss of strength in the French cinema as a whole.

Conclusion

What is particularly striking about these years of the occupation, in terms of average film production, is just how normal everything was. The enormous changes in the society at large, the new conditions imposed on the film industry, appear to have had little effect on the majority of films made during the period. With a pot of gold to be discovered at the end of every film produced, producers and filmmakers had little incentive to experiment with new forms, new subjects, new styles. The French film industry was booming for the first time in a decade—why tamper with success?

So it would seem if the only films had been *Boléro* and *Le Pavillon brûle*. But if such had been the extent of French production, the period would have no more than a sociological interest to us today. That the French film industry managed to survive and to sustain its standards of craftsmanship under difficult conditions is noteworthy but not exceptional. What is remarkable about the occupation period, however, is that it gave birth to a new aesthetic which would dominate the French cinema for fifteen years after the occupation ended. The dramatic change in French production at its highest level is the subject of chapter 6.

A French School
of Cinema

General Tendencies

After the Liberation, when French films of the occupation were seen for the first time by English-speaking critics, the response was one of surprise. The films that emerged from the French cocoon seemed entirely different from those they had remembered. Where once the lined and irregular features of Jean Gabin had suffered in the misty lower depths of the French urban landscape, the classical perfection of Jean Marais's profile now reigned over the countryside of some indefinable era of France's past. Not only the subjects, but the styles of these films had changed. The warmth of the prewar French cinema—the seeming spontaneity of gesture and performance, the *engagé* quality that had emanated an aura of life itself—had been replaced by the iciness of long shots and perfectly composed images, in which actors seemed to be not human beings but well-trained mechanisms, engineered rather than born.

If "average" production during the occupation, particularly in the early years, remained faithful to the genres and styles developed in the 1930s, another group of films surpassed the average, and these films have come to dominate our image of the occupation. A group of filmmakers broke definitively with the styles of the 1930s; by 1944, a new tendency in the French cinema had developed, one which would dominate that cinema for the next fifteen years.

The tendency in the French cinema that characterized the period from 1940 to 1960 was disparagingly labeled the "cinema of quality" by the young critics of the *Cahiers du Cinéma* in the 1950s. Because these iconoclasts denigrated that cinema, subsequent critics have failed, for the most part, to examine it systematically, in order to determine what it was and why it developed. There is no question, however, that the French cinema changed from the 1930s to the 1940s, and that the moment of rupture came during the occupation.

There are many reasons that account for the birth of a new movement in the French cinema. The discussion that follows can only begin to suggest the complexities of its origin. No one element determined the change, but taken together, the conditions of the occupation—both extrinsic and intrinsic to the cinema—necessitated a new response by the cinema. Among these conditions were the change in production practices mandated by material and bureaucratic constraints; the response of French filmmakers to France's defeat and the country's new place in the world; the confused and often contradictory political alignments of the period; and the emergence of a new group of filmmakers. Whatever our critical judgment of it, the new tendency that arose during the occupation has a central place in the history of the French cinema. It merits an extended discussion of its origins and accomplishments.

A question arises concerning the body of films selected to represent the new tendency in the cinema. Of the more than 200 films made during the occupation period as a whole, probably no more than thirty can be said to represent a major stylistic break with the past. Yet, these thirty films are the ones singled out in the critical commentaries of the time, screened at revivals, and written about in general histories.[1] It is inevitable that an era of film history will be characterized by its "prestige" productions—those singled out at the time for critical comment, prizes, and export. The last factor—export—is particularly interesting in terms of this discussion, because the French films that were shown abroad tended to represent the French cinema's own notion of its "prestige" production.[2] Without the opportunity to see the "average" films of both eras, which were primarily intended for domestic consumption, foreign (particularly English-speaking) audiences made a sharper distinction between prewar and occupation-era production. The changes in the French cinema occurred only at a certain level of production, but it is this level with which English-speaking audiences are most familiar.

Of the films released abroad after the Liberation, the one that best exemplified the change in the French cinema was by Marcel Carné and Jacques Prévert. In the late thirties, the two men had been emblems of "poetic realism" with such psychological melodramas as *Quai des brumes* and *Le Jour se lève*. The change from their earlier films to the poeticized allegory of *Les Visiteurs du soir* was undeniable. Doubtless, it was with this film in mind that a British writer criticized French directors of the occupation who concentrated "on the development of the aesthetic side, often at the expense of the human. In fact, a fair general criticism . . . is that the decors are too perfect, the dialogue too witty or too literary, the lighting too subtle and the photography too artistic."[3]

There is no question that the "prestige" cinema of the early 1940s was in many ways, very different from that of the late 1930s. In pointing out these differences, however, the critics failed to recognize that the two cinemas were not really comparable. To judge one by the other is to falsify both, for the origins and purposes of this new style of filmmaking were very different from what had come before. The first question to be asked then is not, "which cinema is better?" but rather "what are the differences between them and why did these changes occur?"

Definitions

The distinctive "thirties' style" originated, in large part, from the political climate of the time and the production circumstances within France.[4] The dominant tone was humanist and despairing, an unconscious reflection, perhaps, of both the values of the Popular Front regime and of its inability to effect any real change in French society. Films like *Pépé le Moko*, *Quai des brumes* and *La Règle du jeu* were films in which change, no matter how ardently desired, was impossible; and the lower-class "hero" was always defeated by the forces of tradition and "rules." Notwithstanding the basic pessimism of these films, however, there is a liveliness about them, a sense of spontaneity of performance and direction that belies the immutability of the protagonists' ultimate fate. If the great films of the late 1930s were characterized by any one element, it was their individualism, the almost anarchic determination of the artists to follow their own vision, regardless of commercial considerations or political pressure. If the society they portrayed was fixed by immutable rules, the films themselves were the opposite; unrestrained by propriety or cinematic conventions, these films emanated an aura of freedom because they recognized few boundaries of expression.

In large part, the freedom of French directors in the thirties to break the rules was due to their system of production. France had one of the few national industries without a rigid studio structure and, consequently, filmmakers could shop around among producers in search of backing for their projects.[5] If one producer objected to a project, they could move elsewhere. For example, when *Quai des brumes* was turned down by its original producer, Ufa, Carné managed to find another, and this one agreed to finance the film without even having read the script.[6] Although France, unlike the United States, had a government-run censorship board, these leftist bureaucrats were far less rigid (in most respects) than the industry-run Hays office. For *Quai des brumes*, the only rule the censor imposed was that the word "deserter" not be used, and that Gabin pile his uniform neatly when he got undressed. If the late thirties were the "golden age of the French cinema," it was because the period allowed a greater artistic liberty than existed in any other major film-producing nation.

By contrast, the forties were a time of absolute constraint—material, cultural, political. The rigidity of the rules imposed from without was mirrored by the rigid forms imposed by filmmakers on their own films. From the Romantic excesses of the thirties, there followed a return to Classicism, with its emphasis on formal perfection and its willing acceptance of rules and restraints. The emblematic films—e.g., *La Duchesse de Langeais*, *Le Baron Fantôme*, *Douce*—shared no common theme or subject, but rather a common tone and style. Many critics have characterized the dominant tendency of the period as the "cinéma d'évasion," but the term is misleading.[7] For what characterizes this cinema is not simply its avoidance of subjects of daily life, but its sense of remove from this life. Although many of these films are set in other times or other worlds, the same tone and style occurs even in films set in a seemingly "realistic" contemporary world: films like *Lumière d'été*, *Les Anges du péché*, and *Le Corbeau*. The dominant tone of the period is, rather, one of hermeticism, what the French call a *vase clos*.[8] It is as if the films of this period were played out under glass, the characters suffocating in an airless environment, observed from a detached, scientific distance.

This tone may, in fact, be a metaphor for France itself—cut off from the world, it turned in on itself. The dramas of individuals exposing their weaknesses and failings led to conflicts of greater ferocity because there were no escape valves. It is not coincidental that Sartre's *Huis Clos* (No Exit) was written during the occupation, for this allegory of French society cut off from the world and exposed to itself was reflected again and again in the cinema of the time.

Two related, but distinctive formal tendencies can be discerned within what I am calling the "cinema of isolation." The first might be labelled "pictorialism," what critic Pierre Cadars describes as "la calligraphie et le romanesque."[9] It can be clearly distinguished in films like *Les Visiteurs du soir*, *Le Baron Fantôme*, and *La Main du Diable*. These films subordinate text, characterization, and other narrative elements to composition of the images, generally composition of a highly stylized kind. The dominant impression made by these films is left by their images—the medieval tableaux of *Les Visiteurs du soir*, inspired by *Les Très Riches Heures du Duc de Berry*; the white scarf floating through a black night in the dream-like images of *Le Baron Fantôme*; the symmetrical grouping of masked figures around a great stone table in a shadowy, Expressionistic chamber in *La Main du Diable*. The pictorialist style is dominated by long shots, by sweeping camera movements, and either highly symmetrical or off-angle compositions. In many ways, it resembles the German Expressionist cinema, combining Lang's grandeur and symmetry with Murnau's camera movement and lighting. But this cinema differs from the German cinema of the 1920s in its lack of subjectivity: its refusal to show the world through the eyes of its characters or to draw the spectator into the drama.

The other trend in filmmaking was equally removed, also creating an emotional distance between spectator and subject. But where the "pictorialist" film placed style over subject, the "literary" film subordinated visual style to the words. In films like *La Duchesse de Langeais*, *Lumière d'été*, and *Pontcarral*, the poetry of images gives way to poetic language. Although this "literary" tendency is not exclusively a question of adaptation, it is noteworthy that the period saw many classics of French literature filmed, including six films based on Balzac alone. The effect of this "literary" style, like that of "pictorialism," was to place the subject of the film one step further removed from lived experience. The fundamental difference, then, between the thirties' and forties' films was that of distance. The "warmth" of the thirties grew from the spectator's sense of observing life itself; in the forties, life was observed through a translucent glass—the conscious "artistry" of image and language standing between spectator and subject.

Origins of a Style

That there was a significant difference between the "prestige" cinemas of the two eras is apparent, but to define the changes is not enough. In order to explain these differences, one must look at the films themselves and at the conditions from which they emerged. Material circumstance was one important factor accounting for the new style. The lack of spontaneity, the studied compositions and technical perfection of this new style were, in part, due to the new bureaucratic forms and channels, the necessity of providing carefully planned budgets and schedules, and of clearing cast and crew for work. All these factors prevented improvisation and spontaneity. Under the new order, all aspects of a film—script, cast, schedule, budgets—had to be planned and approved in advance of filming, so last minute changes in conception, improvisation on the set, or addition of new characters became virtually impossible.

Although the director still maintained, for the most part, ultimate responsibility for the film, he now had a bureaucratic structure looking over his shoulder. The studios themselves were stronger and exercised more control over such basic decisions as budgets and casting. The COIC was the final authority on all questions: no film stock would be provided, no electricity generated without COIC approval of every element. Although the COIC was largely a benevolent autocrat, its very existence deprived the director of much of his former freedom and control.

Another material factor affecting the new style was the scarcity and expense of production necessities. By 1943, a film could receive no more than 16,000 meters of negative stock, and to conserve electricity, total shooting time, including set construction, was limited to seven weeks unless a special dispensation was granted.[10] Thus the number of retakes was severely limited, necessitating not only more careful pre-production planning, but also more rehearsals, which perhaps contributed to the studied quality of many performances. Even shooting style was, in part, dictated by material necessity, as evidenced by Carné's description of his methods for Les Visiteurs du soir. He asserts that one of the reasons he chose to shoot the film predominantly in long shot was because closer camera set-ups would have revealed the ersatz materials used for sets and costumes. Another problem he cites concerned the banquet scene, in which the food was devoured so quickly that it would have been impossible to match shots if the camera had been placed closer to the food-laden table.[11]

The choice of new subjects and styles was only partially determined by new production conditions, however. The "forties' style" was also a response to factors external to the film industry, particularly France's new position in the world. As the thirties had been a period of cinematic despair amidst political freedom, so the forties salvaged hope from the oppression which pervaded it.

The French Style

In 1948, critic Roger Régent wrote of Claude Autant-Lara's *Le Mariage de Chiffon*:

> [The film] served as the first truly conclusive example of this "French style" which would emerge and then fade away from our cinema during those four years of misery . . . It is a paradox that while France had been invaded, subjugated, suffocated by oppression, our screens began to show the foundations of a new French style of cinema. (p. 83)

It is no paradox that a "French style" should have blossomed in the midst of oppression, for this style was the French cinema's response to the shattering of the French spirit. While the filmmakers of the thirties could attack what they perceived to be a moribund culture, in the forties the French nation had literally ceased to exist. Filmmakers during the occupation thus believed their responsibility was to offer renewal and hope for the survival of France.

It must be remembered that during the occupation, the French nation had become a phantasm. In less than six weeks, France had been defeated, divided, and occupied. The French people had rallied around Maréchal Pétain in order to convince themselves that the long and glorious history of France had not come to an abrupt end. But Vichy was not a national government—its military forces were disbanded or powerless, its colonies were politically divided or under the domination of other nations, its laws were inapplicable in the bulk of the country, and even within its own territory, it existed only on sufferance from the enemy. If France were to survive, it was not the government that would save it. All France had left was its past—its centuries of kings and conquests, and the memories of individual French men and women who had given glorious artifacts of culture and art to the world.

To remind the French people of these glories and to sustain these achievements were the goals of most French artists. The time of attack on bourgeois values and culture was past. In the twenties and thirties, the Surrealists and other left-wing artists had delighted in demolishing the traditional icons of French "high culture," in savaging the respectable, safe achievements of the academicians. Now the academy was the source of renewal for the same artists. The dry "perfection" of the academic style— the strictness of form, the "serious" subjects, the literary language and studied compositions—was cultivated in the cinema by avant-gardists like Cocteau and Prévert, by leftists and iconoclasts like Grémillon and Jeanson. What these and other filmmakers hoped to create was a uniquely French film culture, a "French school" of cinema equivalent to the French schools of painting, drama, and literature. According to Claude Autant-Lara, they succeeded: "All French [filmmakers] worked for the French people; as a result, there appeared a true French school of cinema." [12]

The return to the sources was evident not only in filmmakers' choice of styles, but in their choice of subjects as well. Although not all the films belonging to the "cinema of isolation" were set in the historical or legendary past, it is impossible to ignore the large number of films that sought refuge in other eras or other worlds.

Films with historical or fantastic subjects dominated the "prestige" cinema of the occupation. An estimated 16 percent of all films produced during the occupation were set in the historical past, and among the "prestige" films the percentage was closer to 50 percent. [13] Although fantastic films were less numerous, the ten films of this type were particularly influential:

> The most ambitious productions, those most conscious of artistry, closed themselves off from the actual world in the fantastic, the supernatural, the magical and spiritual beyond. It is this tendency that gives its specific coloration to the French cinema of the time. [14]

These two tendencies were analogous, for the choice of historical or fantastic subjects was often made for the same reason. Filmmakers wanted to present subjects that glorified French culture and history, whether adaptations of classic novels (e.g., the many films based on Balzac); biographies of cultural heroes (Berlioz, the nineteenth-century opera star Malibran, a pioneer aviator in Le Mariage de Chiffon); films that took place in periods of French political dominance (Madame Sans-Gêne, Le Destin fabuleux de Désirée Clary, both set in the Napoleonic era); or myths and legends that were part of the French heritage (L'Eternel Retour, La Fiancée des ténèbres). Such subjects offered the French public a reassurance of France's continuity and a hope that new heroes would emerge to lead France from its present troubles.

This notion, that the triumph of French culture could save France politically, was stated quite explicitly in a film by Sacha Guitry, Donne-moi tes yeux. The film, set in contemporary France, opens with an art exhibition, one room of which contains masterpieces by such artists as Manet, Courbet, and Renoir, all painted in 1871.

> Look at these splendors. This is what men of genius could do at a moment when France had just lost the [Franco-Prussian] war . . .
> Before these marvels, one has the impression that what was lost on one side has been regained on the other.
> Because one has the right to consider works like these as substitutes for victories.

The need expressed in these films—for hope, for some small measure of belief that the present suffering would end—was desperate but not always easy to provide. Not all of these films have happy endings; many resolutely pursue their premises to their tragic conclusions (e.g., Douce, La Main du Diable, L'Eternel Retour). Yet, even within tragedy, some measure of hope is conveyed. The message of hope is most clearly seen in Les Visiteurs du soir.

The team of Carné-Prévert had been influential in establishing the emblematic prewar themes of the hopelessness of the human condition. In fact, some Vichy ideologues blamed the pair for causing the mood of defeatism that led to France's fall.[15] In their first occupation-era film, however, the two men offered a different vision to the stunned and despairing people of France. Les Visiteurs du soir has often been read as an allegory: the devil (Hitler) sends two envoys (the army of occupation) to sow discord and misery within a medieval court (Europe). Although the devil defeats humanity physically, he is himself defeated spiritually when one of the envoys falls in love with his victim. Although the devil has the power to turn the bodies of the two lovers to stone, he cannot prevent their hearts from beating. The implication of such an allegory was that although the Nazis could defeat the French physically, the spirit of freedom, the unbreakable heart of France, would live on.[16]

From another perspective, however, the film can be seen as a reworking of the themes of Quai des brumes and Le Jour se lève. But unlike the prewar films, in Les Visiteurs love vanquishes destiny. Where ineluctable death parted the pure hearts of the lovers in the earlier films, in 1942 the people of France needed to believe that destiny was not intransigent, that even death was not the end. The message conveyed in this enormously popular film was not rebellion but reassurance—all is not lost; our destiny has not been determined.

If there is a paradox to the development of a "French school" of cinema in the midst of despair and oppression, it does not lie in filmmakers' desires to counter France's actual condition in the world. Rather, the paradox rests in the new political configuration that led Vichy to promote this new tendency in the French cinema, and the occupiers to contribute to its development.

Political Factors

Of all the external changes that affected the French cinema of the occupation, the most dramatic was the change in France's political status. The abrupt turnaround in governments—from the democratic Third Republic to the combined totalitarianisms of Vichy and the Nazis—could not have failed to affect the cinema in some way. But the effect of the new regimes was not, as one might expect, to make the films more politically reactionary; nor did the regimes directly impose their values on the filmmakers. Rather, the major impact of the new political order in France was to underscore the stylization and distance that were developing as part of the new tendency in the cinema.

Of the two regimes, Vichy had a more direct influence on the French cinema, but the presence of the occupier was not without effect. Some critics have even seen a direct correlation between the fact of German censorship and the tendency of filmmakers to set their films in the historical or legendary past.[17] The implication is that filmmakers chose such settings because they would give the filmmakers a greater freedom to express statements of opposition in allegorical form. While it is true that such historical and fantastic films as *Les Visiteurs du soir*, *La Main du Diable*, and *Pontcarral* have all been read as allegories about resistance, the notion of a direct causal connection between censorship and the tendency toward these subjects cannot be supported, for several reasons.

First, the assumption presupposes that the Germans were incapable of recognizing allegory and were somehow "fooled" by the films' texts. Such obliviousness is not likely and, as the next chapter makes clear, the Germans were not particularly concerned about coded messages of French nationalism or opposition to the German presence in France. If the censors failed to catch messages of opposition, it was because they were not looking for them.

Second, the connection between censorship and allegory is a dubious one, which assumes that filmmakers revert to allegorical expression only because they cannot express their ideas directly. But such an assumption ignores the long, international tradition of filmic allegory, which filmmakers have used to express both opposition to and support of official policies. For example, in prewar France, Renoir made *La Marseillaise* in support of the governing Popular Front coalition; outside of France, such films as Eisenstein's *Alexander Nevsky* and Olivier's *Henry V* used historical subjects for patriotic ends. Allegory is not a form limited to filmmakers who cannot express their ideas directly.

Furthermore, most of the historical films made in France during the occupation had no oppositional intent, other than to remind the French people of the glories of the past. Of the few films made in France between 1940 and 1944 that do seem to contain a statement of opposition, most are not set in the past at all. Such films as Le Ciel est à vous, Nous les gosses, and Adieu, Léonard have all been posited as films that express some opposition to the regime, and all are set in the modern era.

While it is not true, then, that a simple correlation exists between censorship and the tendency to avoid contemporary reality, censorship restrictions did have an indirect effect on the new direction within the prestige cinema. A specific censorship code—a list of rules of what was or was not permitted—was never published by either Vichy or the Germans. In the absence of such a code, filmmakers were obliged to anticipate objections, to exercise self-censorship.

But self-censorship often results in more caution, even rigidity, than external constraints. Any word in a screenplay, any gesture by an actor, could potentially have offended some member of the censorship boards. The degree of caution and restraint exercised by all filmmakers was exacerbated in the case of those individuals who wanted to express sentiments of opposition. The result was that filmmakers chose to couch their political sentiments in such vague terms that audiences of varying political positions could read the messages in accordance with their own beliefs.

Few filmmakers attempted to test the limits of the censors' tolerance; most French filmmakers assumed that any political statement that was contrary to the values of the occupiers or Vichy would be censored. Therefore, when such statements were attempted, they were presented in such ambiguous terms that the debate still continues as to the meaning of such films as Le Ciel est à vous, Le Corbeau, and Pontcarral.

Thus, the effect of censorship was not to create a fashion for allegory but rather to add to the already prevailing trend of indirection, restraint, and distance. Filmmakers hid behind the formal beauty of their mise-en-scène and the elegant construction of their screenplays as if to draw a curtain between their ideas and anyone in the audience who might be offended by those ideas. Censorship did not determine the new styles and subjects that emerged in the 1940s; rather it helped to promote a tendency that was already gaining currency.

Censorship restrictions can be seen as one of the determinants of the new direction in the cinema, although in a way somewhat different from that ordinarily posited by critics. Other critics have insisted on a determinism of a different kind: they maintain that the new development in the cinema was a direct outgrowth of Vichy ideology.

Because the cinema of the occupation tended toward grandiose subjects that celebrated "eternal France," and because this cinema exhibited that "good taste" prized by bourgeois artists and patrons, many recent critics have seen this cinema as being Vichyist.[18] By this accusation, they mean that the values promulgated by Vichy infused the "prestige" cinema of France; that wittingly or unwittingly, filmmakers during the occupation were upholding the ideology of the Pétainist state.

The determinism that underlies this argument rests on two assumptions: that the Vichy regime approved of the new direction in the cinema, supporting it in material ways; and that filmmakers were influenced by the ideological currents of the Pétain regime, particularly its emphasis on nationalism and defense of French culture.

The first of these assumptions is true—Vichy did, in fact, support the new tendency in the cinema. As was the case in other Fascist and proto-Fascist states, the function of art for Vichy ideologues was to unify the French people and to glorify the French nation abroad. The State thus instituted a number of measures to support "prestige" productions and the development of the French film industry. It did not however attempt to impose on filmmakers its own bureaucratic notions of artistry and grandeur, as had Goebbels in Germany. Rather, Vichy entrusted the glorification of the French cinema to filmmakers themselves, through the COIC.

In a speech delivered in September 1941 to the plenary session of the COIC, Raoul Ploquin concluded with these remarks:

> Despite the redoubtable blows it has just suffered, the French cinema has been reborn from the ashes. Everything leads me to believe that its present vitality is as great as ever. Thanks to you, gentlemen, it will carry to the entire world the prestige of the French spirit.[19]

To insure the spreading of French prestige to the world, the COIC instituted a number of measures. The most direct support came from the institution of low-interest loans via the Crédit National. Although some government-sponsored propaganda films were financed by this method, much of the money went to independent producers. In 1942-43 for example, the French government provided 17,400,000 francs for feature films selected by the COIC.[20] The number of films aided in this way was approximately fifteen in 1941 and twenty in 1942, and included many of the films under discussion here: Nous les gosses, Pontcarral, Lumière d'été, Les Visiteurs du soir, Le Baron Fantôme.[21]

Other government measures aimed at aiding the quality of French production included the financing of short documentary films (nearly 400 were produced during the occupation) and reviving the French animated film. These short films, exhibited at special festivals, as well as serving as the first part of the program for regular exhibitors, would result in furthering the career of several important postwar filmmakers, such as Georges Rouquier and René Clément.[22]

Other government measures adopted to assure the "quality" of the French cinema included the institution of a prize, carrying the substantial award of 100,000 francs, for the best film of the year. The Direction Générale du Cinéma awarded it (at the direction of a specially formed committee of critics) to Les Visiteurs du soir in 1942 (with special mention to La Nuit fantastique) and in 1943 to Les Anges du péché (with mention to Douce).

Vichy's policy of raising the quality of film production also led to the establishment of a training center for young filmmakers. This project had first been proposed by Marcel l'Herbier in the 1920s, but it was under Vichy that the director was appointed head of the newly established l'Institut des Hautes Etudes Cinématographiques (IDHEC). It was under Vichy as well that the Cinémathèque Française received its first substantial government support. In 1943, the Cinémathèque was given administrative offices and support funds by the Direction Générale du Cinéma, thus assuring for the State the preservation of France's film heritage.

While it is clear that Vichy approved of the new direction within the French cinema, and helped to further it, it is not accurate to assume that the prestigious films necessarily subscribed to Vichy ideology. Filmmakers had their own reasons for choosing particular subjects and styles, and if these choices often conjoined with Vichyist values, it was because the social and political climate of the time gave rise to certain common attitudes. The austerity and coldness of style was, for filmmakers, a necessary response to scarcity and, perhaps, an unconscious reflection of the isolation of France from the world. Yet this style meshed with Vichy's notions of "high art." Similarly, the refuge that filmmakers sought in history, myth, and allegory served Vichy's interests by promoting the glories of French culture and nationalism. But nationalism was not an exclusive preserve of Vichy. The determination to glorify French culture and to preserve France's past was a commonly held value across the political spectrum.

The Left was as determined as Vichy to glorify France; the Resistance press condemned and applauded the same films as did the Vichy censors. Le Corbeau was excoriated by both groups because it attacked the French bourgeoisie; Le Ciel est à vous was acclaimed by both groups because it showed the "average" French man and woman triumphing over adversity. Nationalism may be supported for different reasons by Left and Right, but it is not easy to distinguish between its manifestations. If the cinema of the occupation was, as some critics claim, a Vichyist cinema, it is not because there was any widespread desire among filmmakers to uphold Vichy's values. That the same tendencies continued after the Liberation, throughout the Fourth Republic, should be evidence enough that the politics promulgated by these films were French rather than specifically Vichyist.

The complexity of political allegiances during the period affected the way filmmakers saw themselves and their films. Most of the important filmmakers in France had been Leftists in the 1930s and supported the Resistance in the forties, yet the films they made were necessarily devoid of clear-cut political meanings. The degree to which political alignments of the period were complex and overlapping can be seen in the possibility of multiple readings of all the films that had any overt political content.

The misdirection of statements which filmmakers adopted to avoid censorship difficulties, combined with the confusion in political values that characterized the era, make it impossible to isolate the exact political meaning of the films made during the occupation. The most striking example of the possibility for multiple readings occurs in *Pontcarral, Colonel d'Empire*, a film that many critics consider the most overtly pro-Resistance film of the period; and yet, it is a film that has also been cited as an example of pro-Vichyist sentiment.

The film was made in 1942, directed by Jean Delannoy based on a script by Bernard Zimmer, and starring Pierre Blanchar, later a leading figure in the Comité de Libération du Cinéma Français (the resistance committee for the cinema). The story, based on a 1937 novel by Albéric Cahuet, concerns an ex-colonel in the Napoleonic army who refuses to recognize the authority of the restored monarchy.

The film opens boldly. The camera tilts down to a large public square, where a crowd is gathered to listen to a speaker extolling the new regime. A medium shot reveals a plaque reading "Place Napoléon" being removed and replaced with "Place Louis XVIII." Suddenly, an arm holding a pistol emerges from a window across the courtyard; gunshots bring down the plaque and knock the hat from the dignitary's head. As the crowd disbands in confusion, the police search out the accused—Pontcarral—who manages to make his escape.

Within the context of the film itself, the thematic value of the politics portrayed is relatively straightforward. Pontcarral's continued devotion to the emperor, even after fifteen years, reveals his strength of character and at the same time his inability to function in a world of compromises. Pontcarral is a complex character, and his unswerving devotion to a lost cause is portrayed by the filmmakers as both noble and pathetic. The politics of the 1820s are also important to the plot, for Pontcarral's rival (his wife's lover) is a Royalist, and the personal conflict between them is reflected in the larger political arena.

If read allegorically, however, the film's politics become extremely confusing. Some recent critics consider it "the only film of the period which was uncontestably a Resistance film."[23] They offer as evidence the very fact of Pontcarral's resistance to the monarchy, such lines as "the place for an honest man today is in prison," and "condemnation to death? it is the only thing left today which dignifies a man. It is the only thing which can't be bought"; and especially the finale, of Pontcarral marching off to conquer Algeria with flags flying and bands playing, a scene which so roused audiences, it was feared the film would be banned.[24]

If the film is indeed a call to Resistance, it is not clear, however, whether the intended enemy is Vichy or Germany. The German censors did not seem to be particularly concerned about the film. Although the Filmprüfstelle reported that it was heavily cut, much of its message was allowed to pass and the Filmprüfstelle mentioned no problem in allowing it through.[25] A postwar English writer claims that, with the offending passages removed, the German censors "looked upon [the film] as anti-Resistance," although for what reason is hard to say.[26] The most objectionable sequence, from the German point of view, would likely have been a long digression that has little bearing on the film's plot but that might have been seen as an allusion to contemporary events. Pontcarral attends a concert where Chopin plays a "Valse Polonaise." Since Chopin had come to Paris in the 1830s following Poland's failed uprising against the Russians, this sequence could be seen as a reference to the occupation of Poland

and Polish martyrdom. However, the sequence could also be seen as a celebration of the French Romantic movement, since Franz Liszt and George Sand are also in attendance. Such an intent would have been less offensive to the Germans and numerous films of the period made similar references.

If the film is meant allegorically, it would seem to be more anti-Vichy than anti-German. Primarily, the film is about power, about who controls the government, about which party sees its interests served while the other waits in the wings. One rather pointed remark, presumably aimed toward Vichy, comes when a noble family discusses a possible scandal arising from their daughter's engagement. "Fortunately, we have a censor in France," remarks the father, calling to mind Vichy's determination to protect France's upper classes.

Pontcarral is feared by the Royalist faction, not for his political beliefs, but because they suspect he is conspiring against them to gain power for his own faction. The domestic nature of the squabble is pointed out in a scene where Pontcarral lunches at a Royalist inn. On entering, Pontcarral is insulted and made to sit at a back table. He overhears his enemies ordering wine. "1815, a very good year," one remarks. (1815 was the year of Louis's accession.) Soon, however, positions are reversed. Pontcarral takes over the best table, tears down the sign honoring the king and orders wine. "1802, a very good year," he retorts.

Pontcarral does indeed join a conspiracy after fifteen years of patient waiting for the proper moment, and in 1830 his faction stages a successful coup which brings Louis Philippe, the Citizen King, to power. It is this benevolent monarch who reconstitutes Pontcarral's regiment and sends him off to fight in Algeria with the words: "It is time to take France out of her humiliation, to render to her flag, our flag, a bit of glory."[27]

If, however, one reads the Royalists as Pétainists, and the Bonapartists as Gaullists, what does one make of Pontcarral's worship of Napoleon? The hero's house is a shrine, a portrait of the emperor rests on an altar and candles burn among the iconic tin soldiers. Such scenes bring to mind the idolization of Pétain, his portrait in every shopwindow. One must remember, as well, that if the little corporal was the hero of the Revolution to the Left, Napoleon I brought France an empire glorified by the Right. The view of *Pontcarral* as a pro-Vichy film is expressed by Raymond Borde:

> Those who loved the film—and there were many—were the same people who acclaimed the Maréchal in his triumphant tours around the country. One too often forgets that Vichy cultivated the glorification of the flag and the troops, and that even beaten and snivelling, patriotism remained as suffocating as ever.[28]

The necessity for equivocation, for not saying exactly what one meant, permeates all of the so-called "political" films of the period, and makes any straightforward political reading impossible. Whatever the filmmaker's intent, all of these antithetical positions are inscribed in the film, and it is this fact that marks these films as belonging to the occupation period.

Borde is probably right in seeing Vichyist values in *Pontcarral*, just as many young critics have seen the whole dominant tendency of the occupation as sharing many of Vichy's cultural assumptions. But the fact that many of these films shared the same values as the State does not necessarily mean that they were instruments of Vichy propaganda. If Vichyist values were present in some of these films, it was because there was a commonality of purpose among most Frenchmen in defense of their defeated nation. Twenty-five years after the occupation ended, at least one leftist filmmaker was willing to admit that the values of the time were not so simple as they had once appeared. In making *Premier de Cordée*, Louis Daquin had intended to convey the freedom and immediacy of nature. Nonetheless,

> the boy-scoutish angle, the return to the earth—all that was no doubt inspired by Pétainist ideology. And here I was a communist and a resister. One should not forget that this was a time of contradictions and confusions. And we can never escape the times.[29]

Films and Filmmakers

The new tendency in the French cinema, the "cinema of isolation," was a product of many factors. The material conditions of filmmaking, the need to provide cultural continuity and a reason for hope to the shattered French spirit, the fear of censorship which promoted obfuscation, and the confusion of political values, all set the stage for the emergence of a new style within the French cinema.

Out of these new conditions, a new group of filmmakers came into the limelight, a group whose ideas and talents meshed with prevailing conditions. In the 1930s, conditions had favored artists like Renoir and Feyder, whose distinctive voices suited the dominant tone of freedom and sympathetic portrayals of the hopeless individual. In the 1940s, there were new themes and new styles, and the leading figures of this movement were, with few exceptions, those whose distinctive voices had not previously been clearly heard.

The discussion that follows briefly examines the work of some of these filmmakers, pointing out how widespread the new tendency was among the major French artists of the time. Some noteworthy exceptions to this tendency are discussed at the end of the chapter.

The Theatrical Influence

One of the factors most often overlooked in explaining the origins of the new style is the influx of theatrical talent into the cinema. The movement of the French cinema from the 1930s to the 1940s—from naturalism to allegory, from the world without to the world within—echoes a similar movement in the French theater of the 1930s. The leading figures of that theater—Jean Giraudoux, Jean Anouilh, and especially, Jean Cocteau—were all forces in the French cinema of the occupation and after.

Although their subjects and styles were very different, these three dramatists used metaphor and allegory as devices for setting forth their thematic concerns, elaborating on contemporary preoccupations through myths and legends in plays like Giraudoux's "La Guerre de Troie n'aura pas lieu," Cocteau's "Orphée" and "La Machine infernale," and, during the occupation, Anouilh's "Antigone" and "Electre." Not only did they bring to the cinema an opposition to naturalism, but they also brought a conviction that cinematic expression, like theatrical expression, should be more evocative than descriptive, metaphysical or spiritual rather than psychological.

Jean Giraudoux was the leading figure in the French theater of the 1930s, the playwright who set the French stage in the direction of poeticism and a definition of man "in metaphysical terms and outside of human institutions."[30] A former novelist, Giraudoux was the most "literary" of French dramatists, and brought to his film work the same concern for elaborately wrought language that had characterized his plays. Of his first screenplay, for La Duchesse de Langeais, Giraudoux wrote:

> My ambition was to create for the French cinema a school of intonation. If I have demonstrated . . . that what the film-going public understands best is language, then it is base to believe that its ears can only recognize stammering, stupidity, banality or solecism. If I have proved that the public responds to the French language by instinct, then I believe my efforts have been well worth the trouble.[31]

La Duchesse de Langeais, based on a story by Balzac (directed by Jacques de Baroncelli), does indeed display a screenplay of unusual literacy. Where characters in most historical melodramas of the period gossip and flirt among the extravagant costumes and scenery, these duchesses and barons trade apothegms on love, friendship, and constancy. The lachrymose plot, to which Giraudoux was assigned, becomes a meditation on freedom versus responsibility. Giraudoux's screenplay does not, however, entirely overcome the limitations imposed by a story in which Edwige Feuillère evolves from a flirt to a woman of substance who dies of love for the stolid Pierre-Richard Willm. (A similar situa-

tion would be more movingly presented eleven years later in Max
Ophuls' *Madame De. . . .*)

Giraudoux completed only one other film before his death
in 1944, providing the dialogue for Bresson's *Les Anges du péché*.
One finds it harder to distinguish Giraudoux's "voice" in this film,
bounded as it is on one side by Father Bruckberger's story and
on the other by Bresson's distinctive style. However, both films
were highly regarded at the time, and Giraudoux's effort to create
a "school of intonation" was very likely a factor in leading the
French cinema toward a more literary tendency.

Jean Anouilh probably had less impact on the development of the occupation-era cinema, because he was less actively
involved in that cinema. His only cinematic effort during the period was as a director (his debut) of his own 1936 play, "Le Voyageur sans bagage." Although the film did not receive wide comment at the time, and is largely ignored today, it is a successful
example of the literary tendency in the cinema.

Anouilh's adaptation of his play, although basically
faithful, improves on the play's structure and makes the situation
less symbolic and more naturalistic. Pierre Fresnay plays Gas-
ton/Jacques, the World War I soldier who has spent eighteen years
without a memory or a past, who is forced to confront a self he
preferred to forget. While the play emphasizes the symbolic nature of Gaston's desire to reinvent himself, "to be the freest being
in the world even if, to be free, I must leave an innocent cadaver
behind," the film makes Gaston a recognizable human being; he
(the film's Gaston) is a man of feeling, an honest, confused person who chooses renunciation of his past more out of shame for
past actions than for some abstract principle. The other characters, particularly Jacques's brother Georges (Pierre Renoir) and his
sister-in-law (Blanchette Brunoy) are no longer simple mechanisms representing sentimentality and desire, but individuals.

Nonetheless, Anouilh had not entirely abandoned his
conception of theatrical distance in the transformation of play to
film. This distance is maintained by denying the audience's expectations, particularly in the sudden appearance of a *deus ex machina*
at the end. "The traditional genres are shown to be false, the al-

lusions are found to be accusations, reality is finally denied by poetry, and the mythical imagination ends by collapsing under the blows of common sense."[32]

If Anouilh's film of Le Voyageur sans bagage had little impact on the cinema of the time, his theatrical work of the period, particularly "Antigone" in 1944, emblemized the tendency within the French theater of the period to escape into myth in order to express a concrete moral position on contemporary political reality (as Sartre also did in "Les Mouches.") The contemporary cinema did not go as far in this direction as did the theater, but both media were impelled by a common desire to turn away from a naturalistic depiction of human conflict in order to pose that conflict on a grander, more universal scale.

It was not the moralistic strain in the French theater, however, that particularly influenced the cinema, but rather its turning away from social reality to concentrate on the spiritual conflict of the individual. "In essence, the virtue of L'Eternel Retour was to show that during this terrible period when one could die an abominable death, one could also die of love."[33] According to this statement by its director, the film served a social function by turning the public's attention away from its everyday problems. But the statement has a deeper significance. In the work of the film's scenarist, Jean Cocteau, there is a consistency of thematic intent, an insistence on death as a metaphor for artistic creation. The abominable deaths of everyday life have no significance unless charged with poetic resonance. The deaths of this modern-day Tristan and Iseult give meaning to the deaths around them because their liebestod is the highest form of art.

L'Eternel Retour was both a popular and critical success, and to many critics it typifies the "cinéma d'évasion" of the occupation. It is a highly stylized film, set in a timeless modernity in which the hero (Jean Marais) drives a car and speaks with the measured cadences of a troubadour. The vacant-eyed heroine (Madeleine Sologne) exists purely as a plot mechanism; there is never any question of watching a real woman. To modern audiences, the film may seem too rigid and stylized, but it is central in Cocteau's oeuvre.[34] For with L'Eternel Retour, Jean Cocteau returned from the periphery of film practice to become a major figure in the French cinema. He brought with him to this cinema his preoccupation with poetry, myth, and allegory.

Cocteau's first occupation-era screenplay was for *Le Baron Fantôme*, in which little of Cocteau's preoccupation stands out.[35] The film is primarily a gothic love story, à la Emily Brontë, and it is only the small role of the phantom baron himself (played by Cocteau) which injects the presence of the poet into this supernatural world. But with Jean Marais standing in as the poet, Cocteau conceived not only *L'Eternel Retour*, but also *La Belle et la Bête*, which was planned for production in June 1944, and belongs to the occupation period in tone and visual style, if not in date of actual production.[36] Even *Les Dames du Bois de Boulogne*, for which Cocteau wrote the dialogue, has elements of Cocteau's preoccupations. Although the film recognizably belongs to Robert Bresson's *oeuvre* of spare, cerebral meditations on sin and redemption, it is also a quintessential occupation-era film which takes place in that timeless eternity of poetic imagination, where both *L'Eternel Retour* and later, Cocteau's *Orphée*, are situated. The narratives of all three films move forward without seeming cause or effect; the events are described with the precision and clarity of dreams. Maria Casarès's avenging Fate in *Les Dames* combines the pure but detached màlevolence of the dwarf in *L'Eternel Retour* with the mysterious Circe of Death of her own role in *Orphée*. The words most often used to describe the cinema of the occupation—cold, detached, composed—are the same which spring to mind in discussing these films by Cocteau. It is apparent that his influence on the cinema of the occupation was profound.

Bresson and Others

These figures from the theater were not the only newcomers to the French cinema during the occupation. Even though there was considerable continuity among film personnel from the 1930s to the 1940s, there was nonetheless a sizable influx of new talent into the industry. The most probable cause of this surge was the absence of trained personnel; certainly, among the approximately two million French prisoners of war, the quarter million Jews, and the large number of emigrés, there were many who had once made their living in the cinema. The most dramatic changeover was the one that affected the "look" of the French cinema: among directors, screenwriters, and actors.[37] Many of these newcomers benefited as well from the ready availability of capital for production and from Vichy's efforts to raise the quality of the French cinema, since these factors allowed producers to gamble on unknown quantities. The newcomer who would achieve the greatest renown was Robert Bresson, who had barely begun his career before he was taken prisoner in 1940. On his release, he proposed the subject of Les Anges du péché to numerous producers

> who all raised their hands to the heavens when confronted by a story of such "extravagance". . . . One of the important directors of Pathé (M. Christian Stengel) who had read Bresson's treatment and sensed its beauty, managed to convince the "Brain Trust" of the rue Francœur and after many hesitations, Pathé bought Les Anges du Péché. But the very next day they bitterly regretted their decision and abandoned the project. . . . The astute M. Roland Tual seized the occasion and bought the rights from Pathé. And thus on the 8th of February 1943, M. Robert Bresson began the first shot of his film which would cost 7½ million [francs].[38]

"The astute M. Roland Tual" was a member of the consultative commission of the COIC, and an aspiring director himself, who had made his own directorial debut in 1942 with Le Lit à colonnes. Tual was willing to gamble, with money provided by the Crédit National, on several projects of less than certain commercial appeal (among his other productions were Claude Autant-Lara's Lettres d'amour, and Bonsoir mesdames, bonsoir messieurs, which Tual directed himself from a script by poet Robert Desnos). Whether the reason for his acceptance of Bresson's project was the near certainty that any film produced would make money (as did Les Anges du péché) or the desire to raise the prestige of the French cinema, it is likely that the unknown Bresson had less difficulty finding financing for his first film than he would later have as one of the established masters of the French cinema.

Perhaps one reason why Bresson found backing for his first effort was because *Les Anges du péché* had much in common with the new "isolationist" tendency developing within the French cinema. Although in his later work Bresson stood apart from dominant styles and trends, his first film reflects many of the stylistic and thematic preoccupations of the period. The glacial compositions of the shots, many in extreme depth of space (the cinematographer was Philippe Agostini, who also photographed *Les Dames du Bois de Boulogne* and *Douce*), the spare and poetic dialogue by Jean Giraudoux, and the controlled performances by Renée Faure and Jany Holt, all reflected the coldness and stylization of the forties' style. An even more apparent parallel was the film's subject—the intensity of passion of those removed from the world. The film is set in a convent of the Order of Bethany, whose mission was to bring faith to female criminals. With the exception of three or four sequences, the entire film takes place within the convent walls. This isolation, this remove from life, was a perfect metaphor of the *vase clos* that was the French cinema, and France itself, at the time.

Not all of the directors who made their debut during the occupation adhered to this new tendency in the cinema. The majority of newcomers came from other positions within the film industry—producer Tual, actors René Lefèvre, Pierre Blanchar, and Fernandel, assistant director André Zwoboda, scenarist André Cayatte. These men, for the most part, broke no new ground. Rather, they created minor commercial films which reflected the styles of their mentors and predecessors.

Nor was the "isolationist" tendency exclusively a creation of *débutants*. The economic conditions which made these debuts possible also gave many veterans a chance to explore styles and subjects that would previously have been considered uncommercial. Marcel l'Herbier, for example, one of the major figures in the experimental movements of the 1920s, had his first opportunity in years to make a film that reflected his personal ideas and style. In *La Nuit fantastique*, l'Herbier rediscovered his roots in the avant-garde movements of the twenties. This comedy-fantasy combines the experimenter's delight in cinematic tricks (to such visual devices as stop and slow motion and multiple exposures, l'Herbier added various kinds of sound distortion) with a surrealistic concern for the marvelous—concretizing the unreal within the real.

Maurice Tourneur, known in the silent period for the atmospheric aestheticism of his films, also returned to his sources with *La Main du Diable*. Abel Gance, one of the pioneers of the French cinema, may, perhaps, have been too influenced by the temper of the times. He directed a version of Gautier's *Le Capitaine Fracasse* in which the dialogue for the duelling scene is recited in verse. The film was disparaged by the critics, as was *La Vénus aveugle*, an odd amalgam of Camille-like sentimentality with a happy ending. The style of the time suited the talents of Sacha Guitry, however, particularly in such historical films as *Le Destin fabuleux de Desirée Clary* and *La Malibran*. And the new emphasis on "pictorialism" led an unheralded veteran, Serge de Poligny, to the highly regarded stylizations of *Le Baron Fantôme* and *La Fiancée des ténèbres*.

Delannoy and Grémillon

The occupation saw the coming to prominence of several directors whose 1930s' works had received little attention, but who found their distinctive voices highly suitable to the new style of the forties. Jean Delannoy was a prolific director during the occupation, evincing no truly distinctive style. However, two of his films—*Pontcarral* and *L'Eternel Retour*—for different reasons, came to emblemize the period.

More highly regarded at the time was Jean Grémillon, who had only begun to emerge as a major figure in the French cinema in the late 1930s. His two occupation-era films—*Lumière d'été* and *Le Ciel est à vous*—were considered "realistic" at the time, perhaps because unlike many "prestige" productions, they were set in a recognizable present. In retrospect, however, one can clearly see the stylization of language and image in these films.

   Lumière d'été, written by Jacques Prévert and Pierre Laroche, is thematically the forties' equivalent of *La Règle du jeu*. In
both there are pairings and re-pairings, as human nature is revealed to be influenced by the passion of the moment and the
masks assumed by all. In *Lumière d'été*, the story centers on Michèle (Madeleine Robinson) who is pursued by three men—a failed
and drunken artist (Pierre Brasseur), a degenerate aristocrat (Paul
Bernard), and a heroic engineer (Georges Marchal), with the cou-
ples forming various permutations until the final fade-out, when
the "proper" match is made. It is not so much the moralizing
ending (the painter is killed in an auto accident he caused and
the aristocrat, surrounded by angry mine workers, falls over a cliff)
which distinctively characterizes it as a forties' film, but rather the
symbolic lighting effects which strikingly contrast the glaring sunshine of the Midi afternoon with the low-key shadows of the aristocrat's chateau. As in *La Règle*, the climatic action occurs at a
masked ball. Unlike the Renoir film, however, the events of the
ball seem to be a dramatic ploy, charged with a symbolic significance which undercuts the human drama. The characters cease to
be individuals, as they don the masks that represent their characters: de Sade for the Count, Hamlet for the artist. And unlike
the Renoir film, the moral is hammered in; as the madness reaches
its climax, each character reveals the truth and is rewarded accordingly.
   Le Ciel est à vous, with a screenplay by Charles Spaak and
Albert Valentin, is less charged with poeticism of language and
image, but this film also creates its effect by allusion and sym-
bolism. The film begins with a crane shot of orphans singing in
an open pasture and ends with the same shot, the pasture now
turned into an aerodrome. This circularity is imposed entirely from
without; the orphans have no intrinsic significance to the narrative, which concerns an artisanal couple (Charles Vanel, Madeleine Renaud) who sacrifice everything in order to break a flying
record. Although the film was based on a true incident, it is not
lifelike. Rather, it reveals its milieu insistently, self-consciously, in
a style Régent describes as the "poetry of the everyday" (p. 239).
   One of the reasons why both these films, despite their

contemporary subjects, appear to share the same distance and stylization of the historical and fantastic films is that they were both intended as allegories. The creators of *Lumière d'été* no doubt wanted to achieve that end which *La Règle du jeu* was often accused of attempting—an attack on France's "best elements" (i.e., the upper classes). The most corrupt figure in the film is the mad and murderous aristocrat, who is driven to his death by a group of mine workers united in a menacing circle around him. The hero is an engineer—not precisely working class, but neither is he a parasite. There is a strong anti-Vichy bias in the film which can be read in its reversal of usual Vichy formulations. Unlike most films of the time where the provinces are celebrated as the place where depraved Parisians come to restore their souls, here the Midi is the locus of corruption, and the redeemable characters (particularly the two women) long to return to Paris. Some observers have even seen anti-German sentiments in the film, particularly in Brasseur's remark, while masked as Hamlet, that "something is rotten in the state of Denmark."

To Georges Sadoul, the whole film was an allegory, both in its "clearly opposing to those society supporters of Vichy, the healthy strength of the workers, the soul of the Resistance," and also by showing "the union of Frenchmen in the Resistance sweeping out the occupiers and their accomplices."[39] Of *Le Ciel est à vous*, Sadoul went even further. It was "the exalting epic of French heroism" (p. 56). The clandestine Resistance paper, *L'Ecran Français*, counterposed *Le Ciel est à vous* to *Le Corbeau*, asserting that the former film "has saved [France's] honor":

> Because to those who are crippled, immoral, corrupted and dishonored in one of our provincial cities in *Le Corbeau*, *Le Ciel* offers characters who are full of French vigor, authentic courage, moral health; in which we find again that national truth which cannot and will not die.
>
> To the dirty little girls born vicious and deceitful which the servile imagination of M. Clouzot has made up as if under Nazi orders, it has answered "No, you are wrong. The true French children, it is I who will show them to you."

> To the club-foot and whorishness of the her-
> oine, it replies with a young mother of France, modest
> and strong, who accomplishes all her duties without
> grandiloquence and whose heart, moreover, is big
> enough to conceive a heroic dream . . .
>
> Here, then, are two films, in which one, pro-
> duced and encouraged by the Germans in camouflage,
> feeds an anti-French propaganda and in which the other
> raises itself against this propaganda by affirming that
> which the former would destroy: that is to say, our con-
> fidence in ourselves.[40]

This glorification is curious for a film which premiered
at a special showing for Maréchal Pétain, and which was proclaimed a film of "exceptional quality" in Vichy's *Presse Information*
of February 9, 1944.[41] Although the filmmakers no doubt intended
the film to be "a message of liberty and of French tenacity, . . .
other Frenchmen saw in *Le Ciel* the illustration of a Pétainist theme:
praise for the artisan class and for the jack-of-all-trades [in coun-
terpoint to] big industry." [42]

Because both of these films comment on contemporary
conditions by allusion, an ambiguity of meaning arises. In part,
this ambiguity lies in the stylization of dialogue and mise-en-scène,
and in the distance from which the characters are observed. As
quintessential occupation-era films, they were both highly praised
at the time. Grémillon continued to be an influential director until his death in 1959.

Autant-Lara and Christian-Jaque

Like Delannoy and Grémillon, two other directors who
would emerge as central figures in the postwar "cinema of quality" had both begun their careers earlier, but first came to prominence during the occupation. Both Claude Autant-Lara and
Christian-Jaque began their careers as set designers in the 1920s,
and directed several films in the 1930s that received little recognition. The film that is considered by most critics to be Autant-
Lara's first important and personal film was *Le Mariage de Chiffon*,

released in 1942. Based on the popular novel by Gyp, with a
screenplay by Jean Aurenche, the film was a nostalgic recreation
of provincial life circa 1900. "It had the deliciously grey tone of
faded flowers and crumbled like the wall paper and frillery of the
fin de siècle."[43] Autant-Lara's next film, *Lettres d'amour* (1942), was
based on an original story, again scripted by Aurenche. It was set
in the Second Empire, and, like *Chiffon*, it was a gentle parody of
the haute bourgeoisie of the provinces. Autant-Lara's last film of
the occupation added a new member to the team—scenarist Pierre
Bost who, with Aurenche, adapted the Michel Davet novel set in
the aristocratic circles of Paris in 1887.

    Douce was one of the most critically admired films of the
occupation and is one of the emblematic films of the period. In
addition to its literate, if slightly stilted, dialogue, and the controlled performances by the largely classically trained cast (Odette
Joyeux, Madeleine Robinson, Marguerite Moreno), the film was
particularly admired for its decor (by Jacques Krauss). It opens with
a tracking shot past a miniature of Paris in 1887, with a half-com-
pleted Eiffel Tower prominently displayed. One of the major leit-
motifs of the film concerns the newly invented elevator installed
in the countess' mansion.

    The film displays the same "coldness" and "lifeless-
ness" of other films of this type, taking refuge in a past cut off
from all audience identification. The emotional distance brings the
filmmakers' political intent into relief, by emphasizing the film's
theme rather than its characters. The story is intended as a com-
mentary on that class struggle Vichy had declared to be no longer
a part of French life. The plot concerns two women—Douce, the
daughter of a count who falls in love with her father's steward,
and Irène, her governess, who was once the steward's mistress and
now hopes to marry the count. The consequences of this min-
gling of classes are disastrous for all, resulting ultimately in Douce's
death. In the final shot, the door to the mansion is implacably
shut on the two servants who tried to rise above their class. Unlike Autant-Lara's two earlier films, the aristocracy is painted here
without nostalgia or sympathy. In the most revealing scene in the
film, the dowager countess pays a Christmas charity call to her

tenants, accompanied by the steward, who carries the countess' gift of a *pot au feu*. In order to warm the gift, the poor couple is obliged to use up their entire winter's supply of firewood. As the countess leaves the peasants' home, she counsels them, "I wish you patience and resignation." To which Autant-Lara added, in a scene shot but not shown until after the Liberation, the steward's parting remark: "I wish you impatience and revolt."

The film's sympathies are clearly on the side of the lower classes, even without the title which Aurenche wanted to add at the end, referring to the two outcasts: "But they lived happily ever after anyway."[44]

Although their work was singled out for attack by the *Cahiers du Cinéma* critics of the 1950s, Autant-Lara, Aurenche, and Bost created a series of films of remarkable stylistic and thematic consistency. Such postwar films as *Le Diable au corps* and *Le Rouge et le noir*, like *Douce*, emphasize the careful observation of the telling detail with a cold, detached view of human relations. One other major figure of the postwar "tradition of quality" was, unlike Autant-Lara, neither thematically consistent nor emotionally detached. What characterizes the work of Christian-Jaque is its insistent "pictorialism," the subordination of subject to style.

Christian-Jaque first came to prominence in 1938, with *Les Disparus de St. Agil*, but his reputation was consolidated during the occupation. He was one of the most prolific directors of the period, creating six films in three years, which ranged in subject from poetic fantasy (*L'Assassinat du Père Noel*, *Sortilèges*) to biography (*La Symphonie Fantastique*) to literary adaptation (*Carmen*) to *comédie sentimentale* (*Premier Bal*) and crime melodrama (*Voyage sans espoir*). In all of these films, the narrative elements are subordinated to the mise-en-scène and the incessantly moving camera. His camera movements can be subjective, as in the dance scenes in *L'Assassinat* and *Sortilèges*, where the camera whirls with the rhythms of the dancers, communicating the emotional frenzy of the characters. Generally, however, his camera movements are descriptive, like the tracking shot through the trees which ends *L'Assassinat* and pinpoints the couple's isolation from the real world. For Christian-Jaque, camera movement, sets, lighting, camera angles serve to define his characters in terms of their emotional states or their environments: the off-angle shots which express Berlioz' inner passion in *La Symphonie Fantastique*, or the extreme high angle of the final shot, which signifies his ascent to the gods. *Sortilèges* opens with a stark white landscape and a tiny cabin visible in the rear-ground, symbolic of nature's primacy over man which will emerge as a major theme of the film. As a self-conscious stylist, Christian-Jaque's talents were apposite for the new emphasis that developed during the occupation.

The Exceptions: Becker et al.

Whatever the merits of Autant-Lara and Christian-Jaque, there can be no question that they were among the most influential figures in the postwar French cinema. In fact, with the exception of Jacques Tati, all of the major French filmmakers of the period between the Liberation and the New Wave first came to prominence during the occupation.[45] Most of them conformed, to varying extents, to the dominant style of this "isolationist" cinema.

The one significant exception was Jacques Becker, whose three occupation-era films were very different in spirit from those which characterized the era. Perhaps it was Becker's long association with Jean Renoir that led him to emphasize character over style. Certainly, among the films released abroad after the Liberation, Becker's *Goupi Mains Rouges* was one of the most enthusiastically received, for it was among the few that reminded critics of the prewar style.

Becker had been an assistant to Renoir on such films as *Boudu Sauvé des eaux*, *Les Bas Fonds*, and *La Marseillaise*. He began his first film, *L'Or du Cristobal*, during the *drôle de guerre*, but it was finished and signed by Jean Stelli when Becker was mobilized. On his return from a prisoner of war camp in 1941, he was hired by André Halley des Fontaines, who had produced *Le Crime de M. Lange*, and Becker made his debut in 1942 with *Dernier Atout*.

The film was a fast-paced comedy of cops and robbers, recognizably American in subject and style. But it was set in a

mythical Latin American country, in order not "to give the Pro-
pagandastaffel [sic] the satisfaction of telling us once again that
the U.S. was a country of bandits."[46]

Becker's next film, *Goupi Mains Rouges*, was released in 1943
and was adapted by Pierre Véry from his own novel. Unlike the
films Christian-Jaque made from Véry adaptations (*Les Disparus de
St. Agil*, *L'Assassinat du Père Noel*), *Goupi Mains Rouges* emphasized
character over environment. In fact, the decor was unexceptional;
the two or three interior sets were purely functional and lacked
the symbolic significance with which Christian-Jaque infused his
decor. Becker's revelation of character traits was the heart of the
film and, contrary to Vichyist practice, he refused to indulge in
sentimentality in his study of a well-to-do peasant family.

> [The film] is a scathing picture of peasant customs, de-
> tailing the way a family, after having become masters of
> their village, surrender themselves to the search for one
> of those mysterious treasures which make up the ro-
> mantic element of French provincial life. It is not, in any
> case, the plot line which holds the film's chief interest,
> but rather the collection of portraits which are painted,
> from that of the patriarch, nicknamed l'Empéreur
> [Maurice Schutz] to the young man who left to seek his
> fortune in Paris and only succeeded in becoming a
> salesclerk: Goupi-Cravates [Georges Rollin], by way of
> the soldier who served in the colonies, Goupi Tonkin
> [Robert le Vigan] and the poacher, Goupi Mains Rouges
> [Fernand Ledoux]. There are not many peasants in French
> films, and those there are either fall into the "George
> Sand category" or in the "Zola category" . . . Those of
> Pierre Véry and Jacques Becker are certainly the most
> authentic peasants who have ever come to life in a
> French studio.[47]

Barthélemy Amengual compared the realism of *Goupi*'s
milieu to that of Renoir's *Toni*, while Maurice Bardèche asserted
that some scenes in the film had the authenticity of a painting by
Courbet.[48] The film was praised by the critics and proved extremely popular with audiences.

Becker's third film was begun in March 1944, and not released until after the war. While *Falbalas*, with its melodramatic love triangle, lacks the verisimilitude of character of Becker's previous film, it has the singular distinction of being the only film of the period to sketch the daily life of the Parisian *haute bourgeoisie* during the occupation itself. Given the resolute atemporality of almost every film of the period, it is striking to see in *Falbalas* the nearly empty *grands boulevards*, and the wealthy heroine running her errands by bicycle. The film's setting in a *maison de haute couture* is sketched in great detail, providing an almost documentary view of the preparations necessary for each new collection. The carefully observed detail of these films, the "realism" of character and milieu, set Becker apart from his contemporaries and place him as the direct descendant of Jean Renoir.

Becker's films, *Goupi* in particular, recall the "warmth" of close observation, the sense of life as it's lived of such Renoir films as *Boudu* and *Une Partie de campagne*. Another director would provide a film in the Groupe Octobre spirit of *Le Crime de M. Lange*, a film filled with the same high spirits, camaraderie, and freedom. It is not surprising that this spirit should infuse a film written and directed by the founders of the Groupe Octobre: Jacques and Pierre Prévert. What may be surprising is that the original scenario for *Adieu Léonard* was written in 1930, but the film was not made until 1943.

Adieu Léonard is one of the many paradoxes of the occupation period. The film's creators were well-known Leftists. Their only previous collaboration, on the 1932 production of L'*Affaire est dans le sac*, had ended in a commercial disaster which had prevented Pierre Prévert from directing any commercial projects in the interim. The subject of their film was liberty. And most of the cast and crew were political or religious outcasts, some wanted by the police, most banned from the profession. Under the circumstances, a less likely opportunity for filmmaking cannot be imagined, and yet Prévert maintains he had no difficulty whatever in making the film.[49]

The film was produced by the same Halley des Fontaines who had financed Becker's *Dernier Atout*, and it was distributed by Pathé, who imposed Charles Trenet, a singer with little acting experience as the star. In an interview in 1968, Prévert asserted that the film was made in order to give work to his friends,[50] a story confirmed by Simone Signoret in her memoirs.

> Pierre Prévert was the first of the Préverts to come back to Paris. He came with a scenario by Jacques called *Adieu Léonard* which was the biggest find for the paperless persons of the [Café de] Flore . . . There was a whole host of small parts, all those unusual minor roles that Jacques loved so: [Roger] Blin was a Gypsy, along with Vitsoris, a Greek Trotskyite in hiding. I was a Gypsy. My hair was curly and I wore a very beautiful dress. I didn't say a word; I made baskets . . . There was also a girl from the October Group, whose name I have forgotten: She was Jewish, her husband was in a concentration camp, she had left her kids behind in Paris in order to do the film on location and earn a little money. She cried all the time. (p.60)

Many of the technicians involved in the film were active in the Resistance, including the cameraman, who later joined the maquis and was shot by the Germans.

Yet none of the tensions of the time show up in this free-spirited comedy which begins with an inept thief, Léonard (Carette), being blackmailed by his intended victim, Bonenfant (Pierre Brasseur), into murdering Bonenfant's cousin Ludovic (Trenet). Most of the film takes place at Ludovic's newly inherited estate in the provinces, where this simple, good-hearted soul invites every passing peddler and tradesman to live and teach him their *métiers*. The hapless Léonard fails in his half-hearted attempts to become an assassin, and after a wildly farcical finale with gunshots punctuating the dialogue and the villains finally locked in the closet, Léonard goes off with Ludovic, his girlfriend (Jacqueline Bouvier), and the tradesmen to pursue the carefree life of the open road.

Roger Régent justifiably saw parallels between this anarchic fantasy and Clair's *A Nous la liberté*, although the characters of Léonard and Bonenfant strongly recall Lange and Batala in *Le*

Crime de M. *Lange.* The freedom celebrated by the screenplay is echoed by the expansiveness of the performances. As in *Lange*, the camera often seems to be merely capturing a group of actors enjoying themselves, which was, in fact, the case.

> The film was made in Dax, in the southwest. The weather was beautiful, we were working—it was a breather. Above all, it was the Café Flore on holiday. What luck to be young, with these people, and in that production where there wasn't the slightest discrimination between actors, extras, technicians and stars. Brasseur and Carette supplied a nonstop stream of stories . . . Trenet was the only one among us who had any money. He would buy the hams cured in the region and we would all throw ourselves upon them greedily . . . We would all gather around him, sitting in the grass, and on the spur of the moment he'd compose songs . . . What with Brasseur's and Carette's stories, Jacqueline Bouvier's humor, and [the] concerts, we were entertained by a constant show.[51]

Yet, despite the high spirits, despite its paean to liberty, *Adieu Léonard* was one of the few commercial failures of the occupation. The problem may have been the loosely structured narrative which was difficult to follow, or the broadly drawn characters who repelled audience sympathy. Perhaps the film was simply too different from others of the period to be fashionable. Whatever the case, the film proved that the anarchic spirit of the early 1930s was not entirely dead.

The work of Becker and Pierre Prévert skirted the mainstream of contemporary filmmaking by looking back to the styles and subjects of the great thirties' works. Two other films stood outside the dominant tendencies of the early 1940s by anticipating styles that had not yet become current.

When Louis Daquin's *Nous les gosses* was released in late 1941, it was "like a joyous cry which resounded in that darkened auditorium. The film had freshness, spontaneity, a wonderful surge . . . Even the best films made since the exodus provided nothing that had not been done before . . . But in Nous les gosses there was a style that the French cinema had never been able to capture before."[52]

In a style that would later be called neorealistic, the film is constructed around the daily incidents in the life of a group of children living in a working-class suburb of Paris. The film was shot mostly in exteriors (albeit on constructed sets) and the simple story revolves around the efforts of the children to get money to replace a broken window. Thematically, the film is a celebration of the unity of the children in the face of adult authority, and was clearly intended as a parable for adults as well.

Nous les gosses illustrates not only a departure from the stylization and rigidity of the dominant tendency, but serves as another of those paradoxes that the period seemed to give rise to. For the film was not only fairly clearly about the efficacy of united action in the face of stronger authority, but it was also made by a group of men whose left-wing politics were well-known. The writers Maurice Hiléro and Gaston Modot (better known as an actor) had both been leaders in the Communist-controlled Ciné-Liberté movement of the thirties. Louis Daquin, for whom Nous les gosses was the first major directorial assignment, had joined the clandestine Communist Party in 1941 and later became a leader of both the Comité de Libération du Cinéma Français and the clandestine trade union movement. Yet, ironically, Daquin had more difficulties with French censors on such postwar films as Bel Ami (1954) than he encountered from the Germans. In fact, Daquin deliberately inserted several anti-authoritarian statements into Nous les gosses, with the hope that at least some would be overlooked by the German censors. Much to his surprise, the film was passed without cuts.[53]

"Like Nous les Gosses, Marie-Martine impressed those who saw it in the fall of 1942 as bringing something new to the French cinema."[54] The "sleeper" of the occupation period and a casualty of the auteur theory, this film by Albert Valentin is periodically rediscovered by critics and then, just as inevitably, forgotten. In narrative structure, it is the equivalent of Citizen Kane, without Welles' bravura style. But its complex use of multiple points of

view and flashback techniques seemingly had no influence whatever on other films of the period which are resolutely linear in
their unfolding.[55] The story by Jaques Viot (who is often credited
with "inventing" the inverted structure of present to past narration in *Le Jour se lève*) begins in a bookstore in a provincial town.
An author, meant by his dress to suggest André Gide (Jules Berry),
enters to discuss his new novel which is displayed in the window.
He discovers that the subject of his novel, Marie-Martine (Renée
St. Cyr), lives in this very town and he proceeds to wrest from her
the postscript to the tale he wrote (but which has not yet been
revealed to the audience). In flashback, she tells of her imprisonment and of the kind man (Bernard Blier) who befriended her
after her release. The story then shifts to Blier's point of view, as
he visits an uncle (Saturnin Fabre) to seek advice on proposing
marriage to Marie-Martine. As this part of the narration goes forward, he discovers the book, whose contents—the first meeting
between Marie-Martine and the author, and his betrayal of her to
the police—are revealed in flashback.

The story continues to move both forward (the engagement of Marie-Martine and the young man) and backward (the
events leading to Marie-Martine's meeting with the author are revealed by an old woman who knew the heroine as a girl). The events
of the past assure the viewer of the essential innocence of the
heroine, allowing for a happy resolution of the forward-moving plot.

Marie-Martine's present obscurity is hard to explain, since
it was not only highly praised by contemporary critics but was also
extremely popular with audiences. The recent critic who asserted
that the standard histories have ignored unusual films such as
these is incorrect.[56] But our image of the films of the occupation,
inasmuch as we have one, has certainly been shaped far more by
Les Visiteurs du soir and *L'Eternel Retour* than by *Nous les gosses* or *Marie-
Martine*. Among the more than 200 films made between 1940 and
1944, other works may, perhaps, be hidden whose merits were not
recognized at the time, because they did not conform to the style
then in vogue. Yet now, modern critics may find themselves more
drawn to the exceptions than to the rules, our changing tastes in

film having consigned what was once a dominant tendency to present-day obscurity.

Conclusion

Few of the films made during the occupation are widely seen and discussed today. The new style that developed at that time has passed from fashion, largely because of attacks leveled at it in the postwar years. When the critics of the *Cahiers du Cinéma* launched their attack on the "tradition of quality" in the early 1950s, they were reacting against what they saw as a moribund stylistic tendency, one which had come to represent "the" French cinema and which had been overpraised. Their objection to this tradition was based on both political and stylistic antagonism to a group of films which they believed exalted the scenarist at the expense of the director, and which created a cold distance between the filmmaker and his subject. "This school which aspires to realism destroys it at the moment of finally grabbing it, so careful is the school to lock these things in a closed world, barricaded by formulas, plays on words, maxims, instead of letting us see them for ourselves, with our own eyes."[57] The iconoclasm of these attacks served as a corrective—by challenging the very concept of "quality," the *Cahiers* critics established a new standard of judging cinematic worth.

Although a redefinition of cinematic quality may have been a necessary breakthrough in 1954, we should not allow the needs of that moment to forever determine our attitudes toward the "cinema of quality." When the tendency first appeared, during the occupation, it was applauded by most critics, including André Bazin (the founder of the *Cahiers du Cinéma*), as a valid response to the political and social conditions of the time.

It is even possible to believe that the health and probably the quality of our production has remained sound, in spite of terrible economic and technical conditions. French cinema is putting up an almost miraculous fight,

with a vitality and energy that may perhaps surprise its
historians . . .[58]

Summing up the period as a whole, Bazin wrote in 1944:

> For two years now critics have unanimously and un-
> ceasingly been congratulating themselves on the prog-
> ress of French cinema. Just think back to 1940–41 film
> production, the nothingness of which skirted disaster.
> We were ready to believe that our cinema was con-
> demned. But even as we listened to the demon of de-
> spair, there was already being erected under the sky of
> Provence the great white chateau that Marcel Carné was
> to make the bastion of our hopes [in Les Visiteurs du soir].
> They were not to be disappointed: three years of war-
> time production today reveal themselves as not only
> honorable but of an exceptional richness. (p.95)

Whatever our judgments of this cinema today, the great
films of the occupation turned the period's liabilities into assets.
The material shortages became challenges to filmmakers' ingenuity; the bureaucratic oversight spurred the development of a
cinema that was rigorous, restrained, and formal. The French cinema of the occupation turned inward, returning to its sources in
the French cultural tradition because it needed to give hope and
reassurance to the French public and because filmmakers believed the development of a distinctively French style was a proper
response to a time of upended political values. Marcel Carné's
white chateau was among the first bastions constructed in defense of the French cinema. The newcomers and veterans who followed his example formed the front ranks of a new cinematic tradition that had been born from the destruction of France.

Chapter 7

Goebbels and German Film Policy in France

With whatever sophistries they disguised their actions, the fact of writing an article, even a neutral one, in a newspaper that was nothing but a propaganda sheet for Hitler, of acting in a theater that was authorized to reopen only because it suited the needs of the nazis, of making a film—of behaving oneself, in brief, as if the war hadn't happened, as if the country were not in mourning, as if the new order did not exist—all these things constituted an indirect way of serving German interests . . . Jean Cocteau's words, "Long live shameful peace," could have been the national motto.[1]

T here are those who believe that in making films at all, the French were morally culpable; that essentially, if not literally, they were collaborating with the enemy. Those active in the film industry during the occupation would not agree, however. They did not see their work as in any way supportive of German interests. Rather, they saw their activities as honorable efforts to sustain the national film industry, and to bring comfort and hope to the French people.

Producers and filmmakers believed it was important to keep the French film industry alive, both for national prestige and to provide jobs. Of course, there was a great deal of money to be made during the period, and producers did not act entirely for selfless ends. Nevertheless, with new productions, film companies provided work for artists and technicians, for employees of distribution companies and movie theaters. If production had simply shut down, many thousands of people would have been unemployed, some of them with highly specialized skills not easily transferable to other professions.

Far from being viewed as greedy exploiters, French producers were regarded by many filmmakers as allies. Louis Daquin, a militant Communist, maintains that there was no class struggle in the film industry during the occupation. "There was a kind of solidarity [between filmmakers and producers] against the common enemy. The producers were small entrepreneurs and they supported our activities. We got money from them to give to the maquis. In terms of working conditions at the time, we had nothing to complain about."[2]

It was well known that some producers, like André Paulvé, employed Jews and members of the Resistance. André Halley des Fontaines hired both Jacques Becker and Pierre Prévert, well-known leftists whose films served as vehicles for Resistance activities. Raoul Ploquin, once head of the COIC, produced Le Ciel est à vous, considered a pro-Resistance film at the time, and another vehicle for Resistance activities. This list (and other producers can be added to it) is not meant to suggest that all French producers were heroes or that financial considerations were not their primary concern. But it is worth pointing out that concern for profit could coexist with social and political ethics, and that making money was not, in itself, a sign of collaboration.

Filmmakers across the political spectrum—from active collaborators to active resisters—made films because they needed the money. Some, it is true, didn't much care who paid their salaries. Actor Léonce Corne traveled from roles in proto-Resistance films like Pontcarral and Lumière d'été, to a leading part in the overt Nazi propaganda film Forces occultes (1943), an anti-Freemasonry tract that was the only feature-length fiction film made in France at the Germans' behest.[3]

On the other side, René Lefèvre, who spent much of the occupation in the active Resistance, helping downed English flyers escape, admits the films he made during the period were done simply for the money.[4] Even resisters had to eat.

Filmmakers did not exclusively see their work in material terms, however.

> We wanted and needed to divert ourselves, to escape from reality. It was very important because all around us there was a misery that encouraged us to make films that would engage the public without totally distracting them, films that could give them a different sense from their day to day lives . . . The French needed to see films. There was no other distraction . . . Films and theater were the only outlets for people who were dying of hunger, who had no shoes except wooden clogs, whose normal lives no longer existed.[5]

There was, then, a social reason for continuing to make films. To lift the spirits of a disheartened people, to provide some small measure of hope, sympathy, or even simple fantasy, seemed to be an unexceptionable goal.

But for many filmmakers, amusing the audience was not enough. By reminding audiences of a glorious past, by creating a film culture that reflected the heights of the French nation, filmmakers also saw themselves as defending France. The "French school" which developed during the occupation was, in part, a political response to the time. By making films that would be recognized for their high quality. French filmmakers were answering those who believed France and its institutions were dead, that the leadership of the cultural world had passed to the eastern side of the Rhine. The heart beating within the petrified body of France was its art, its culture, its cinema.

French filmmakers believed that by making films, by making the best films they could, they were helping their nation. But this view of French filmmakers' actions overlooks a vital question: if the French film industry worked for the benefit of

France, why did the Germans allow the French film industry to function?

The answer to this question is not to be found in any of the accounts of the period, nor was it generally understood among those who were active in the film industry of the time. Yet the answer to the question is of fundamental importance, both for understanding the conditions of filmmaking of the time and for arriving at a judgment about the activities of filmmakers. When it is understood why the Germans allowed the French film industry to continue relatively unimpeded, the actions of those who were responsible for the French cinema may be seen in an entirely different light.

It was suggested in chapter 3 that the main reason the Germans allowed French production to resume in the North was because audiences would not go to German films in sufficient numbers to maintain the livelihoods of theaters and distributors; that without new French features, the French film market would simply dry up. Although undoubtedly true, this answer is insufficient. There were other occupied countries, notably Poland, where the Germans simply shut down film production. Although it is true that overall German policy in Poland was far more brutal than in France, the point is that if the Germans had wanted to prevent the French from making films, they would have done so notwithstanding the economic consequences.

Another possible reason suggested in chapter 3 concerns the Germans' own financial stake in the French film industry. Undoubtedly, this was an important motive. German interests controlled companies in all branches of the film industry—from studios to laboratories, from film manufacturing to theaters. According to postwar documents, Gaumont, France's third largest film production company, was also controlled, in part, by German interests.[6] And of course, the Germans had established their own, 100 percent German-owned company in France, Continental Films.

Notwithstanding the economic advantages of taking over a large portion of the French film industry, however, the issue of what the Germans expected to gain from this investment is not immediately apparent. For one thing, it is not clear that Conti-

nental made a profit—its enormous initial investment would have
required many years to amortize and, in its first year of operation
(1941), the firm showed a loss of 21 million francs.[7] Second, if
Continental was intended to be a way of channeling French box
office receipts into German hands, its effectiveness was questionable. Unlike films made in Germany, production costs for Continental's films were channeled into the French economy. Technicians' salaries, purchase of material, post-production costs, all took
money out of the German economy and put it back in France.[8]

Furthermore, even if Continental was expected to turn a
profit, it would have been in a far better position to do so had
there been no competition. Yet, the Germans did allow, even encourage, private French firms to produce films. In order to determine why, it is first necessary to dispel one common assumption
concerning the Germans' attitude toward the French film industry.

Goebbels's Diary

In those portions of Joseph Goebbels's diaries published after the war, the Minister for Propaganda and Public En-
lightenment addressed the question of French film on three separate occasions. These sections, reprinted in Hull, Sadoul, and other
commentaries, have colored most perceptions of the Germans'
intent in France.[9]

The first entry was written on May 13, 1942:

> I took a look at another French movie [sic], *Annette et la
> Dame Blonde*. It is of the same levity and elegance as the
> Darrieux movie, *Caprices*. We shall have to be careful
> about the French so that they won't build up a new
> moving-picture art under our leadership that will give
> us too serious competition in the European market. I
> shall see to it that especially talented French film ac-
> tors are gradually engaged for the German movie.[10]

What is immediately puzzling about this remark is that
both films named in the passage were produced by Continental,

a firm owned and operated by Goebbels's own RMVP, via Cautio. Did Goebbels really think of the firm's products as French? Surely, it was good business for this German company to make "elegant" films that would do well at the box office.

The remarks concerning "a new moving picture art" and the "competition in the European market," are equally puzzling and will be discussed below. Of the plan to co-opt the French industry by stealing its talent, Goebbels reiterated his determination on May 15, 1942:

> All actors of more than average talent in the French movies should, as far as possible, be hired by us for German film production. I see no other possibility of achieving a satisfactory result in this matter. We might well worry about the consequences that might result if we did not take a hand. (p. 215)

Goebbels did, in fact, attempt to engage French personnel, but his efforts were a failure. Although "goodwill" trips to Berlin were organized, and such important stars as Danielle Darrieux, Viviane Romance, Junie Astor, Suzy Delair, and Albert Préjean went to Berlin, of their own accord in March 1942, and met with Goebbels in a highly publicized encounter, most of the French film community simply refused to go.[11] For the March 1942 trip, all of Continental's personnel had been invited, as well as others such as Pierre Renoir. But these actors, directors, and writers found excuses. Pierre Blanchar asked for "more information"; André Luguet suddenly took sick.[12] Although Goebbels may have enticed a few stars to provide propaganda material for Franco-German unity, no major star, director, or writer (with the exception of Harry Baur) ever worked in Germany throughout the period.

That same May 15, 1942, entry contained two other passages concerning French film. The first concerned Christian-Jaque's La Symphonie Fantastique:

> In the evening, we viewed a new motion picture produced by our Continental-Gesellschaft in Paris, after a scenario written around the life and activity of Hector

> Berlioz. The film is of excellent quality and amounts to
> a first-class national fanfare. I shall unfortunately not
> be able to release it for public showing. (p. 215)

But the film had already been released in Paris, on April 1, 1942,
and was, by May 15, enjoying a successful run throughout France.
It is not likely that Goebbels was unaware of what Continental
was doing. In any case, the Filmprüfstelle mentioned La Symphonie
Fantastique in its report to Berlin in March 1942. In fact, they considered it "an excellent film artistically and culturally, and it should
be used for educational purposes" (R142/F539).

Goebbels' pique at the nationalism of La Symphonie Fantastique led him to formulate the most often-cited of his dicta. The
passage reads in full:

> I am angry to think that our own offices in Paris are
> teaching the French how to represent nationalism in
> pictures. This lack of political instinct can hardly be
> beaten. But that's the way we Germans are. Whenever
> we go into another country, be it ever so strange to us
> or even an enemy, our first task seems to consist in
> getting order into that country regardless of the fact that
> perhaps in several years or decades it may go to war
> against us. The lack of political instinct among the Ger-
> mans is the result of their passion for work and of their
> idealistic enthusiasm. You have to put on the brakes
> constantly so that evil and damaging consequences may
> not result. I ordered Greven to come to Berlin from Paris,
> to give him absolutely clear and unmistakable direc-
> tives to the effect that for the moment, so far as the
> French are concerned, *only light, frothy and, if possible corny
> pictures* are desired. No doubt the French people will be
> satisfied with that too. There is no reason why we should
> cultivate their nationalism. (p. 215, emphasis mine)

It is not known what Goebbels had in mind by "light,
frothy, and corny," but it is unlikely he was thinking of films like
La Main du Diable or Le Corbeau, both of which went into production at Continental after May 1942. Of the non-Continental films

made in France, a more unlikely characterization could not be made. The cinema of the occupation—the cinema of Les Visiteurs du soir and Douce—may be many things, but it is not "light, frothy, and corny."

Since the portions of Goebbels' diary that have been published are excerpted, it is not known whether these entries represented a consistent attitude on Goebbels' part or merely a temporary peevishness brought on by the evident superiority of French production. Since all the evidence suggests that German policy was contrary to that outlined in the diary, one must either assume that the Propaganda Abteilung and Continental operated against Goebbels' wishes, or that his own attitude was ambivalent and that only the negative aspect has been preserved.[13] In any case, these diary entries run entirely against the facts, as can be seen in the last entry, on May 19, 1942:

> In the afternoon I had a long argument with [Fritz] Hippler [the head of the film division of the Propaganda Ministry] and with Greven about the aims to be pursued in our French film production. Greven has an entirely wrong technique in that he has regarded it as his task to raise the level of the French movie. That is wrong. It isn't our job to supply the Frenchmen with good pictures and it is especially not our task to give them movies that are beyond reproach in their nationalistic tendency.
>
> If the French people on the whole are satisfied with light, corny stuff, we ought to make it our business to produce such cheap trash. It would be a case of lunacy for us to promote competition against ourselves. We must proceed in our movie policies as the Americans do in their policies toward the North and South American continents. We must become the dominating movie power on the European continent. In so far as pictures are produced in other countries they must be only of a local or limited character. It must be our aim to prevent so far as possible the founding of any new national film industry, and if necessary to hire for Berlin, Vienna or Munich such stars and technicians as might

be in a position to help in this. After I talked to him for
a long time Greven realized the wisdom of this course
and will pursue it in the future. (p. 221)

In this passage, Goebbels again refers to the French cinema as a "new national film industry." Yet it was an industry older
and more prestigious than Goebbels' own. His desire to treat the
French film industry in a way analogous to the American domination of Latin America may have been, in fact, his hope, but the
analogy has severe limitations. Unlike the Latin American film industry, French film was not strictly "of a local or limited character." In fact, France had had a much stronger position on the international export market than Germany before the war. It had been
the chief supplier of films to Switzerland, Belgium, Egypt, and
French Canada, and before 1936, it had been second only to the
United States in Spain and the Balkan countries. France had also
had important export relations with Sweden, Turkey, and Latin
America before the war.[14]

Thus, with the exception of Italy, France was the only
country under German domination whose film industry could
provide a real competition to the German film industry. But contrary to Goebbels' statements, German film policy in France was
neither obstructive nor imperialistic in the way Goebbels envi-
sioned in the diaries.

The New Europe

That Goebbels' remarks concerning the French film industry have been accepted at face value by film historians is puzzling, since it is obvious that such a policy was never carried out.
Perhaps historians have been willing to credit these remarks because the malevolence of Goebbels' intentions accords with our
preconceptions of Nazi brutality. But if the functionaries of the
Third Reich were cruel, they were not dimwitted. In fact, far from
seeking to destroy the French cinema, the Nazis found it to their
advantage to encourage French filmmakers to produce their best
efforts. The reasons for the Germans' seeming benevolence are
varied and complex.

A consideration of German film policy in occupied France must first take into account the conditions that existed at the time. During the first two years of the occupation (1940–42), overall German intentions toward France were not primarily destructive.[15] Whatever the goals of Nazi policymakers in Berlin, the military's overriding need for cooperation from the French necessitated a policy that would create the least amount of dissension. In order to free German armies for the active fronts, it was essential that France be given a certain amount of latitude; if the Germans imposed harsh conditions on the French people, they would need to divert more personnel to enforce these policies.

The Germans sought to engender cooperation among both producers and consumers. In the film industry, this meant allowing French production companies to resume work. Once Continental's production schedule was in place and its French personnel under contract, competing French firms could be allowed to begin production once more. By permitting French production in June 1941, the Germans not only alleviated the problems of unemployment and capital losses for the French film industry, but they also hoped to satisfy French audiences' demands for French films. Continental alone could not have provided sufficient numbers of films to satisfy the French market, but with French firms in operation, the Germans had enough French films available to pacify the public.

That pacification was one of the goals of German film policy in France is stated explicitly in the Film Section reports:

> The Kodak-Pathé company has been forced to cut production in half, because they lack raw material. But in the interest of the public, the Propaganda Abteilung has decided to allow them to make as much film as they can, in order to quiet the average citizen and to give the people entertainment. (R142/F745)

and

> Because of the heavy bombings, many buildings have been partially destroyed. We have ordered them to be

La Fille du Puisatier (The Well-Digger's Daughter), directed by Marcel Pagnol, was the first film to begin production after the French defeat of 1940. With (*from left*): Josette Day, Raimu, Fernandel. Courtesy Museum of Modern Art, Film Stills Archive.

L'Assassinat du Père Noël (Who Killed Santa Claus?) was the first film produced in the German occupied zone. It was directed by Christian-Jaque with a French cast and crew for the German-owned production company, Continental Films. The star, Harry Baur (*shown here*), was the only major French film artist to work in Germany. He was also the only important film star to die as a result of Nazi persecution. Courtesy Museum of Modern Art, Film Stills Archive.

The occupation saw the birth of a new film style in France. Criticized by some as cold and artificial, the new style was celebrated by many critics as the birth of a specifically "French school of cinema." Its champions included both veteran filmmakers like Marcel L'Herbier and newcomers like Robert Bresson. ABOVE: *La Nuit fantastique* (The Fantastic Night), directed by Marcel L'Herbier, with Micheline Presle and Fernand Gravey. BELOW: *Les Anges du Péché* (Angels of the Streets), directed by Robert Bresson. Courtesy French Cultural Services.

"The virtue of L'*Eternel Retour* [The Eternal Return] was to show that during this terrible period when one could die an abominable death, one could also die of love." Jean Marais, as the contemporary Tristan will soon be joined by Madeleine Sologne, his Iseult. The film, directed by Jean Delannoy, was based on a screenplay by Jean Cocteau. Cocteau's influence on the cinema of the occupation was profound. Courtesy French Cultural Services.

The Devil (Jules Berry) rants in despair as the hearts of the lovers (Alain Cuny, Marie Déa), whom he has turned to stone, continue to beat. To many in France, *Les Visiteurs du Soir* (The Devil's Own Envoys), directed by Marcel Carné, with a screenplay by Jacques Prévert and Pierre Laroche, was an allegory of France's indomitable spirit. Courtesy Museum of Modern Art, Film Stills Archive.

Contrasting styles of filmmaking in two dinner table scenes. ABOVE: Claude Autant-Lara's *Douce* (Love Story) typifies the ornate style of the "French school." With Roger Pigaut (back to camera), Odette Joyeux (*far left*), Marguerite Moreno, Jean Debucourt, Madeleine Robinson. BELOW: Jacques Becker's *Goupi Mains Rouges* (It Happened at the Inn) recalls the warmth of Renoir's prewar films. FROM LEFT: Marcelle Hainia, Blanchette Brunoy, Germaine Kerjean, Arthur Devère and Guy Favières. Courtesy Museum of Modern Art, Film Stills Archive.

The lavishness of production despite material scarcity. ABOVE: Jean Grémillon's *Lumière d'été* (Summer Light). BELOW: Marcel Carné's *Les Enfants du Paradis* (Children of Paradise), the most expensive film produced in France up to that time. Courtesy Museum of Modern Art, Film Stills Archive and French Cultural Services.

Le Corbeau (The Raven) directed by Henri-Georges Clouzot, the most controversial of all occupation films. ABOVE: Pierre Fresnay as Dr. Germain; from moral certainty to an acceptance of ambiguity. BELOW: Ginette Leclerc as Denise; a symbol of that "degeneracy" that weakened the moral fiber of France and led to its defeat. Courtesy Museum of Modern Art, Film Stills Archive.

> repaired immediately, so the film industry will not be
> held up for too long. There is a great need among the
> common people for entertainment, especially now that
> food rations have been cut. (R142/F800)

A relatively liberal film policy met the Germans' immediate needs to pacify the French. But the liberalism also served
the Germans' long-range goals. It must be kept in mind, that in
the period 1940–42, it appeared likely that the Germans would
win the war and that France would be permanently attached to
Germany. The exact nature of France's place in the "new Europe"
was never formulated, but what evidence exists indicates that the
Germans expected France to continue to be a major industrial
nation, in a subsidiary relationship to Germany.[16] Unlike Eastern
Europe, the occupied countries of Western Europe were expected
to maintain a strong industrial base that would work in conjunc-
tion with Germany. In other words, France was no longer to be
regarded merely as a defeated enemy, but was to be a future part-
ner (albeit, a junior one) in the creation of a continent-wide industrial giant.

For the Germans to gut French industry would have been
counterproductive in the long run. After all, France was no longer
producing goods for its own benefit, but for that of the "new Europe." In the film industry, this policy meant overcoming the sim-
plistic assumption of a French/German rivalry. The French were
now citizens of Europe, and if they produced critically admired
films, the prestige these films generated would reflect not on French
culture, but on the culture (and prosperity) of this "new Europe."

Even Goebbels publicly supported such a policy. In July
1941, the first congress of the International Moving Picture Association was held in Berlin. Not only were the occupied countries represented, but invitations were extended to such neutral
countries as Switzerland and Sweden. The purpose of the association was to formulate an overall film policy in Europe, with Germany naturally taking the leading role. Although France was not
represented at the conference, one of two vice-presidencies of the
association was reserved for a member of the French delega-
tion.[17]

In his speech to the delegates, Goebbels evinced the same ambivalence as was seen in his diary. "He said that after the war, the Germans would encourage production in the smaller European countries, unlike the U.S. which suppresses the production of its competitors. Since only a few films can be made, they should be of high quality." [18]

The ambivalence arises from Goebbels' continued viewing of non-German production as "competition," while at the same time assuring these competitors that they were working for the benefit of a new European order. Among the German film officials in France, however, no such ambivalence occurred, at least in their public statements.

> A group of actors—among them Danielle Darrieux and Fernandel—were told [by officials of the Propaganda Abteilung] that they were not making French or German films, but European ones. There is no greater art, nor any with more influence—especially on the young—than film. Its influence can be good or bad, so rigid control must be exercised over the industry. The most important thing is to find talent, and to promote works that are worthy of French culture in the European frame. (R141/F900)

Even discounting the rhetoric of the "new Europe," there was an immediate propaganda benefit to be gained for the Germans from promoting French film production. By using the French film industry as a showcase, the Germans could prove the benefits of following the German line to the French themselves and to other nations of Europe. This point was made by Dr. Diedrich of the Propaganda Abteilung in a speech to film producers:

> The French must make films of quality, bearing in mind the moral and educational importance of their production.
> Formerly, French films contained negative values and were made by Jews . . . . The French people are now waiting for films that show its true character, films

that are healthy, worthy of the artistic heritage of the
nation, and which show the mark of the new order.[19]

The Germans could afford to be generous in their French
film policy, for the benefits of their liberality accrued to themselves. Films that promoted French nationalism, such as La Symphonie Fantastique or Pontcarral, showed other occupied and neutral
nations just how much could be accomplished by working side by
side with Europe's new masters. Even political opponents of the
Nazis could serve the Germans' propaganda ends, and the Germans did not hesitate in hiring (or trying to hire) left-wing filmmakers, as long as their work exemplified the best that could be
accomplished. For example, following the critical and commercial
success of Les Visiteurs du soir, Alfred Greven made a special trip to
unoccupied France for the purpose of signing Jacques Prévert for
Continental. According to Pierre Prévert, "they knew he was a leftist, but they also knew he had a great deal of talent. At that time,
they were extremely tolerant; they wanted to demonstrate their
liberalism."[20]

Thus, far from wanting to undermine French production,
the Propaganda Abteilung made special efforts to promote the
quality of French films. In terms of technical equipment, the Film
Section made many requests for additional film stock for France,
and France was the only occupied country equipped to process
Agfacolor. The Epinay Tirage labs in Epinay received the equipment in 1942, although no French color features were produced
during the occupation.[21]

In production levels, the Propaganda Abteilung seemingly favored France over Germany. In 1941, production in the two
countries was nearly equal (59 French films, 71 German films). In
1942, French production actually exceeded the German output by
77 to 64.[22]

The Real Competition

Three reasons have been proposed thus far to explain
the seeming benevolence of German film policy in France. First,

there is the direct economic benefit to the Germans that resulted from their investment in the French film industry. Second, the Germans saw a propaganda benefit in encouraging French production, as a way of demonstrating to occupied Europe and the world that countries under German domination could continue to thrive artistically. Finally, there is the long range view of France as an integral part of the "new Europe," whose production would glorify not merely France, but the new order as a whole.

All of these factors were of secondary importance to the Germans, however. The major goal of German film policy in France during the first two years of the occupation was to encourage the highest level of production in order to compete in the international market. German film policy in France was determined, not by the Germans' attitude toward the French, but rather by their determination to overcome the international filmmaking dominance of the United States.

The United States had been the leading exporter of motion pictures since World War I. The international acceptance of American movies had roused chauvinistic outrage in many countries long before World War II. During the 1920s and 1930s, most European countries had unsuccessfully attempted to stem the tide of American films in their theaters, both because the popularity of American films created insurmountable competition for their own national film industries, and because European political leaders resented the Americanization of their national cultures. In the case of Nazi Germany, this opposition to American economic and cultural imperialism was intensified, in part because the Nazis viewed Americans as a mongrelized race, anathema to their notions of racial purity.

Goebbels' diaries contain numerous statements denouncing American culture and specifying his determination to rid Germany and Europe of the American taint. This same obsessive hatred of the United States crops up repeatedly in the Filmprüfstelle reports. For example, even before the United States and Germany were at war, the Filmprüfstelle had not only banned American films, but had also forbidden the press from even mentioning the names of American film stars.

> American or English film people are not to be men-
> tioned, even negatively, and critical or comparative
> considerations should not be made. That English film
> people should not be mentioned goes without saying,
> as they are enemies of France. The American film is being
> squeezed out of Europe, as well as from France. No more
> American films are being shown in the occupied zone
> and it can be taken for granted that within a short time
> the same thing will happen in unoccupied France.[23]

Given Nazi attitudes toward Americans and American films, the primary goal of German film policy was to promote filmmaking that was superior to that of the United States: "The protection of Western civilization makes it indispensable to defend cinematographic production against all dependence on a foreign continent and to create within Europe itself the beginnings of a continental film industry."[24]

German opposition to the American presence was not merely chauvinism, however, but rather an expression of a concrete economic goal. The Germans wanted not only to dominate the film markets of Europe, but also to compete successfully with Hollywood in neutral areas such as Latin America. In order to do so, however, they had to provide a product which could stand up to American competition, something German films, despite their often high production values, could not do.

In order to convince Spain, Turkey, Sweden, Latin America, and other neutral markets to purchase "European" rather than American productions, the Germans had to offer a product the audience wanted—popular stars, literate screenplays, and a political orientation that was not suspect. The French film industry, led by its own Continental Films, was admirably suited to the purpose. With the conquest of France, the Third Reich had come into possession of the most prestigious and internationally popular film industry in Europe. Far from wanting to destroy the French film industry, the Germans hoped to exploit its popularity for their own ends. As long as it appeared that the Germans were winning the war, they had tangible reasons for encouraging the French to maintain the prestige of their cinema.

The French would supply the commercially appealing films that were necessary for the Germans to compete successfully with the Americans on the international market. This was, probably, a short term goal. Once the markets of Latin America and elsewhere had been penetrated by European (i.e., French) films, the Germans could use their market position to force purchase of their own films. The Germans thus saw that by encouraging French film production, they could use French films as an economic wedge to force the purchase of German films.

Both these short and long term goals were explicitly expressed at a "Meeting of the Ministry of Propaganda of the German Reich concerning the export of French film" held in Paris on July 16, 1941. In attendance were the heads of the Propaganda Abteilungen of Belgium and France, and representatives of Dr. Winkler's office, the German Propaganda Ministry, Ufa, the Reichsfilmkammer and the Reichskommisar.

> Subject to the approval of the Minister for Propaganda and Public Enlightenment [Goebbels] the following has been agreed upon for 1941–42:
>
> Continental Films, Paris, is appointed worldwide distributor of all films produced by them. In addition, Continental Films will acquire from other French producers their export visas for their good films and those usable for export. In short, the total export of French films for all practical purposes will be reserved for Continental Films.
>
> Eventually, Continental Films is to form an export company, controlled by Continental, for the express purpose of exporting films produced by the French film industry.
>
> Continental Films will grant all rights to their own films and those films acquired by them (hereinafter referred to as "our French films") to those German distribution companies with branches in foreign countries.

> These firms can only have films from Continental after they have supplied their own branches [with German films] and have exhausted their source of supply.
>
> For those German distributors that are now forming branches in Sweden, Denmark, Portugal, and Bulgaria, French films must be reserved for them.
>
> In countries without foreign branch operations, those customers who are primarily customers of the German film industry will get preferential treatment—that is, they will get "our French films" before anyone else.
>
> Only those distributors who formerly bought extensive amounts of German films will be entitled to "our French films." These branches and customers should distribute more German than French films . . .
>
> In general, the use of "our French films" is a palliative, its purpose being to supplement the still inadequate (in terms of numbers) German film supply, to channel film into the European film markets, to squeeze out the Americans, and in certain territories, to serve as a pioneering introduction to French film. (R141/F948)

It is obvious from the tone of this report, that the Germans were well aware that French films were more marketable than their own. While they may have regarded the use of "their" French films as a short-term measure to induce foreign buyers to purchase German films, they recognized the value of French films as a device to counter the Americans. As early as May 1941, before the above export policy had been formulated, the Filmprüfstelle reported that they had received many inquiries from abroad concerning the import of French film. Although at that time they had decided to limit French exports to Holland and Belgium, they made an exception of providing ten (prewar) French films to Spain and Portugal, "in order to counteract the influence of American films" (R141/F849).

Because external conditions changed so rapidly, the export policy formulated in 1941 was never actually carried out, and few French films were distributed outside of France. The largest markets were Belgium and Switzerland, where even a few non-Continental productions, like *Premier Bal* and *Histoire de rire* were shown.[25] The rest of French export (primarily Continental) was scattered throughout Europe. Some French films were shown in Holland, Sweden, Czechoslovakia, and three were even shown in Germany (*Premier Rendez-Vous, Caprices, Le Dernier des six*).[26] Of the Latin American market, it is known that twenty French films were shown in Argentina in 1941, and twelve in 1942, but whether these were previously held or arranged through Vichy is not known.[27] It is worth noting that French export to Italy was specifically banned because the Germans hoped to institute a tripartite agreement among the three largest film-producing countries on the continent, and refused to send French films until such agreement was reached.[28]

Even though the export policy formulated in 1941 was not carried out, when this export policy was formulated at the beginning of the occupation, it was advantageous for the Germans to encourage the French to maintain prewar standards of quality for both economic and propaganda reasons. The reports of the Filmprüfstelle underline the importance to the Germans of encouraging high production values and developing stars and stories with popular appeal. The censorship reports on individual films, for example, are not primarily concerned with political questions, but are rather critical summaries of the film's plot and style, its suitability for export, and its artistic quality. Scattered throughout these reports are such comments as "this film is rated technically and artistically impossible"; "in poor taste, technically and artistically primitive"; "the film is poor in content, poor in technique. It is filmed theater, [the director] is totally unaware of the broader horizons filmmaking offers. The only bright spot is the performance of Pierre Renoir"; and "an excellent film—it should make Micheline Presle a star."[29]

Further evidence that these film "critics" of the Propaganda Abteilung were determined to maintain France's prewar reputation for quality cinema was their effort to convince the emigré actors and directors to return.

There are several French film people who, by emigrating to the U.S. or by signing contracts with American companies, have demonstrated that they no longer represent the French film. Among them are: René Clair, Julien Duvivier, Michèle Morgan, Jean Gabin. Negotiations are in progress concerning the return of these people. We must wait for the results. (R141/F1024)

German Censorship

The Propaganda Abteilung's obsession with America was not limited to its economic competition with Hollywood. The Filmprüfstelle noted in its report of December 12, 1942, that "in order to counteract French sympathies for the U.S., a [short] film called *Amerikanische Unkultur* (American Unculture) has been made" (R142/F1017). Though they might be citizens of the new Europe, the French were still suspected of harboring pro-Allied sentiments. The major goal of German censorship policy in France, therefore, was not to prevent the French from glorifying their own culture, or even to sniff out possible resistance sentiments, but rather to try to make the French forget that America or England had ever existed.

The anti-American and anti-British obsession led to some petty decisions. Christian-Jacque, for example, was told to cut all references to Clark Gable and Carole Lombard from *Premier Bal* (R141/F1121). A production from the unoccupied zone, André Berthomieu's *La Neige sur les pas*, was criticized by the Filmprüfstelle because

> the continual mention of England, even as a vacation goal for Frenchmen, is intolerable. Accordingly, the following cuts are ordered:
> 1) . . . the scene where Remeny recommends to Mme. Acker that the child be taken to England on vacation.
> 2) The word "England" in the scene where the housekeeper relates that she has just returned from England with the child.

German sensitivity in other matters is indicated by a third cut ordered for the same film in "the scene where the child insists that the capital of Switzerland is Berlin. We must certainly expect that every child knows the capital of Germany" (R142/F605).

Bertrand Fabre reports that the Germans were so sensitive to references to the Allies that even inadvertent reminders were forbidden. In Albert Valentin's A *la belle frégate*, the only ship available for filming was named *La Tamise* (The Thames). The Filmprüfstelle demanded that any scene in which the ship's name was visible be cut.[30]

Since few Frenchmen had the temerity to offer pro-Allied or anti-German sentiments in their films, the Filmprüfstelle had less reason to censor the films' political sentiments than to concern themselves with the political actions of those involved in production. Producers found, to their dismay, that films initially cleared for showing were later banned because the stars had provoked German ire. Michèle Morgan's prewar films were all banned in November 1942, because she had made an anti-Nazi film in the United States. Jean Gabin's films were prohibited in April 1944, for the same reason.[31] The luckless producers who financed *L'Histoire comique* (*Félicie Nanteuil*) and *La Belle Aventure* never saw them released at all during the occupation. The star of both films, Claude Dauphin, had fled to London in 1943 to join the Free French, and had particularly angered the Germans by broadcasting resistance messages over the BBC.

Not all the German censorship activities were directed against the Allies, however. Because the Germans wanted to consolidate all filmmaking in France under their direct supervision, most Vichy-made films were prohibited in the North until 1942. Three early pro-Vichy films—*La Troisième Dalle*, *L'An 40*, and *La Nuit merveilleuse*—were never released in Paris at all. German determination to prevent a Franco-Italian film alliance which excluded Germany was undoubtedly the reason for German failure to issue exhibition visas to two co-productions, *La Vie de Bohème* and *Carmen*.

The only other occupation-era film banned after having been cleared for production was Jean Dréville's *Les Cadets de l'océan*.

It, too, was a victim of circumstance. The film was about a group of young men training for careers in the Navy. It had been cleared for production in spring 1942, and was shot on location in Toulon, site of the French naval fleet. But by the time the film was ready to be released in late 1942, Toulon had become a sore subject for the Germans: to prevent the Germans from seizing the fleet after they occupied southern France in November 1942, the French had scuttled their own ships. Les Cadets de l'océan was not released until November 1945.

The Filmprüfstelle was not, of course, totally indifferent to outbursts of French nationalism, particularly when it appealed to the insurrectionary spirit. Pontcarral was heavily cut, as was the singing of the "Marseillaise" in Andorra (R142/F876). And, not surprisingly, Roger Richebé was ordered to eliminate the following lines of Robespierre's from Madame Sans-Gêne:

> "Prudence and discipline. One cannot improvise an insurrection. One meditates on it and one executes it, as with a military campaign."
> "I wasn't there, citizen Fouché. Neither were you. And at the moment, it does not concern the taking of a château, but the destruction of a tyrant."
> "Citizens, the people are never vanquished if they retain the will to conquer. Victory goes to the relentless." (R141/F1117)

Outright revolution was seemingly no worse than disrespect for authority, however. Claude Autant-Lara was confounded when the Filmprüfstelle objected to a plot element of what he had taken to be an innocuous subject. In Le Mariage de Chiffon, the heroine chooses to marry a young aviator, rather than an elderly colonel, but the Germans objected. "A colonel cannot be defeated, even in love."[32]

Bertrand Fabre reported that the Germans censored an essential plot element in Christian-Jaque's Premier Bal, in which a monkey was to be dressed in a sailor costume, on the grounds that it tended to ridicule the army, "or more exactly, to avoid ridiculing a German admiral who really looked like a monkey" (p. 19)

Although there is no mention of this incident in the Film Section reports, an order was issued by the Direction Générale du Cinéma in 1944 which confirmed that "all films in which the action would tend to ridicule the prestige of agents of public order or representatives of the magistrature will be immediately banned."[33]

With the above exceptions, almost all the films submitted to the Filmprüfstelle were passed without revision. This relative leniency can, in part, be explained by the degree of self-censorship exercised by producers, and by the COIC who served as intermediary between producers and the German censors. Nonetheless, as Louis-Emile Galey pointed out, the German film officers in Paris were not ideologues but bureaucrats who treated the French "with neither passion nor goodwill."[34] One too easily forgets that in the early years of the occupation, the German goal was not to crush French resistance but rather to encourage a collaborative spirit that would free their armies for engagements in Russia, North Africa, and other theaters of war. If the French could be mollified with a relative liberalism of artistic expression, it was militarily and economically advantageous to encourage their best talents to produce the best possible effort. Far from the Draconian supervision one might expect, the Germans allowed relatively free expression to French nationalism, left-wing ideology, and aesthetic individuality, so long as they did not call up public antipathy to German aims in France or remind the public that somewhere beyond the Atlantic coast Edward G. Robinson was still battling the G-Men; or that France's former ally carried on a war that the French had long ago thought lost.

Conclusion

If, as the Filmprüfstelle reports appear to bear out, the Germans *wanted* the French to continue making films, to make films that would generate critical respect and audience response, then the whole question of collaboration and resistance must be recast. For then the filmmakers who did the most to distract their audience, and to uphold the standards of the French cinema, were the most culpable of working for the Germans' own ends. What the French cinema accomplished during the occupation was not the upholding of French culture, but the glorification of the new Europe. Had Germany won the war, these filmmakers' defense of the national film industry would have been turned against them, used to drive a wedge into foreign markets in order to sell the Germans' own products.

French filmmakers did not, of course, see matters in this light. Because Germany lost the war, the French were free to recriminate among themselves from an entirely different perspective. As the outside war returned to the Western front, the war within France became more heated. The battles waged on both fronts are the subject of chapter 8.

Chapter 8

The War Without
and the War Within

On October 24, 1942, Le *Film* announced production of a new film to be called *Destin*
(Destiny). Co-directors Marc Didier and Charles Boulet were to
begin location shooting in the Sahara desert on November 2.

The destiny of *Destin* was unique in film history. As Le
Film laconically reported on November 12: "the *Destin* team, made
up of 29 people, has been stranded in North Africa . . . The last
word received from the group was from Oran on November 7."

What Le *Film* failed to mention was the event that caused
the stranding. On November 8, 1942, Allied troops had landed in
French North Africa, marking the beginning of the campaign that
would eventually lead to the liberation of Western Europe. *Destin*,
which was never finished, was the first film to be a casualty of the
new turn in the war. But before the Allies liberated Paris in August 1944, every film made in France would in some way be affected.

The landings in Algeria and Morocco were the most dramatic event to signal a turning point in the war, but by the winter
of 1942–43, there was sufficient evidence that the period of "normalcy" was over. In response to the African landings, the Wehrmacht occupied the former "free" zone on November 11, 1942, ir-

revocably destroying the myth of an autonomous French state. The large number of Frenchmen who had supported Pétain as the last hope of French nationalism began to turn against him. When a new Free French government was established in Algiers in the spring of 1943, the French public had a new leader who seemed to be ascendant. The public that had ignored Charles de Gaulle's appeal from London in June 1940 had now become the general's ardent supporters.

Other factors contributed to the changing of allegiance among Frenchmen. In January 1943, the German armies suffered their first major defeat, at Stalingrad. Although German losses were minimized in the media, the French had enough information to begin to hope that the German army was not invincible. As the eventual defeat of the Axis became more plausible, the small groups of active resisters scattered throughout the country began to see their numbers swell. In the isolated areas of the mountains and countryside, guerilla bands, known as the maquis, were formed. Although many of the recruits to these units were drawn to the Resistance for ideological reasons, many more came to escape conscription for forced labor in Germany.

By early 1942, Germany had begun to suffer from a labor shortage. Although slave laborers from the Eastern occupied territories took up part of the slack, as did the French and other prisoners of war already held in Germany, various German industries coveted the skilled labor pool seemingly available in the West. The first efforts to tap this pool called for volunteers. Initial efforts to convince French workers to sign up for German factories were supplemented in the summer of 1942 by a program called La Relève (the Relief). French workers were told that they would be changing places with their imprisoned compatriots: for every three skilled French workers who volunteered to go to Germany, one French prisoner of war would be released.

In the film industry, these efforts seem to have had some success. Although the first call for volunteers was not published in Le Film until October 10, 1942, by January 1943, the Filmprüf-stelle reported that 1,400 French film industry personnel were working in Germany.

> All housing for French film workers in Germany is now full. No additional workers can be accommodated. A total of 1,400 workers are employed in film production companies. They are lodged in clean, well-equipped military barracks, close by their factories. They are fed in the factory canteens . . . (R142/F1034)

It was probably not the factory canteens that induced workers to sign up for Germany, but rather the certainty that if they didn't volunteer, they would be conscripted. This was made plain in the announcement in Le Film (October 10, 1942) which quoted the German official in charge of the program: "Those who sign up immediately will be assured of equivalent work in Germany . . . Otherwise, you may find yourself drafted into work other than that which you are accustomed to doing."

Notwithstanding the threats and the blandishments, La Relève soon proved to be supplying insufficient numbers of workers. Therefore, in February 1943, the Germans instituted a forced labor policy, supported by Vichy law, called Le Service du Travail Obligatoire (S.T.O.). In each industry, a certain number of workers were deemed essential; all the others were subject to conscription. In general, the Comités d'Organisation cooperated with the S.T.O., and nearly 700,000 French workers were sent to Germany.[1] In the film industry, however, the officials seem to have been more obstructive. According to Roger Richebé, then head of the COIC, his organization resisted the S.T.O. by registering large numbers of men as essential and by providing forged identity cards listing male workers as female.[2] According to Louis-Emile Galey, head of Vichy's film service, few film workers were conscripted. He claims the method employed to protect them was to send the list of indispensable workers to each firm—those who didn't see their names on the list immediately fled, many to join the maquis.[3]

One indirect and unexpected consequence of the S.T.O. was to cause cinema receipts in France to fall. Not only was a large percentage of the movie-going public now living in Germany, but for those who remained cinema-going became a dangerous activity.

In those theaters that still continued to hold afternoon showings [in 1944], young men were no longer to be seen; numerous roundups had been conducted in the cinemas during the afternoon, since the Germans considered any young person with time on his hands to be fodder for the factories of the Reich. In order to avoid the S.T.O., or any interrogation, the "under 40's" simply avoided going to any form of public entertainment. The receipts dropped accordingly.[4]

The disappearance of young filmgoers was not the primary reason for the fall in cinema receipts in the final years of the occupation, however. By 1943, it was clear that the war had returned to France and that the film industry would suffer the consequences.

Effects of the War

The most direct effect of the war on the film industry, as on the rest of France, was from Allied bombing. Although the targets were military and war-industrial installations, civilians and non-military industries located nearby unavoidably fell victim. The massive bombing of Boulogne-Billancourt in March 1942, for example, though aimed at a Renault factory, destroyed the GM Film Laboratory and with it the films it was processing (R142/F429). By October 1943, Le Film was calling for donations for those hurt or killed in bombing attacks. They asked that 10 percent of the theaters' net receipts for a week be donated to the victims of the destruction, which included six theaters in the Paris region and a large number of theaters on the northern coast.[5] When the Photosonor studio was hit on December 31, 1943, thirty-seven workers were killed, including those reshooting scenes requested by the censorship office for La Collection Ménard.[6] By the end of the war, five studios were totally destroyed in Paris and Nice, and the Victorine studio in Nice was badly damaged.[7] There were 166 movie theaters partially destroyed, 156 totally destroyed. France's northern coast was particularly hard hit and the cities of Brest, Caen, and Le Havre lost all of their downtown theaters.[8] The loss of theaters contributed to the falling off of receipts, as did the curfews which accompanied the bombings. Theaters in Nice, for example, lost 50 percent of their normal receipts when a 7 P.M. curfew was instituted in August 1943.[9]

Other direct effects of the war on production included restrictions on location shooting. The Filmprüfstelle declared the seacoasts of France off-limits in August 1943. They had already turned down Jean Delannoy's request to shoot scenes for L'Eternel Retour on the Mediterranean, so he had to substitute Lake Annecy for the sea. Christian-Jaque, who began filming Voyage sans espoir in August 1943, was forced to reconstruct Le Havre in a studio. In a period of absolute material scarcity, the production required the building of a tank holding 100,000 liters of water, a full size ship's hull made of 12 tons of plaster, 163 cubic meters of wood, and 29,000 rivets, and masts made of 800 meters of rope and 2 tons of iron.[10]

That so much material could have been procured is astonishing, given the increasingly stringent limits on all material by 1943. By that time, the relative leniency of the early years of the occupation had given way, as Germany found itself faced with material restrictions it had previously avoided. Germany did not begin to operate on a total war economy until late 1942, but from then on occupied France found itself little more than a conduit for the German war machine.

Restricted materials for filmmaking included not only building supplies, coal to heat theaters and studios, and film stock, but most crucially, electricity. To conserve energy, as early as December 1942, studios were forced to shut down altogether for two weeks, and thereafter for one day a week. All movie theaters were to be closed on Tuesdays.[11] By March 1944, the supply of electricity had become so erratic that André Cayatte could film Le Dernier Sou for only about an hour at a time, whenever the current was on. Jacques Becker took advantage of the greater supply of electricity at night when he filmed Falbalas, but this necessitated paying his crew a differential, as well as entailing difficulties in getting everyone safely home.[12]

Attending the movies was not much easier than making them. According to Roger Régent:

> every film we were shown from [March] until the summer [of 1944], we were to see with a kind of surprise, in transit, between alerts. And, if by some miracle the showing ended without our being sent to the cellars [by an air raid], it seemed that with the last meters of film, the last drop of electricity had run out. (pp. 249–50)

All of these difficulties no doubt contributed to the decline in box office receipts in 1944—because production was more difficult and expensive, the number of new films in production declined sharply. In 1943, new film starts dropped from 77 to 59, the majority of these productions beginning early in the year. Between July 1943 and May 1944, only 37 films went into production, less than 4 per month compared to nearly 7 per month during the period of "normalcy." The shortage of new production starts inevitably led to a shortage of finished product. New releases in Paris dropped from an average of 7 per month in 1943 to under 3 per month between January 1944 and the Liberation.[13]

Many producers with completed films deliberately held back their premieres, since the risk of not recouping their investments under prevailing exhibition conditions was greater than the cost of holding unreleased films. Nonetheless, there were a few without trepidation. In an often-cited passage, Roger Régent described the premiere of the Franco-Italian production of *Carmen* on August 8, 1944:

> The evening of the showing an enormous crowd pressed up against the doors of the Normandie, where the autograph hunters hoped to glimpse Jean Marais and Viviane Romance. While the stars' fans, pens in hand, searched for Carmen and Don José by moonlight, the Champs-Elysées was covered with tanks, trucks filled with men and heavy materiel, camouflaged under newly cut branches which gave to this strange convoy the air of a motorized forest. The soldiers of the Wehrmacht, weighed

> down by their gear, drained by nights without sleep,
> unending combats and successive "disengagements,"
> looked without comprehension at these young men and
> women pursuing the cinema stars through the crowd.
> All those who were there are not likely to soon forget
> this extraordinary spectacle which will remain one of the
> oddest visions of occupied Paris. (p. 257)

Of the few films that were made in the last year of the occupation, what is particularly striking is the lavishness of production in the face of the enormous difficulties these films encountered. The most expensive production in French film history (to that time) began filming in Nice on August 17, 1943. Les Enfants du Paradis, undoubtedly the best-known of all films made in France during the occupation, fell victim to a series of war-related disasters while shooting that significantly added to the production's expense. Given conditions at the time, it is astonishing the film was completed at all.

Production began in August 1943 at the Victorine studios in Nice where the massive exterior sets for the Boulevard of Crime had been constructed. As they were about to begin filming on those sets

> like a thunderbolt from a calm sky, the news broke that
> the Americans had disembarked in Sicily.
> It would take them a year to get to the North
> of the peninsula, but at that moment of chaos, every-
> one imagined them flooding the "Baie des Anges" in a
> few hours.
> To add to the panic, we received a telegram
> from Vichy a little later ordering us to leave for Paris
> immediately, with all our equipment and even our film.[14]

The dislocation in Carné's shooting schedule was less serious than the Badoglio Armistice which was signed in September. At that point, the Germans occupied Nice (previously under Italian occupation) and forbade further Franco-Italian co-production. Since the producer of Les Enfants, André Paulvé, had been

financed by Scalera, production of the film was shut down altogether.

Louis-Emile Galey finally managed to arrange for Pathé
to take over production, but at the price of Paulvé's removal. There
is some question as to why the Germans insisted that Paulvé be
fired—Carné believes it may have been Greven's revenge for the
success of *Les Visiteurs du soir*. A more likely reason, suggested by
film historian Armand Panigel, was that Jews and resisters were
working for Paulvé and that he had been living with a Jewish
woman.[15] However, Paulvé did produce one more film in 1944—
Mademoiselle X—which makes his removal from *Les Enfants* all the
more puzzling.

Production on *Les Enfants* resumed in Paris in November
1943, with one cast member absent. Again, it is not clear exactly
what happened to Robert le Vigan. Carné claims the actor fled
France after the Allied landings in Italy, fearing post-Liberation
reprisals for his anti-Semitic broadcasts over Radio-Paris (p. 228).
However, le Vigan is listed in the credits for *Les Enfants* published
in *Le Film* as late as February 1944, and he was in the production
of *Bifur III* which began shooting in May 1944.[16] In an interview in
1978, Arletty maintained that le Vigan did shoot several scenes
on *Les Enfants* in Paris. But he refused to return to Nice with the
company when filming resumed there, because he had received
death threats.[17] Whatever the reason, Carné was forced to reshoot
le Vigan's scenes, substituting Pierre Renoir.

Les Enfants du Paradis may have been the most elaborate
and difficult production of the late occupation period, but Carné
and his colleagues were not the only filmmakers to create a fantasy world of luxury and plenty as an antidote to the daily priva-
tions of real life. Other late occupation films—Becker's *Falbalas* and
Bresson's *Les Dames du Bois de Boulogne*, among them—were set in
the haut monde and emphasized lavish costumes and sets. Historical epics, popular throughout the period, became even more
grandiose. In January 1944, Jean Delannoy began production of *Le
Bossu*, a lavish swashbuckler set in the era of Louis XIV. In March
1944, Serge de Poligny began production, in Carcassonne, of a
historical epic in modern dress, *La Fiancée des ténèbres*. According

to Le Film, "despite present difficulties . . . this film will reconstruct in modern times the picturesque climate of the Albigen-
sian heresy" (April 1, 1944). As late as May 2, 1944, Pierre de Hérain began work on Paméla, an expensive reconstruction of the
Directory period.

    None of these projects could match the production en-
visioned by Marcel l'Herbier, along with writers Nino Frank, Alexandre Arnoux, Jean Aurenche, and Marcel Achard.

> Between the spring and summer of 1944 when all of
> Europe began to crack apart, a producer [André Paulvé]
> was found in France to undertake the preparation of a
> monumental [life of] Louis XIV, in two parts, no less,
> to which it was proposed that 80 million [francs] be
> consecrated and for which it was expected that they
> would renovate the Grand Canal at Versailles, recon-
> struct the staircase of the Ambassadors, make 100 sets
> and 1,000 costumes.[18]

    The incredible difficulty in finding supplies for these films,
not to mention the problem of finding a way to exhibit them,
seemingly did not deter French producers. Even after the Normandy landings threw the country into total chaos, film production continued. The last film to go into production was Pierre Billon's Mademoiselle X on May 23, 1944. He somehow managed to
continue shooting until early July, when, like all other productions, the film was halted until late fall.

Resistance Activities

    One of the oddest cases of production continuing de-
spite external circumstances involved screenwriter Charles Spaak.
Spaak was arrested by the Gestapo in late 1943, because they
wanted information on his brother Claude, an active resister.[19] At
the time of his arrest, Spaak had been working on the screenplay
for Les Caves du Majestic for Continental. It was a mystery, based on
a Simenon novel, but Spaak had changed the identity of the murderer.

> One day two members of the Gestapo appeared, asking me, very politely, if I would finish work [on the screenplay]. I asked for several things—food, cigarettes, books. They agreed to all my conditions. Every three days, through the bars, they came to collect 3 or 4 pages of the scenario; during a time when there was terrible fighting—on the ground, the sea and in the air—the Gestapo continued to want to know who the killer in Simenon's novel would be. What was even more amusing was that the "Majestic" was one of the hotels in which the Germans were most securely installed and organized.[20]

Although accused of aiding the Resistance, Spaak continued to work. Other, more active resisters, would use their film activities as vehicles for carrying on clandestine resistance activities. As early as 1940, for example, a clandestine grouping of film technicians was founded in Nice by director Léonide Moguy, before he left for the United States.[21] When Becker made *Dernier Atout* in 1942, he deliberately chose Nice as a location in order to make contact with this resistance group. Among the activities of this Nice-based syndicate were helping French p.o.w.'s in the cinema. They were also instrumental in aiding Claude Dauphin to escape to England.

Another filmmaker based in the South who was active in the Resistance was René Lefèvre. His activities were not limited to those concerning the cinema—among his duties as a registered British agent were unloading arms and ammunition dropped from English planes and helping downed pilots escape. Lefèvre's cinematic activities made him especially useful to the British, however. As an actor/director, he had been given an official safe conduct to cross the demarcation line. He often carried secret papers on these trips and once found himself in jeopardy when engaged in conversation by a German officer. As it turned out, however, the German was only interested in knowing whether Lefèvre knew actor Heinrich George. Because Lefèvre had worked in Germany in the 1930s, he exploited his contacts with the German filmmakers he knew for the benefit of the Resistance.[22]

Not all who took part in clandestine activities remained undetected, however. Actor Robert Lynen, who had starred as a child in Duvivier's *Poil de Carotte*, was arrested in February 1943 for resistance activity, not long after completing the Vichyist *Cap au large*. He was shot in April 1944.

Poet Robert Desnos had worked on only one film, Man Ray's *Etoile de Mer* in 1928. He returned to the cinema in 1943 with the scenario for *Bonsoir mesdames, bonsoir messieurs*, a satire about radio. One week after the film was released in February 1944, Desnos was arrested for resistance activities. He died of typhus contracted while in a German concentration camp.[23]

At least one film-related victim of German anti-Resistance activity was no more than an innocent bystander. According to the clandestine newspaper, *La Cinématographie Française*, an assistant cameraman named Savvia was on vacation when he was taken hostage and shot in reprisal for some resistance act against the Germans.[24]

Few well-known filmmakers engaged in active combat against the occupiers, but by 1944 passive resistance was widespread. There were several filmmakers who found ways to use their filmmaking as devices to help the Resistance. Both Christian-Jaque with *Sortilèges* and Louis Daquin with *Premier de Cordée* took advantage of location shooting in the French Alps to provide cover for those trying to get across the border into Switzerland.[25]

For *Le Ciel est à vous*, producer Raoul Ploquin managed to convince the Germans to allow shooting at Le Bourget, which was camouflaged. Not only did the crew remove the camouflage, but they also lit the airport for night scenes, making it an easy target for Allied bombers. The airport was bombed during shooting and production had to be moved to a safer airport near Lyon.[26]

Jacques Becker and his crew hid film and equipment in various caches around Paris during shooting on *Falbalas*. These provisions were put to use during the fighting for the city that preceded the Liberation. The resulting film, released as *La Libération de Paris*, served as a documentary record of the last days of Paris under the occupation.[27]

La Libération de Paris was one of the rare examples of

clandestine filmmaking during the occupation. The Germans kept a close eye on film stock and equipment, forestalling such activity. Furthermore, the results of any clandestine production could not, of course, have been shown publicly. Nonetheless, there were at least three other films made that showed aspects of the occupation not seen in the official cinema of the time.

Cameramen Robert Godin and Albert Mahuzier filmed scenes of life in occupied Paris in the spring of 1944 that were included in a film released after the Liberation as La Caméra sous la botte.[28] A group of officers in a French p.o.w. camp in Austria managed to hide an 8 mm camera in a hollowed-out dictionary and exposed fourteen reels detailing the life in the camp, later released as OFLAG XVII A. Finally, documentary filmmaker Félix Forestier, accompanied by cameramen Weill and Coutable, filmed scenes among the maquis of Vercors which were later used in Jean-Paul le Chanois's Au Coeur de l'orage.

The clandestine filming in Paris and among the maquis was carried out at the behest of the Comité de Libération du Cinéma Français (CLCF). This committee was initially established by journalist René Bleck in 1943 and was attached to the Communist-dominated resistance group, the Front National. Five resistance organizations in the cinema were amalgamated into the CLCF, including the reconstituted trade union movement of the Confédération Générale du Travail.[29] The president of the CLCF was actor Pierre Blanchar; other active members of the committee included documentarian Jean Painlevé (who was appointed head of the Direction Générale du Cinéma in the provisional government after the Liberation), directors Louis Daquin, Jean Grémillon, André Zwoboda, Jacques Becker, Jean-Paul le Chanois, and actor Pierre Renoir.

In addition to promoting clandestine filmmaking, the CLCF published a clandestine newspaper, titled L'Ecran Français. Among the contributors were Jean Delannoy, Bernard Zimmer, and critic Georges Sadoul. L'Ecran Français first appeared as a mimeographed leaflet in December 1943, but it was subsequently incorporated into Les Lettres Françaises, an underground literary journal whose contributors included Jean-Paul Sartre and Paul Eluard. The four issues of L'Ecran Français published between March and July 1944, and the single issue of La Cinématographie Française put out by the C.G.T. in May 1944, consisted mainly of accusations against collaborators, including officials of the COIC and those working for Continental. The post-Liberation program set out in the newspapers called for the "purification" (épuration) of the film industry of collaborators, the dissolution of the COIC and its replacement with an organization less biased toward the interests of producers, and a number of noncontroversial measures aimed at promoting the film industry.

As was true of the Resistance overall, the resistance groups in the cinema fought among themselves. In April–May and August 1944, a clandestine newspaper titled Opéra appeared, which represented various resistance groups in the arts including the "comité de résistance de l'industrie cinématographique." This committee was associated with the non-Communist Mouvement de Libération Nationale (also known as Combat). Opéra was attacked by L'Ecran Français and La Cinématographie Française, who claimed that it was being published by "agents provocateurs" and did not represent the official resistance committee of the cinema. Nonetheless, the program proposed in Opéra was nearly identical to those published in the other papers.

Libération

Until August 1944, none of the resistance movements in the cinema joined in active combat. The immediate activities were limited to planning and organizing, although there were a few practical measures taken. The gala Carmen premiere described earlier had been organized by the CLCF as a benefit to finance resistance activities. Among the contributors was Pablo Picasso, who donated a painting.[30]

With the general uprising in Paris on August 19, 1944, however, the CLCF put their plans into action. The offices of the COIC were among the first occupied by the group. Union members had already staged sit-in strikes at the major studios and laboratories; members of the CLCF proceeded over the next two days to take over the offices of such organizations as the Direction Générale du Cinéma, France-Actualités, Continental, and Tobis. Some CLCF members took part in the street fighting of those pre-Liberation days. Fifteen of their number were wounded and three killed, including the well-known character actor Aimos.[31]

Nino Frank recalled that the coordinator of the takeovers was Jean-Paul le Chanois. Frank claimed his own duties were to provide food to the buildings' occupiers, which he arranged by emptying Alfred Greven's cellar.[32]

Louis-Emile Galey described the final days of Paris' occupation as "Ubuesque." On the 19th, his assistant Robert Buron (who was active in the Resistance) phoned him to say that Galey's office had been taken over by a Christian-Democratic group of resisters. On the 21st, this group was evicted by another (presumably Communist) group. Although the CLCF officially considered him the enemy, Galey was greeted on the street by the Resistance leader Boulanger, who was in fact Jean Painlevé, an old friend of Galey's. Painlevé arranged for Galey to get into his former office "and even hinted that I should remove any incriminating papers."[33]

Louis Daquin remembered that he received a phone call informing him that the takeover of the COIC had begun. The offices of the COIC were on the Right Bank, Daquin lived on the Left—every bridge in Paris was barricaded and manned by German soldiers. Daquin scurried up and down the banks of the Seine, trying to get across, all the while dodging German bullets. Finally, he ran into an old friend who suggested Daquin give up for the moment and join him for tea. And, in the midst of all the fighting and confusion, Daquin was refused admission to a restaurant because he was not wearing a tie.[34]

Nino Frank described in his memoirs the absurd image of director Christian-Jaque leading an attack on Propaganda Abteilung headquarters at the Hotel Majestic. The ultimate absurdity, however was reserved for "Henri Langlois, shadowy, shrivelled, more tattered than ever, who undoubtedly took himself for

Marat, because he installed himself in Painlevé's office and called for executions in the name of the Cinémathèque" (p. 199).

"Purification" of Collaborators

If no executions were carried out in the name of the Cinémathèque, the victors of August 25 were quick to institute a questionable justice to those they believed had betrayed France. By September 1944, the first "épuration" committees had been established in the cinema, to decide which colleagues had been guilty of helping the enemy.[35] These first committees, ad hoc bodies without official legitimacy, appear to have served as little more than platforms for personal vendettas, and justice tended to be arbitrary. Few in the film industry suffered the extreme penalty of execution. But the reprisals were often unjust in that they tended to be visited upon the most celebrated of the film community, rather than the most guilty.[36]

Many well-known film and theatrical figures were arrested by Resistance groups and jailed for months without any charges being brought. Although some, like Sacha Guitry and Tino Rossi, had been seen publicly with the occupiers at receptions and nightclubs, few had aided the enemy in substantial ways. One example of the injustice of many of these arrests is mentioned in Jean Marais's memoirs. Marais was instructed by the Resistance committee in the theater to demand a large sum of money from actors Alice Cocéa and Pierre Fresnay, in exchange for immunity from arrest. Marais refused to be party to this extortion, and joined General Leclerc's division to avoid future dealings with the Resistance.[37] Fresnay was arrested in September 1944 and spent six weeks in prison, although there were never any charges levelled against him.[38]

Maurice Chevalier was another figure who was subjected to the arbitrary measures of the post-Liberation frenzy. The singer had been condemned over the BBC early in 1944 because he had sung publicly in Germany. According to his own account, Chevalier had appeared in Germany only once, having entertained French prisoners of war in a prison camp where he himself had been incarcerated during World War I. The commander who arrested Chevalier in September 1944 told the singer he would have summarily executed him if he had not just received orders calling for all executions to be approved by the central committee in Paris. Chevalier was later cleared of all charges.[39]

The proceedings against collaborators soon followed a more legal procedure, and the "épuration" committees were permitted to exact only minor punishments. All serious cases of collaboration were remanded to the courts. The official proceedings against collaborators in the film industry were instituted in the summer of 1945. Very few of their cases were sent to the courts. Nonetheless, the determination of who was to be punished and to what extent continued to be arbitrary.

Those who had helped the occupier economically—the administrators of Jewish-owned businesses, the suppliers of materials for the German film industry—were seldom punished. Yet Arletty, whose crime consisted of having had an affair with a German officer was imprisoned for four months and then placed under house arrest for an additional eighteen months before she was finally "purified" in November 1946.[40] Perhaps she was punished for her lack of repentance. She is reported to have said at her trial, "My heart is French, but my ass belongs to the world."[41] As she noted, there were others who were not condemned for equivalent crimes or worse. For example, the actresses who traveled to Berlin in 1942—Danielle Darrieux, Junie Astor, and Suzy Delair—were not punished.

Roger Richebé, former director of the COIC, was cleared of all charges at his "épuration" hearing, despite what he claims were the efforts of his "communist accusers" (he singles out Daquin) to "get" him.[42] Daquin himself had to pass before the committee, since he had briefly been involved with the Vichy newsreel service. He had, of course, no difficulty in gaining clearance.

In general, the épuration proceedings in the cinema were relatively mild. According to Robert Aron, the total number of persons suffering any sort of sanction reached only 171.[43] However, this number did not include those individuals associated with the cinema whose cases did not pass through the "épuration" committee. Some such cases did result in the ultimate penalty.

Two figures associated with the film industry are known to have been executed. Critic and novelist Robert Brasillach had been highly visible in collaborationist circles and worked closely with Jean Luchaire (also shot) on the collaborationist paper *Les Nouveaux Temps*. Director Jean Mamy was also executed, not primarily for his work on the pro-Nazi film *Forces Occultes*, but rather because he had denounced several members of the underground labor movement to the Gestapo.[44] Novelist Lucien Rebatet [François Vinneuil], the vitriolic film and theater critic of *Je Suis Partout*, was condemned to death, but his sentence was commuted to life imprisonment and he was eventually paroled. Actor Robert le Vigan, who had fled to Germany at the end of the occupation, was imprisoned for four years and fled France when he was released on parole in 1949. He went into exile in Argentina, where he died in 1972.

According to Georges Sadoul, the only serious sanctions were applied to le Vigan, actor Roger Duchesne, who was suspected of working for the Gestapo, and a producer, Muzard, who was sentenced to three years in prison for making propaganda films for the enemy.[45]

The "épuration" committee in the cinema did not handle these cases. Rather, they dealt with those filmmakers accused of "having collaborated with the enemy by making films."[46] Primarily, the targets of these charges were those who had worked for Continental, but even within this category, justice was far from even-handed.

Marcel Carné was censured by the "épuration" committee for "having favored the designs of the enemy in signing a contract with Continental,"[47] even though he had never made a film for them. On the other hand, Christian-Jaque, who had made two films for Continental, had become active in the Resistance in 1944, and not only escaped censure, but served as one of the judges, according to the possibly biased account of Maurice Bardèche.[48]

The penalties exacted against those who had "made films

for the enemy" were highly inconsistent. The most common penalty was "censure with posting [of the censure] in the workplace," a somewhat difficult proposition for peripatetic filmmakers. Charles Spaak, one of those thus censured, claims some "épurés" posted their censure in their favorite cafes;[49] Nino Frank (censured for having worked on Les Nouveaux Temps) noted, "I was to post notice in my place of work, which I could never understand because my place of work was wherever I chose. I am placing it here [in his memoirs] in the hope of finally giving satisfaction, better late than never, to my excellent 'épurateurs.' "[50]

Among the personnel thus censured were directors André Zwoboda (who had nonetheless been a member of the CLCF), Richard Pottier, Georges Lacombe, and Jean Boyer (the last for having worked for Scalera); set decorators Georges Wakhevitch and André Andrejew, cameraman Roger Hubert, and a number of technicians.[51] More serious penalties were leveled at director Jean de Limur for "having collaborated with the enemy on the direction of films." He was "forbidden to occupy a managerial post in the profession" and was ordered to publicize his penalty in three film trade journals "at his own expense."[52]

The most serious penalties were imposed on the three directors whose films for Continental had been singled out by L'Ecran Français as enemy propaganda: Henri Decoin, director of Les Inconnus dans la maison, was banned from the profession; Albert Valentin, director of La Vie de plaisir, was banned from the profession and had his case remanded to the courts.[53] The same penalty was applied to Henri-Georges Clouzot.

Of all the crimes committed by the film industry during the occupation, seemingly the most serious was having worked on Le Corbeau. While few who made Vichy propaganda films or newsreels for the Germans suffered penalties, nearly everyone associated with Le Corbeau was treated with unusual severity: Clouzot and screenwriter Louis Chavance were banned from the profession "in perpetuity"; the stars, Pierre Fresnay and Ginette Leclerc were imprisoned; other actors—Micheline Francey, Noel Roquevert, and Jean Brochard—were banned from the profession for various terms, ranging from two to twelve months.[54]

To understand the degree of animosity generated by this film, it is necessary to examine it in detail. Such an analysis reveals more than the political divisions of the time. The story of *Le Corbeau* encapsulates the paradoxes of the French cinema of the era: its strengths and weaknesses, its idiosyncracies and accomplishments. It is a film that has been called "the best French film of the occupation, perhaps of the whole decade and certainly the most significant," and "one of the half-dozen greatest French films ever made,"[55] yet it continues to stir controversy to this day.

Le Corbeau

"I do not regret having condemned *Le Corbeau*," said Louis Daquin in 1979, unregenerate thirty-six years after the film's release.[56] Daquin and other members of the Comité de Libération du Cinéma Français remained convinced that the film was a direct attack on French character and patriotism and so served to further the enemy's cause.

The unpleasantness of the film's subject was the primary reason for the attack by the Resistance press.[57] *Le Corbeau* is a character study of a town under siege from a flood of anonymous letters. The letter writer, who signs himself "le corbeau" (the raven or crow), reveals disquieting facts about the various townspeople, who respond to the letters with cowardice and malignity. After causing one suicide, along with collective suspicion and hysteria, the culprit is finally murdered by the mother of the man who had committed suicide.

It was not only the film's subject which aroused the Resistance, however, but also the time and place of the film's production. To make an "anti-French" subject during the darkest period of the occupation, for a German company, was an act of collaboration, whether witting or not.

Was *Le Corbeau* an "anti-French" film? Vichy certainly thought so. When it was released, Louis-Emile Galey lodged a formal protest with Alfred Greven and demanded that the film not be distributed abroad.[58] The Church also saw the film as an attack on its values; the Centre Catholique du Cinéma condemned the

film as blasphemous and gave it the lowest possible rating—
"pernicious" and "not to be seen."[59]

That the leftists in the Resistance should ally themselves with Vichy and the Church in condemnation of *Le Corbeau*
is one of the many paradoxes of the occupation. So concerned
was the Left with protecting France's image, that it failed to see
that the film stood firmly in the tradition of such other *films mau-
dits* as Bunuel's *L'Age d'Or* and Vigo's *Zéro de Conduite*. But as Roger
Régent aptly pointed out, it was for that very reason that the film
could have been made at no other time and in no other place.

> Not since Vigo had French filmmakers gone so far in
> expressing their most direct thoughts, nor in treating with
> such virulence our trials and heartbreaks. Our censors
> were on guard against such expression. Whether it was
> the censorship of M. Edmond Sée before 1939, that of
> Vichy or of the IVth Republic, the result was the same;
> the censorship office stood vigil lest a scenario were to
> show adulterous relations, suicide, immoral characters,
> social workers who were not angels, bureaucrats who
> were not models of conscience and professional virtue,
> mothers who did not represent the purest image of ma-
> ternity.
> One can be sure that no French producer would
> ever have obtained permission to make *Le Corbeau* be-
> tween 1940 and 1944, and most likely not before '39 or
> after '44 either . . . The author, who believed in the worth
> of his script, could find only one producer for his proj-
> ect, French censorship naturally having no say over the
> affairs of Continental. (pp. 194–195)

The Resistance committee did not see the film in this
light. To buttress its case against Clouzot and Chavance, *L'Ecran
Français* accused the filmmakers of having made the film under
German orders. But this charge proved to be untrue. Far from acting at the Germans' behest, Louis Chavance had first drafted the
screenplay in 1931 and had deposited a version of it with La Société des Auteurs in 1938. It was based on a true incident that
had scandalized French newspaper readers in the 1920s, involving

a series of anonymous letters in the town of Tulle. When the culprit was finally revealed, it was estimated that Angèle Laval had written more than a thousand letters, not to mention those written by her mother.

This "scandalous" subject appealed to Henri-Georges Clouzot, who had become one of Continental's most successful directors with L'*Assassin habite au 21*. Alfred Greven had agreed that for his next project Clouzot could film anything he liked, so long as it was a mystery. For both Clouzot and Chavance, the subject of Le *Corbeau* provided a way of breaking free from the typecasting of their work.[60] They were both seeking an *éclat* of the kind that Carné and Renoir had achieved with their bitter visions of French society during the prewar period. They succeeded.

Le *Corbeau* was released in Paris on September 28, 1943, to general critical acclaim. French audiences, despite the increasing hardships of war, were undoubtedly tired of the vacuousness of most films released. Le *Corbeau* was triumphant at the box office throughout France, despite the denunciations of the film by both Vichy and the Church. What these audiences saw in the film was an attack on "work, family, country," the watchwords of Vichy ideology. This film was no ironic allegory, like *Pontcarral* or Les *Visiteurs du soir*, but a frontal assault on Vichy bastions.

The milieu of the film is the haute bourgeoisie: doctors, government and school officials, the high clergy. Although a few petit bourgeois are indicted in passing for their prejudices and willingness to condemn without evidence, the working class is excluded from the film's attack.

The first target of the film is the medical profession. Dr. Vorzet (Pierre Larquey), the psychiatrist, has a free hand in investigating the case which he pursues with scientific detachment, constructing meaningless graphs showing the temperature of the town. Vorzet also provides a "scientific" explanation for the character of the raven, applying his psychological terminology:

> In all the cases I've studied, the guilty parties have exhibited the same psychological symptoms. They are al-

ways inhibited and more or less sexually unbalanced . . . old maids . . . widows, impotent men, cuckolds, cripples.[61]

Vorzet's scientific methods fail to catch the criminal because the raven is none other than Vorzet himself. The least likely suspect is all the more surprising, given the weight his observations carried throughout the film. More than a surprising plot twist, however, this revelation serves retroactively to undermine his scientific detachment, and, by implication, that of the entire medical profession. Such a sense is bolstered by the behavior of the other doctors. The chief of staff drops his investigation into the accountant's misuse of funds when confronted by a letter accusing him of being the lover of the accountant's daughter. These symbols of detached authority are ready to condemn their colleague Dr. Germain (Pierre Fresnay), and conspire to entrap him into committing the crime of abortion. Certainly, the medical staff is not the voice of reason controlling the mounting hysteria of the town.

The representatives of the State fare no better. Although the film presumably takes place during the prewar period, the government officials serve as general symbols of the petty self-protective bureaucrats of any regime.[62] Neither the sub-prefect nor the assistant prosecutor is able to control the town or to catch the criminal. They themselves behave criminally by setting the trap for Germain. The assistant prosecutor hypocritically justifies this conspiracy by maintaining: "Germain is the raven's principal target. Since we cannot rid ourselves of the guilty party, let us get rid of Germain. Perhaps with this stroke we will end the letters."

Throughout the film, the raven's attacks on symbols of authority are justified by the behavior of his targets. The raven's blasphemous behavior—attaching a letter to a coffin, sailing another letter from the balcony in the middle of Mass—are justified by the hypocrisy of the priest, who condemns Marie Corbin without evidence in the same lynch mob spirit as the rest of the town. It is during his self-congratulatory sermon that the letter falls clearing Marie Corbin and signed, "Your brother in Jesus Christ."

The two objects of particular veneration in Vichy ideology—women and children—were targets of special scorn in the film. Vichy idealized women as the repositories of family virtue, as the providers of the new generation of new men. Women could serve but one function in the National Revolution—as the keepers of the moral order.

The women in *Le Corbeau* are direct challenges to this notion. Marie Corbin is a particularly unsympathetic nurse, who refuses to comfort the sick and dying, and steals morphine from pain-wracked patients in order to feed the habit of her former fiancé, Vorzet. The cancer patient's mother, far from embodying the maternal virtues of patience, resignation, and humility, is the avenging angel who murders the raven in cold blood, in repayment for the death of her son. But it is particularly the dichotomy of Laura/Denise that sharply illustrates the film's political position.

Laura (Micheline Francey) is the physical symbol of virtue—blonde, modest, devout, a devoted wife to an aging husband. She is introduced as a contrast to her cruel sister, Marie Corbin, who refuses to comfort the cancer patient which Laura happily does. But beneath the virtuous exterior, her sexual frustration soon becomes apparent. She either is, or wishes to become, Germain's mistress; she once stole her sister's fiancé and attempts to frame her rival, Denise, in order to sustain Germain's attention. Knowing full well the identity of the raven, she allows her sister to be accused and almost lynched, her lover to be hounded, and shares responsibility for the death of the cancer patient whom she so patiently nursed. It no doubt caused Vichy particular discomfort that Laura is identified early in the film as a social worker.

In contrast to Laura, Denise (Ginette Leclerc) is patently "the bad girl." She is introduced lounging in bed in a revealing negligee, with painted lips, smoking a cigarette and polishing her toe nails (certainly the ultimate degeneracy for an era when even soap was rationed). Denise's sexuality is no repressed secret. Unlike Laura, Denise's seduction of Germain is open and direct. She is, in short, a symbol of that "degeneracy" that weakened the moral fiber of France and led to its defeat.

Yet Denise is the heroine of Le Corbeau, the proud cripple who resists the town's hysteria and is willing to defend Germain against his accusers. It is Denise, alone, who maintains a sense of justice, refusing to condemn a suspect without proof, and it is she who puts the matter in its proper perspective. In a key dialogue between Denise and her parting lover, Denise expresses the filmmaker's contempt for bourgeois morality:

> Germain: My poor girl, people are what they are: an honest man remains an honest man, a philanderer remains a philanderer and a . . .
> Denise: whore remains a whore. Perhaps you're right, doctor, but in that case I feel sorry for you because you will always remain the saddest and strangest thing in life.
> Germain: A fool?
> Denise: Oh, no. A bourgeois.

If it was not sufficiently shocking to the good burghers of Vichy to find that the only honest woman in a town full of vipers was a physical cripple (Vichy, too, admired the Aryan ideal of physical strength and wholeness) with an undisguised sexuality, Clouzot and Chavance would go even further. In attacking childhood, they were treading upon one of the fundamental precepts of Vichy—that France would achieve full moral regeneration only through its children.

The primary accusation against Germain in Le Corbeau is that he is an abortionist. Although the accusation, strictly speaking, is proved false, Germain openly and even proudly admits that in doubtful cases he saves the mother rather than the child. Such an act is not only a violation of Catholic doctrine, but a violation of the fundamental principles of the National Revolution.

The physical and moral health of France and its youth is highly questionable on the evidence of Le Corbeau. Every child who appears in the film projects a malevolent image. Rolande, Denise's sinister fourteen-year old niece, eavesdrops at doorways and lies with calm assurance. An angelic-looking child tells Germain she has not seen his letter, only to draw it out from under her dress as soon as Germain turns away. In this atmosphere of thorough corruption, even the children are not above suspicion.

No other film made during the occupation was so fundamentally opposed to all the values and principles of the Vichy regime. The Resistance press that attacked the film was undoubtedly correct in seeing it as an anti-French film—it was opposed to the France of Vichy, authoritarian France with its bourgeois moral codes and hypocrisies. But to claim that the film was pro-German is absurd.

Another of the charges made against the film was proved totally false. *Le Corbeau* was not released in Germany under the title "A Little Town in France," or any other title, because the German distributor, Ufa, turned it down for being "too morbid." In his defense of the banned film in *La Rue* in 1945, Louis Chavance wrote that the Gestapo was furious when they discovered the subject matter of the film, and demanded that the advertising slogan—"the crime of the century. Is the law strong enough to punish writers of anonymous letters?"—be changed. Although neither Chavance nor Clouzot ever claimed the film was conceived as an attack on anonymous letters, the Germans had no wish to see this pervasive practice discontinued. That such letters were commonplace is demonstrated by the frequent editorials against them:

> The appalling flood of anonymous letters and denunciations increases daily . . . you'd swear every Frenchman regards his neighbor as an enemy to be got rid of. (*Aujourd'hui*, Jan. 14, 1941)

> Too many of our contemporaries are revenging themselves for their present misfortunes by denouncing, on some trifling score, their enemies; and if they haven't got enemies, they pick on their fellow workers, neighbors or concierges." (*Les Nouveaux Temps*, Dec. 23, 1940)[63]

Whatever its makers' intentions, it is doubtful the film stemmed the tide of anonymous letters. Nevertheless, Continental dismissed Clouzot because "the Kommandantur complained that we were discouraging these letters."[64] He did not work again until 1947.

Le Corbeau may have been the most controversial film of the occupation, but in most ways it was similar to the dominant trend in filmmaking of the time. The film's atmosphere, its sense of self-enclosure and isolation from the world are typical of the "isolationist" tendency of the French school.

St. Robin, the mythical town of Le Corbeau, is France in microcosm. The opening shot defines the boundaries of the town and its isolation. A panoramic traveling shot reveals the hills and meadows which surround the town, and the specific geography of the city's streets. The camera tracks down toward a cemetery, through whose gates the camera enters. With the exception of the subsequent scene in the farmyard, the camera does not leave the town again.

St. Robin is a town of narrow streets, with high stone buildings walling them in on all sides. Every exterior space is enclosed by a fence or a wall. Deep shots, such as those from within the classroom, clearly show the fences in the rearground. The physical barriers which surround Marie Corbin in flight or Germain in the schoolyard, are symbolic correlatives of both France's physical entrapment and of that human condition drawn by Sartre in Huis Clos. The impossibility of escape is most vividly symbolized by Marie Corbin's terrified race through the empty, endless maze of the town, but no character in the film ever escapes the town's boundaries. Germain, the most determined to leave, gets to the point of packing his bags, but he does not escape. Vorzet, at the beginning of the film, has just returned from Paris, but if people can enter the town, they cannot leave. The subprefect, informed of his transfer by the Paris paper (whose news seems to be entirely about the affairs of St. Robin) is still in this hated assignment at the end of the film. Germain has come to St. Robin seeking to escape his past, but he brings his past with him. No one will let him forget what he was and, like the others, he is trapped. This hell is, indeed, other people.

If *Le Corbeau* differs from the other "prestige" films of the occupation only in the bitterness with which it views bourgeois attitudes and behavior, it is surprising that it aroused so much antipathy from the Resistance press. But it was not simply Clouzot's and Chavance's attacks on French hypocrisy which so angered the Left. Rather, the underlying problem was their world view, their refusal to acknowledge that moral positions were clear-cut.

The theme of the film is stated quite explicitly in a scene between Vorzet and Germain:

> Vorzet: You are incredible. You think that people are all good or all evil. You think that good is light (he lifts the lamp) and darkness is evil. But where is darkness (he pushes the lamp and it begins to swing), where is light? Where is the border of evil? Do you know which side you are on? Think about it and examine your conscience. You will perhaps be astonished.
> Germain: I know myself.
> Vorzet: Pride. Since a whirlwind of hate and denunciation has blown into this town, all moral values are more or less corrupted. You have been afflicted like the others. One only has choices you know.[65]

The moral ambiguity which Vorzet verbalizes in this scene is certainly Clouzot's. Through the course of the film, Clouzot attempts to impose his moral perspective on the viewer by showing the action through the viewpoint of Dr. Germain.

Germain is the first character shown, washing blood off his hands after an unsuccessful delivery. This Lady Macbeth gesture is no doubt ironic, for Germain feels no remorse for having lost the child to save the mother. As the film will reveal, Germain feels absolutely justified in his moral values. The audience tends to accept his judgments because they correspond to liberal, humanistic principles (his anger that Marie Corbin is stealing morphine intended for the cancer patient, his repugnance at the doctor's jokes about the case of gangrene). Thus, the viewer tends to accept not only Germain's view of the action, but his condemnation of each suspect in turn.

The raven, rather than being merely a malevolent force is, in fact, an agent of Germain's transformation, finally forcing him to see the truth of Vorzet's moral relativism. The surprise of discovering the raven's identity is due to the fact that Vorzet has been, throughout the film, the voice of moderation and reason. That his benign exterior hides a force of deep evil forces Germain to reexamine his values, a process that culminates with Vorzet's murder.

From Germain's morally certain position at the film's opening, which includes not only his position on childbirth, but his rejection of Denise as a proper love object, his willingness to accept circumstantial proof of first Marie's and then Denise's guilt, to his outraged condemnation of the mother's plan for revenge ("you have no right to do that, none at all"), Germain ignores the weakness of his own position, preferring to see himself as a kind of *Übermensch* who alone has the right to decide what is good and what is evil. Despite the fact that his judgments become increasingly suspect, he maintains this posture until the scene where Denise finally forces him to see the truth about himself. ("You rationalize too much. Your brain is full of reasoning but you feel nothing. If you want to know the truth, look into my eyes.") In a series of extreme close-ups (the first in the film), Germain for the first time feels doubt. By the end of the film, the moral ambiguity of Clouzot's universe has become Germain's and the viewer's. Faced, like Germain, with a moral dilemma, do we condemn or applaud the mother's murder of Vorzet? Clouzot provides no answer.

That men are neither all good nor all evil seems a platitude to us now. But in occupied France, a Manichean view of human nature was almost a necessity. In order to risk one's life by distributing newspapers, assassinating German soldiers, or blowing up troop trains, one had to believe that one was on the side of justice and virtue, and that the enemy shared no common humanity with oneself. By casting that certainty into doubt, Clouzot

undermined more than bourgeois complacency. To those members of the Resistance who still cannot forgive him, Clouzot's *Le
Corbeau* was the most dangerous film of its time.

Conclusion

The moral and political issues raised by *Le Corbeau* ex-
emplify the larger questions that surround the period as a whole.
The need for clear-cut villains and heroes, for a sharp distinction
between "us" and "them," was the motivating force for the reprisals against collaborators and the concurrent heroization of any
who had helped those trying to drive the occupier out.

What the "épuration" failed to see was the very ambiguity Clouzot insisted upon. The line between the heroes and villains was not so clear as the Resistance would have liked to believe. The distinction between those who had worked for
Continental and those who had worked for French firms was more
apparent than real. Both groups continued working because they
needed the money and because they believed that they were
helping to save the French film industry. The personnel at Continental, as much as those working for French producers, saw their
work as bringing entertainment and hope to a despairing people,
and glory to French culture. Both groups chose to ignore the banning and arrests of their Jewish colleagues, and both groups preferred not to understand the reasons for the occupier's liberality
toward the French film industry. For it was not only those who
worked at Continental who unwittingly provided propaganda for
the New Europe and an economic wedge for the German film industry. All of the filmmakers who worked through the occupation
did so with the express permission and encouragement of the occupiers, and, by working, they legitimized the occupier's presence.
Yet, neither group can be blamed, for they both believed that by
making films they were helping France.

Even today, the complexity of moral responsibility for
French filmmakers during the occupation has not been fully
understood. Young French critics, themselves free of the taint of
collaboration, look at the work of the previous generation in or-

der to find the ideology of the conqueror or of Vichy. The accusations of moral culpability go on. But Clouzot's insistence that there are no final answers, "only choices," is as true of the occupation as a whole as of the world of *Le Corbeau*. We can neither condemn nor applaud those choices. We can only seek to understand.

Conclusion

In many ways, the French film industry suffered more after the Liberation than it had during the occupation. Although political freedom returned to France, economic conditions continued to deterioriate. The provisional government was neither strong enough nor sufficiently interested in the film industry to oversee its reconstruction. The Comité de Libération du Cinéma Français took over many of the COIC's functions, but internal disputes and the hunt for collaborators weakened its economic purpose. The bombings and destructions continued until the war ended in Europe in May 1945; even after the Allied victory, material scarcity remained critical in France.

All of these economic problems were insignificant, however, in comparison to the one overriding threat to the French film industry; with the arrival of American soldiers came the return of American films. Four years of Hollywood production were waiting to swamp the French market; and the market for French films collapsed.[1]

Throughout most of its history, the French cinema has verged on economic collapse. From the moment it lost its international predominance during World War I, the French film industry has staggered from crisis to crisis: the coming of sound, the Depression, the financial scandals of the thirties, the war, the occupation. After the war, the crises continued: changing international markets, the need for expensive technologies (color, wide screen) to hold audiences; the competition with television. If the long history of the French cinema is marked by any continuity, it is a continuity of survival in the face of imminent disaster.

Given its history, we should not be surprised that the French cinema survived the occupation. Yet, of all the events in the history of France during the twentieth century, surely the defeat and occupation were the most serious threats to the survival of the nation itself and to the survival of its cultural production. During the occupation, the film industry faced two totalitarian regimes, the loss of its most highly regarded talent, and severe shortages in all areas of production. That it did not collapse is testimony to the paradoxes of the era.

Vichy, and its creature, the COIC, were determined to keep the French cinema functioning at the highest possible level for the prestige of France and for its economic well-being. The Germans, too, wanted the French film industry to survive, because they needed it to carry out their own economic plans. Producers, with COIC support, poured money into the industry, because there was a great deal of money to be made. And so filmmakers found themselves encouraged on all sides. In response, they made films that were well-crafted and popular; many even tried to make films that would help restore pride to a defeated nation.

But the French cinema's survival came with a price. In order to continue making films, the industry had to sacrifice the freedom, the near anarchy, that had prevailed in the 1930s. Although the freedom of the thirties had made the cinema economically insecure, it had also given many individualistic artists the opportunity to make films, and it had infused the films that were made with a spirit unlike those of any other nation. In the 1940s, Jews and dissidents could not make films at all; those who wished to protest the new era had to speak *sotto voce*, hiding their ideas in vagueness and contradiction. And although many newcomers were welcomed into the French cinema, most of their work would be regarded by a later generation of Frenchmen as a diminution of that cinema's accomplishments.

The debate over the significance of the French cinema of the occupation will continue, as will the debate over the moral responsibility of those who contributed to it. There is no way to objectively measure the cinema's failures and accomplishments, because what were failures to some were accomplishments to others. That the French cinema survived at all is an accomplishment—unless one considers that the cinema survived because two of the most odious regimes in history wanted it and aided it to survive. That the French cinema lost its spirit of freedom is a failure—unless one is willing to consider a new style of filmmaking, with roots in French cultural traditions, a valid and even praiseworthy development.

Even if we cannot come to ultimate judgment, we can at least isolate the criteria by which we might judge. Two antithetical positions on the problem of the French cinema during the occupation are inscribed in two images drawn from the films of the period. In one, the devil rants in despair as the hearts of two lovers continue beating beneath their petrified bodies. The body turned to stone by defeat and occupation is France; the heart that continues beating is the French spirit. The cinema of the occupation carried on the French spirit. By refusing to die, it showed itself and the world that France was stronger than the forces that would have destroyed it.

The other image is of two Frenchmen standing under a swinging lamp. As the light swings back and forth, the line between good and evil is cast into shadow. The cinema of the occupation also eludes moral definition. Its failures and accomplishments cannot be separated; its achievements were also defeats.

Les Visiteurs du soir and Le Corbeau were both made by talented artists whose primary goals were to create films of lasting value. Nearly all French film artists placed their devotion to the cinema over any immediate political or moral consideration, and that devotion is what saved the French cinema from destruction. But both films were also expressions of deeply held world views. The era cannot be characterized by either alone.

Feature Film Production, June 1940–August 1944

C ontrary to normal practice, films of the occupation are generally considered by their dates
of production, rather than their dates of release. The list that follows is taken from the one published in Le Film, July 22, 1944.

Several points should be noted about this list. First,
notwithstanding the generally accepted count, there are 219 (not
220) films on the list. Second, four films are included on the list
that began production before June 1940 but were completed after
(marked by *). In addition, the list includes one film, Bifur III, that
was in production in July 1944, when the list was compiled, but
was never completed.

Three films are missing from the list for various reasons.
Christian-Jaque's Franco-Italian co-production of Carmen was shot
in Rome beginning May 18, 1942 (its first Paris showing was on
August 8, 1944). Forces occultes (director: Jean Mamy) cannot really
be considered a feature film at forty-three minutes, although it
was released in March 1943 in an exclusive first-run showing. It
may have been left off the list because it was an overt propaganda tract against Freemasonry. Finally, a feature-length film titled Finance noire (director: J. Vitry) was released in Paris on November 24, 1943. No additional information is available on this
film.

Title	Director	Production Start[a]	Paris Release[b]	P/C[c]	American Release Title
A la belle frégate	A. Valentin	April 24, 1942	April 1, 1943		
A vos ordres Madame	J. Boyer	June 15, 1942	Oct. 16, 1942		
Ademaï bandit d'honneur	G. Grangier	Feb. 9, 1943	Sept. 1, 1943		
Adieu Léonard	P. Prévert	Jan. 7, 1943	Sept. 1, 1943		
Adrien	Fernandel	April 1, 1943	Dec. 22, 1943	C	
Les Affaires sont les affaires	J. Dréville	June 8, 1942	Sept. 10, 1942		
L'Age d'or	J. de Limur	June 30, 1941	Jan. 28, 1942		
Les Ailes blanches	R. Péguy	Aug. 21, 1942	March 10, 1943		
L'Amant de Bornéo	J-P Feydeau	Feb. 9, 1942	May 28, 1942		
L'An 40	Y. Mirande	Oct. 21, 1940	n.r.		
Andorra	E. Couzinet	Aug. 14, 1941	July 27, 1942		
L'Ange de la nuit	A. Berthomieu	Nov. 13, 1942	Jan. 19, 1944		
L'Ange gardien	J. de Casembroot	Feb. 16, 1942	July 1942		
Les Anges du péché	R. Bresson	Feb. 8, 1943	June 1943	C	Angels of the Streets
Annette et la dame blonde	J. Dréville	Sept. 20, 1941	March 16, 1942		
L'Appel du bled	M. Gleize	March 25, 1942	Oct. 21, 1942		
Après l'orage	P.-J. Ducis	July 31, 1941	Feb. 4, 1943		
L'Arlésienne	M. Allégret	Aug. 11, 1941	Sept. 4, 1942		
Arlette et l'amour	R. Vernay	April 12, 1943	Sept. 22, 1943		
L'Assassin a peur la nuit	J. Delannoy	March 4, 1942	Sept. 2, 1942		
L'Assassin habite au 21	H.-G. Clouzot	May 4, 1942	Aug. 7, 1942	C/P	The Murderer Lives at 21
L'Assassinat du Père Noël	Christian-Jaque	Feb. 17, 1941	Oct. 16, 1941	C/P	Who Killed Santa Claus?
Au Bonheur des Dames	A. Cayatte	Feb. 1, 1943	July 2, 1943	C/P	Shopgirls of Paris
L'Auberge de l'abîme	W. Rozier	Aug. 3, 1942	Feb. 24, 1943		
L'Aventure est au coin de la rue	J. Daniel-Norman	Sept. 6, 1943	Feb. 18, 1944		
Le Bal des passants	G. Radot	Oct. 23, 1943	April 1, 1944		
Le Baron Fantôme	S. de Poligny	Sept. 21, 1942	June 1943		
Béatrice devant le désir	J. de Marguenat	June 7, 1943	March 8, 1944		

Title	Director				English title
La Belle Aventure	M. Allégret	Aug. 22, 1942	Dec. 20, 1944		
Le Bienfaiteur	H. Decoin	Sept. 7, 1942	Dec. 11, 1942		
Bifur III*	M. Cam	Aug. 1939/ May 10, 1944	n.r.		
Blondine	H. Mahé	Nov. 8, 1943	May 16, 1945		
La Boîte aux rêves	Y. Allégret	July 26, 1943	July 11, 1945		
Boléro	J. Boyer	Nov. 17, 1941	March 25, 1942		
La Bonne Étoile	J. Boyer	Sept. 14, 1942	March 24, 1943		
Bonsoir mesdames, bonsoir messieurs	R. Tual	May 10, 1943	Feb. 16, 1944		
Le Bossu	J. Delannoy	Jan. 10, 1944	Dec. 6, 1944		
Le Brigand Gentilhomme	E. Couzinet	Sept. 20, 1942	Dec. 22, 1943		
Le Briseur de chaînes	J. Daniel-Norman	Aug. 23, 1941	Dec. 23, 1941		
Les Cadets de l'océan	J. Dréville	April 27, 1942	Nov. 14, 1945		
La Cage aux rossignols	J. Dréville	March 22, 1944	1945		Cage of Nightingales
Le Camion blanc	L. Joannon	Aug. 8, 1942	March 24, 1943		
Cap au large .	J.-P. Paulin	June 8, 1942	Sept. 25, 1942		
Le Capitaine Fracasse	A. Gance	Aug. 10, 1942	June 1943		
Caprices	L. Joannon	June 27, 1941	Feb. 10, 1942	C/P	
Le Carrefour des enfants perdus	L. Joannon	Oct. 8, 1943	April 26, 1944		
Cartacalha	L. Mathot	Aug. 28, 1941	Jan. 21, 1942		
La Cavalcade des heures	Y. Noé	Jan. 6, 1943	Nov. 10, 1943		
Les Caves du Majestic	R. Pottier	Feb. 16, 1944	Oct. 31, 1945	C	
Ce n'est pas moi	J. de Baroncelli	Sept. 15, 1941	Dec. 23, 1941		
Cécile est morte	M. Tourneur	Dec. 20, 1943	March 8, 1944	C	
Ceux du rivage	J. Severac	May 12, 1943	Oct. 20, 1943		
Chambre 13	A. Hugon	Aug. 14, 1940	Jan. 31, 1942		
Le Chant de l'exilé	A. Hugon	Nov. 5, 1942	April 21, 1943		
Un Chapeau de paille d'Italie	M. Cammage	Nov. 7, 1940	Jan. 26, 1944		
Chèque au porteur	J. Boyer	July 21, 1941	Dec. 24, 1941		

Title	Director	Production Start[a]	Paris Release[b]	P/C[c]	American Release Title
La Chèvre d'or	R. Barberis	Aug. 25, 1942	March 31, 1943		
Le Ciel est à vous	J. Grémillon	May 31, 1943	Feb. 2, 1944		The Woman who Dared
Le Club des Soupirants	M. Gleize	April 20, 1941	Sept. 26, 1941	C	
La Collection Ménard	B. Roland	April 19, 1943	April 12, 1944		
Le Colonel Chabert	R. le Hénaff	April 28, 1943	Dec. 1, 1943		Colonel Chabert
Le Comte de Monte Cristo	R. Vernay	Aug. 15, 1942	Jan. 21, 1943		
Le Corbeau	H.-G. Clouzot	May 10, 1943	Sept. 28, 1943	C/P	The Raven
Coup de feu dans la nuit	R. Péguy	July 9, 1942	March 3, 1943		
Coup de tête	R. le Hénaff	Sept. 9, 1943	Oct. 3, 1944		
La Croisée des chemins	A. Berthomieu	July 6, 1942	Dec. 2, 1942		
Croisières Sidérales	A. Zwoboda	Nov. 12, 1941	April 29, 1942		
Les Dames du Bois de Boulogne	R. Bresson	May 2, 1944	Sept. 20, 1945		Ladies of the Park
Défense d'aimer	R. Pottier	July 27, 1942	Oct. 30, 1942	C	
Départ à zéro	M. Cloche	May 12, 1941	n.r.		
Dernier Atout	J. Becker	March 24, 1942	Sept. 2, 1942		
Dernière Aventure	R. Péguy	Oct. 2, 1941	March 26, 1942		
Le Dernier des six	G. Lacombe	Feb. 28, 1941	Sept. 16, 1941	C	
Le Dernier Sou	A. Cayatte	Dec. 8, 1943	Jan. 23, 1946	C	
Le Destin fabuleux de Désirée Clary	S. Guitry	Dec. 5, 1941	Sept. 4, 1942		Mlle. Desirée
Les Deux Timides	Y. Allégret	March 25, 1941	July 28, 1943		
Domino	R. Richebé	March 15, 1943	July 28, 1943		
Donne-moi tes yeux	S. Guitry	Feb. 11, 1943	Nov. 24, 1943		
Douce	C. Autant-Lara	April 11, 1943	Nov. 10, 1943		Love Story
La Duchesse de Langeais	J. de Baroncelli	Nov. 28, 1941	March 27, 1942		The Wicked Duchess
Echec au Roy	J-P. Paulin	Oct. 28, 1943	May 16, 1945		
L'Enfant de l'amour	J. Stelli	Feb. 16, 1944	July 19, 1944		
Les Enfants du Paradis	M. Carné	Aug. 17, 1943	March 22, 1945		Children of Paradise

Title	Director				English Title
L'Escalier sans fin	G. Lacombe	March 4, 1943	Aug. 25, 1943		
L'Eternel Retour	J. Delannoy	March 15, 1943	Oct. 13, 1943	P	Eternal Return
Une Etoile au soleil	A. Zwoboda	July 20, 1942	Feb. 24, 1943		
L'Etrange Suzy	P.-J. Ducis	Feb. 26, 1941	Aug. 29, 1941		Paris Frills
Falbalas	J. Becker	Mar. 1, 1944	Jan. 20, 1945		
Farandole	A. Zwoboda	Jan. 17, 1944	Jan. 10, 1945	C/P	
La Fausse Maîtresse	A. Cayatte	May 1, 1942	Aug. 14, 1942		
Félicie Nanteuil	M. Allégret	April 25, 1942	June 27, 1945		
Une Femme dans la nuit	E. Gréville	June 19, 1941	Jan. 13, 1943		
La Femme que j'ai le plus aimée	R. Vernay	Jan. 26, 1942	Sept. 6, 1942		
La Femme perdue	J. Choux	April 19, 1942	Aug. 5, 1942		
La Ferme aux loups	R. Pottier	Aug. 19, 1943	Dec. 14, 1943	C	
Feu Nicholas	J. Houssin	March 29, 1943	Nov. 17, 1943		
Feu sacré	M. Cloche	Nov. 17, 1941	Oct. 12, 1942		
La Fiancée des ténèbres	S. de Poligny	March 11, 1944	March 22, 1945		
Fièvres	J. Delannoy	Sept. 8, 1941	Jan. 21, 1942	P	
La Fille du puisatier*	M. Pagnol	May 1940/ Aug. 13, 1940	April 24, 1941	P	The Well-Digger's Daughter
Florence est folle	G. Lacombe	March 15, 1944	Nov. 8, 1944		
Forte tête	L. Mathot	Jan. 5, 1942	June 10, 1942		
Fou d'amour	P. Mesnier	Nov. 13, 1942	June 1943		
Frédérica	J. Boyer	Aug. 5, 1942	Nov. 18, 1942		
Fromont Jeune et Risler Aîné	L. Mathot	June 10, 1941	Oct. 8, 1941		
Goupi Mains Rouges	J. Becker	Oct. 10, 1942	April 14, 1943	P	It Happened at the Inn
Graine au vent	M. Gleize	March 22, 1943	March 16, 1944		
Le Grand Combat	B. Roland	June 29, 1942	Dec. 23, 1942		
La Grande Marnière	J. de Marguenat	Aug. 28, 1942	Jan. 14, 1943		
La Grande Meute	J. de Limur	May 3, 1944	July 18, 1945		
Haut-le-Vent	J. de Baroncelli	April 27, 1942	Dec. 23, 1942		
Histoire de rire	M. l'Herbier	Aug. 7, 1941	Dec. 18, 1941		

Title	Director	Production Start[a]	Paris Release[b]	P/C[c]	American Release Title
L'Homme de Londres	H. Decoin	Jan. 14, 1943	Aug. 5, 1943		
L'Homme qui joue avec le feu	J. de Limur	March 30, 1942	Aug. 5, 1942		
L'Homme qui vendit son âme	J.-P. Paulin	Feb. 24, 1943	Sept. 22, 1943		
L'Homme sans nom	L. Mathot	Sept. 1, 1942	Feb. 4, 1943		
Les Hommes sans peur	Y. Noé	May 2, 1941	Oct. 7, 1942		
L'Honorable Catherine	M. l'Herbier	June 25, 1942	Feb. 4, 1943	P	
Huit Hommes dans un château	R. Pottier	April 13, 1942	Dec. 9, 1942		
Ici l'on pêche	R. Jayet	Aug. 18, 1941	Dec. 17, 1941		
L'Ile d'amour	M. Cam	Sept. 8, 1943	May 24, 1944		
Les Inconnus dans la maison	H. Decoin	Dec. 9, 1941	May 16, 1942	C/P	Strangers in the House
L'Inévitable M. Dubois	P. Billon	Nov. 2, 1942	Aug. 3, 1943	P	
Je suis avec toi	H. Decoin	Aug. 2, 1943	Dec. 22, 1943		
Jeannou	L. Poirier	April 28, 1943	Nov. 10, 1943		
Des Jeunes Filles dans la nuit	R. le Hénaff	Aug. 10, 1942	April 10, 1943		
Le Journal tombe à Cinq heures	G. Lacombe	Jan. 23, 1942	May 21, 1942		
Les Jours heureux	J. de Marguenat	Aug. 25, 1941	Dec. 24, 1941		
Lettres d'amour	C. Autant-Lara	June 22, 1942	Dec. 23, 1942		
Le Lit à colonnes	R. Tual	March 16, 1942	July 9, 1942		
La Loi du printemps	J. Daniel-Norman	Feb. 16, 1942	May 20, 1942		
Le Loup de Malveneur	G. Radot	July 27, 1942	May 12, 1943		
Lucrèce	L. Joannon	May 11, 1943	Dec. 15, 1943		
Lumière d'été	J. Grémillon	Aug. 17, 1942	May 26, 1943		
Lunegarde	M. Allégret	May 16, 1944	Jan. 16, 1946		
Madame et le mort	L. Daquin	May 25, 1942	April 21, 1943		
Madame Sans-Gêne	R. Richebé	June 3, 1941	Oct. 7, 1941		
Mademoiselle Béatrice	M. de Vaucorbeil	Sept. 10, 1942	May 19, 1943		
Mademoiselle Swing	R. Pottier	Nov. 17, 1941	June 12, 1942		
Mademoiselle X . . .	P. Billon	May 23, 1944	June 17, 1945		

Mahlia la Métisse*	W. Kapps	1939/ Nov. 13, 1942	Dec. 15, 1943		
La Main du Diable	M. Tourneur	Aug. 21, 1942	April 21, 1943	C/P	Carnival of Sinners
La Maison des sept jeunes filles	A. Valentin	Oct. 15, 1941	Feb. 6, 1942		
Malaria	J. Gourguet	Nov. 9, 1942	June 30, 1943		
La Malibran	S. Guitry	July 12, 1943	May 3, 1944		
Mam'zelle Bonaparte	M. Tourneur	Sept. 1, 1941	Jan. 16, 1942	C/P	
Mariage d'amour	H. Decoin	April 27, 1942	Dec. 22, 1942	C/P	
Le Mariage de Chiffon	C. Autant-Lara	Aug. 20, 1941	Aug. 6, 1942		
Marie-Martine	A. Valentin	Nov. 11, 1942	May 11, 1943	P	
Mélodie pour toi	W. Rozier	July 14, 1941	Nov. 11, 1942		
Le Merle blanc	J. Houssin	Feb. 28, 1944	Dec. 6, 1944		
Mermoz	L. Cuny	Sept. 10, 1942	Nov. 3, 1943		
Le Mistral	J. Houssin	July 25, 1942	Nov. 5, 1942		
Mon Amour est près de toi	R. Pottier	May 11, 1943	Sept. 29, 1943	C/P	
Monsieur des Lourdines	P. de Hérain	Sept. 21, 1942	June 9, 1943		
Monsieur la Souris	G. Lacombe	June 29, 1942	Oct. 14, 1942		
Montmartre-sur-Seine	G. Lacombe	Aug. 18, 1941	Nov. 19, 1941		Midnight in Paris
Le Mort ne reçoit plus	J. Tarride	May 10, 1943	July 7, 1944		
Le Moussaillon	J. Gourguet	Sept. 25, 1941	Feb. 6, 1942		
Les Mystères de Paris	J. de Baroncelli	May 5, 1943	Sept. 8, 1943		
Ne bougez plus	P. Caron	July 22, 1941	Oct. 31, 1941	C	
Ne le criez pas sur les toits	J. Daniel-Norman	Nov. 16, 1942	July 14, 1943		
La Neige sur les pas	A. Berthomieu	July 7, 1941	June 3, 1942		
Nous les gosses	L. Daquin	July 10, 1941	Dec. 2, 1941		Portrait of Innocence
La Nuit fantastique	M. l'Herbier	Dec. 1, 1941	July 10, 1942		
La Nuit merveilleuse	J.-P. Paulin	Dec. 2, 1940	n.r.		
Opéra-Musette	R. Lefèvre	Sept. 18, 1941	Feb. 18, 1942		
Paméla	P. de Hérain	May 2, 1944	May 2, 1945		
Patricia	P. Mesnier	May 26, 1942	Nov. 12, 1942	P	

Title	Director	Production Start[a]	Paris Release[b]	P/C[c]	American Release Title
Patrouille blanche*	C. Chamborant	1939/ Sept. 29, 1941	March 5, 1942		
Le Pavillon brûle	J. de Baroncelli	Aug. 18, 1941	Dec. 17, 1941		
Péchés de jeunesse	M. Tourneur	May 12, 1941	Nov. 16, 1941	C	
Pension Jonas	P. Caron	Sept. 25, 1941	March 6, 1942		
Le Père Goriot	R. Vernay	April 15, 1944	March 22, 1945		
Les Petites du Quai aux Fleurs	M. Allégret	June 15, 1943	May 27, 1944		
Les Petits Riens	R. Leboursier	Feb. 3, 1941	Dec. 16, 1942		
Picpus	R. Pottier	Oct. 28, 1942	Feb. 12, 1943	C/P	
Pierre et Jean	A. Cayatte	Aug. 30, 1943	Dec. 29, 1943	C	
Pontcarral, Colonel d'Empire	J. Delannoy	June 1, 1942	Dec. 11, 1942	P	
Port d'Attache	J. Choux	Aug. 9, 1942	Feb. 10, 1943		
Premier Bal	Christian-Jaque	June 9, 1941	Sept. 17, 1941		
Premier de Cordée	L. Daquin	June 15, 1943	Feb. 23, 1944		
Premier Rendez-Vous	H. Decoin	April 22, 1941	Aug. 14, 1941	C/P	Her First Affair
Le Prince charmant	J. Boyer	Sept. 25, 1941	May 26, 1942		
Promesse à l'inconnue	A. Berthomieu	Feb. 16, 1942	Oct. 2, 1942		
La Rabouilleuse	F. Rivers	Sept. 17, 1943	Feb. 2, 1944		
Retour de flamme	H. Fescourt	Sept. 23, 1942	May 26, 1943		
Romance à trois	R. Richebé	April 7, 1942	June 17, 1942		
Romance de Paris	J. Boyer	June 3, 1941	Oct. 3, 1941		
Les Roquevillard	J. Dréville	Feb. 15, 1943	Aug. 25, 1943		
Le Secret de Madame Clapain	A. Berthomieu	April 5, 1943	Aug. 11, 1943		
Secrets	P. Blanchar	Sept. 7, 1942	March 17, 1943		
Service de nuit	J. Faurez	May 8, 1943	April 19, 1944		
Un Seul Amour	P. Blanchar	June 25, 1943	Nov. 25, 1943		
La Sévillane	A. Hugon	Oct. 10, 1941	March 10, 1943		
Signé:illisible	C. Chamborant	Feb. 16, 1942	July 17, 1942		
Simplet	Fernandel	Feb. 7, 1942	Nov. 11, 1942	C/P	

Title	Director	Production start	Paris release		English title
Six Petites Filles en blanc	Y. Noé	Sept. 15, 1941	July 21, 1943		
Le Soleil a toujours raison	P. Billon	June 9, 1941	Jan. 27, 1943		
Le Soleil de minuit	B. Roland	Jan. 20, 1943	June 30, 1943		The Bellman
Sortilèges	Christian-Jaque	Feb. 22, 1944	Dec. 5, 1945		
La Symphonie Fantastique	Christian-Jaque	Oct. 17, 1941	April 1, 1942	C/P	La Symphonie Fantastique
Tornavara	J. Dréville	April 17, 1943	Oct. 6, 1943		
La Troisième Dalle	M. Dulud	Aug. 25, 1940	n.r.		
Le Val d'enfer	M. Tourneur	June 14, 1943	Sept. 22, 1943	C	
Le Valet maître	P. Mesnier	July 24, 1941	Oct. 30, 1941		
La Valse blanche	I. Stelli	Feb. 22, 1943	Dec. 15, 1943		
Vautrin	P. Billon	June 17, 1943	Jan. 12, 1944	P	Vautrin the Thief
Vénus aveugle	A. Gance	Nov. 11, 1940	Oct. 1, 1943		
La Vie de Bohème	M. l'Herbier	Nov. 30, 1942	Jan. 17, 1945		
Une Vie de chien	M. Cammage	March 7, 1941	June 1943		
La Vie de plaisir	A. Valentin	Sept. 27, 1943	May 16, 1944	C	
Vie privée	W. Kapps	Dec. 8, 1941	May 29, 1942		
Vingt-cinq Ans de bonheur	R. Jayet	Jan. 13, 1943	May 25, 1943	C	
Les Visiteurs du soir	M. Carné	April 27, 1942	Dec. 3, 1942	P	The Devil's Own Envoys
Le Voile bleu	J. Stelli	April 15, 1942	Nov. 18, 1942	P	
Voyage sans espoir	Christian-Jaque	Aug. 5, 1943	Dec. 15, 1943		
Le Voyageur de la Toussaint	L. Daquin	Sept. 26, 1942	April 8, 1943		
Le Voyageur sans bagage	J. Anouilh	Oct. 4, 1943	Feb. 23, 1944		

[a] Production start dates are drawn from the original production notices in *Le Film* (1940–1944). In some cases, they differ from the dates given in *Le Film*'s list of July 1944.

[b] Paris release dates are drawn from notices in *Le Film*, and for films released after the Liberation, from *La Cinématographie Française*. Films marked n.r. were never released in Paris (although some were released in the unoccupied zone).

[c] C = Continental Production; P = one of the 27 films listed in *Le Film* as being extremely popular or breaking box office records.

* Production began before June 1940.

Appendix B

Tables

Table 3.1 First Quarter Receipts—Paris

Year	Gross Receipts (francs)	Percentage of 1938	Percent Increase/Decrease over Previous Year
1938	118,629,600	100.00%	—
1939	131,241,800	110.63%	+10%
1940	89,460,600	75.41%	−32%
1941	89,498,000	75.44%	+.04%
1942	139,134,000	117.28%	+55%
1943	239,233,000	201.66%	+72%

SOURCE: Le Film, May 20, 1944

Table 5.1 Average Production Cost by Year (in francs)

1938[a]	2,900,000
1941[a]	3,400,000
1942[b]	4,500,000
1944[c]	13,400,000

Notes: The figures are drawn from different sources, so they are not entirely comparable. However, in those cases where two sources provide figures for the same year, they are in agreement.

Figures for 1943 are not available, but Chéret (p. 27) gives the following figures for the 1942–43 and 1943–44 seasons:

1942–43 (first half)	5,100,000
1942–43 (second half)	8,300,000
1943–44	13,000,000

[a]The figures are an average taken from the range given in Le Film, August 7, 1941.

[b]CNC, p. 18.

[c]Dommages, p. 27.

Table 5.2 Gross Receipts by Year (in francs)

Year	France[a]	Paris[b]
1938	1,300,000,000	452,513,000
1940	n.a.	257,114,000
1941	n.a.	416,500,000
1942	2,504,000,000	707,079,000
1943	3,805,000,000	1,077,322,000
1944	3,215,000,000	n.a.

[a]The figure for 1938 appeared in *Le Cinéma Français*, 1945, p. 24. Figures for 1942–1944 in CNC, p. 18.

[b]*Le Film* May 20, 1944, corrected July 1, 1944.

Table 5.3 Number of Films Released (Paris) by Year and Country of Production

Year	French	German	Other[a]	Total	Percent French
1941	50	39	—	89	56%
1942	74	43	14	131	56%
1943	82	30	15	127	65%
1944 (Jan.–Aug.)	21	9	2	32	66%

SOURCE: CNC, P. 23

[a]According to *Dommages* (p. 23), 32 films were imported from countries other than Germany during the occupation: 30 from Italy, 1 each from Spain and Japan. A chart published in *La Cinématographie Française*, December 29, 1945, gives a figure of 35 Italian films released in France between 1941 and 1943, and 3 "other." The difference in totals may be accounted for by the fact that not all of these films were necessarily released in Paris.

Notes

1. War and Defeat

1. A detailed discussion of German wartime propaganda films can be found in Siegfried Kracauer, *From Caligari to Hitler* (Princeton: Princeton University Press, 1947), pp. 275–331. Of the psychological effects of these films on foreign audiences, Kracauer notes: "as to export, the effort of the Nazi authorities to flood foreign countries with their official pictures is sufficiently characterized by the fact that the Propaganda Ministry prepared versions in sixteen different languages . . . Of particular interest is the well-known use Hitler diplomats made of propaganda films to undermine the resistance of foreign peoples and governments. In Bucharest, Oslo, Belgrade, Ankara, Sofia—to mention but a few—official showings of these pictures served as psychological holdups" (p. 277).

2. There is some question as to whether French filmmakers worked in Italy at their own initiative or at the government's instigation. Renoir claims in his memoirs that he was sent at government orders and "being in uniform, I had no option but to obey." Jean Renoir, *My Life and My Films*, p. 175. L'Herbier, in his memoirs, says he accepted the Italian offer voluntarily, but that the French government encouraged the effort: "Our ambassador [to Italy], André Francois-Poncet, secretly desired that the most binding ties of cooperation be maintained with Italy." Marcel l'Herbier, *La Tête qui tourne*, pp. 276–277.

3. See editorials in *La Cinématographie Française*: February 3, 1940, Feb. 17, 1940 and March 2, 1940.

4. *La Cinématographie Française*, December 9, 1939.

5. Marcel Carné, *La Vie à Belle Dents*, pp. 171–172.

6. Collaborationist newspapers in the North would soon be publishing outraged articles denouncing these producers' intentions to take over the French film industry in the South. Anti-Jewish measures on the part of the Vichy government were quickly instituted, however, and most of these producers continued their exile, fleeing to North Africa (Jacques Haik) or the United States (Robert Hakim). See chapter 4 for a discussion of these anti-Jewish measures.

7. Jean-Pierre Aumont, *Sun and Shadow*, p. 51.

8. Renoir, p. 181.

9. Renoir, p. 182. Renoir's first impulse was to stay. In a letter to Flaherty on August 8, 1940, Renoir wrote, "I would be ashamed to leave my fellow countrymen when everything goes wrong." Letter in the Robert Flaherty collection, Columbia University; cited in Robert Paxton, *Vichy France: Old Guard and New Order, 1940–1944*, p. 45.

10. Published in *Le Film*, November 15, 1940. This weekly took over the offices of *La Cinématographie Française*, and was the major film trade journal during the occupation. Clair's citizenship was returned to him in March 1941.

11. According to Suzanne Bidault's (then Borel) account, the Vichy Minister of Information, Paul Marion, threatened to forbid the actress permission to work in the unoccupied zone unless she agreed to make films for the Germans. Suzanne Bidault, *Souvenirs de guerre et d'occupation*, p. 113.

12. Rosay, in her memoirs, does not mention the incident with Marion, although she says that the Vichy government made every effort to prevent the couple from leaving. Françoise Rosay, *La Traversée d'une vie*, pp. 255–273.

13. "Evocation: Louis Daquin," *Cinéma 79* (January 1979), 241:29. Daquin is probably mistaken about Becker, who was then in a prisoner of war camp.

14. For example, the Scala in Lyon, the Olympia in Bordeaux, the Capitole and Odéon in Marseille. In Paul Léglise, *Histoire de la politique du cinéma français, Entre deux républiques 1940–1946* 2:29.

15. Author's interview with Pierre Prévert, Paris, October 16, 1979.

16. Madeleine Ozeray, *A Toujours Monsieur Jouvet*, pp. 164–184.

17. For a complete account of the fate of *Sierra de Teruel*, see Walter G. Langlois, "Malraux's *Sierra de Teruel*: A Forgotten Treasure of the Library of Congress Film Collection," *The Quarterly Journal of the Library of Congress* (January 1973), 30:1–18.

18. Information provided by Jay Leyda.

19. Hervé Le Boterf, *La Vie Parisienne sous l'occupation*, 1:20. Approximately one million had returned by mid-July, and most of the rest by the end of the year.

20. *Le Film*, October 12, 1940.

21. *Le Film* estimated on October 12, 1940, that 450 films had been cleared for exhibition, mostly German or documentary films. Among the French films authorized for showing in the occupied zone were Pagnol's *Angèle* and the Marius trilogy, and Duvivier's *Carnet de Bal*.

22. Figures published after the war indicate a drop in German imports from 60 films in 1935 (17 percent of total imports) to 26 films in 1939 (9 percent). In France, Commission Consultative des Dommages et des Reparations, *Dommages subis par la France et l'Union Française du fait de la guerre et de l'occupation ennemie (1939–1945), Emprise Allemande sur la pensée française* 8:15. Hereinafter referred to as *Dommages*.

23. The Germans did not succeed in forcing Vichy to ban these American films until October 1942.

24. The exact number of employees in film-related industries cannot be precisely determined. The figure of 60,000 (mostly employed in the area of exhibition) is taken from contemporaneous sources. Later observers, like the compilers of the *Dommages* series, claim the figure was closer to 80,000. It is likely, however, that all of these figures are inflated.

2. Filmmaking in Vichy

1. Betty Daussmond was replaced by Line Noro.

2. My discussion of Vichy policies is derived largely from Robert O. Paxton, *Vichy France: Old Guard and New Order, 1940–1944*, passim.

3. Henry W. Ehrman, *Organized Business in France*, p. 17.

4. Alan S. Milward, *The New Order and the French Economy*, p. 67; and Ehrman, p. 51.

5. In 1935, 158 new production companies were formed, mostly for the production of a single film. In 1936, 175 came into existence, according to the figures in Francis Courtade, *Les Malédictions du cinéma français*, p. 129.

6. Roger Richebé, "L'Activité cinématographique sous l'occupation," in Hoover Institute on War, Revolution and Peace, *La Vie des Français sous l'occupation* 2:963. On the double meaning of "cleansing" see discussion later in this chapter.

7. Cited in Paul Léglise, *Histoire de la politique du cinéma français, Entre deux républiques 1940–1946*, 2:28. No source given.

8. The best account of the organization and function of the COIC may be found in Léglise, pp. 43–82. Unless otherwise specified, all information presented here on the COIC comes from Léglise, *Histoire de la politique*.

9. Law of December 2, 1940, reprinted in *Dommages*, Annexe 3.

10. Galey had been an architect and set designer for films in the 1920s, before becoming a journalist and minor functionary in the Popular Front government. (Author's interview with Louis-Emile Galey, Paris, October 1, 1979). It is worth noting that when the Socialist-leaning Galey was selected by Vichy's Minister of Information, Paul Marion, his rival for the post had been the Fascist writer and critic Robert Brasillach. See Philippe Amaury, *De l'information et de la propogande d'état*, p. 226.

11. Jacques Siclier, *La France de Pétain et son cinéma*, p. 30.

12. Reprinted in *Le Tout Cinéma* (1942), p. 58.

13. *Le Tout Cinéma* (1942), pp. 58–59.

14. Law of October 26, 1940, reprinted in *Dommages*, Annexe 2.

15. *Le Tout Cinéma* (1942), pp. 58–59.

16. *Le Tout Cinéma* (1942), p. 46.

17. Jean A. Gili, "La Vie cinématographique à Nice de 1939 à 1945," p. 180.

18. Cited in Gili, p. 183. Rocher's call for turning Nice into a "French Hollywood" resurrected an idea that had been first proposed in the 1910s.

19. Gili, p. 183.

20. Some examples include: *L'Assassinat du Père Noël*, filmed in Châmonix; *Histoire de rire* on the Côte d'Azur; *Le Pavillon brûle* in a copper mine in Caen; *Le Baron Fantôme* and *Goupi Mains Rouges* outside of Bordeaux; and *Lumière d'été* in the countryside near Nice.

21. Information from the weekly reports of the Filmprüfstelle (Film Control Board), Militärbefehlshaber in Frankreich, which are contained in the U.S. National Archives Series T-501, Rolls 141 and 142. All references to these reports will be cited by roll and frame numbers. R141/F1060.

22. Gili, p. 186.

23. Estimates of Italian participation from *Dommages*, p. 30.

24. Author's interview with Galey.

25. *Le Tout Cinema*, pp. 66–67.

26. Léglise, pp. 21–23. Léglise does not give the full list of films aided, but mentions that approximately 15 received financing in 1941 and 20 in 1942.

27. *Dommages*, p. 15.

28. *Dommages*, p. 19.

29. *Le Film*, February 28, 1942.

30. *Le Film*, May 9, 1942, and May 8, 1943.

31. Author's interview with Galey; Roger Richebé, *Au-Delà de l'écran*, p. 144.

32. Marc Allégret interview in Armand Panigel, "L'Histoire du cinéma français par ceux qui l'ont fait," 1975.

33. No figures are available on the relative popularity of French and American films in the unoccupied zone. However, since many of the American films were 1939 releases and had not previously been exhibited in France, one must assume that their popularity was equal to or greater than their prewar counterparts.

One impressionistic indication of the popularity of American films can be gathered from Simone de Beauvoir's account of her first visit to the unoccupied zone in the summer of 1941: "The cinemas on the Cannebière were showing American films, and some of them opened at ten o'clock in the morning. We once saw three shows in the same day. We watched Bette Davis, Edward G. Robinson and James Cagney [sic] in *Dark Victory*, hailing them like very dear, long-lost friends. We went to literally anything, from the sheer joy of seeing an American picture again." *The Prime of Life*, Peter Green, tr. New York, Harper & Row, 1962, p. 392.

34. Cited in Paxton, p. 166.

35. Bidault, *Souvenirs de guerre et d'occupation*, pp. 111–112. Bidault (Borel) could not remember the title of the American film about divorce.

36. Unsigned article in L'*Atelier*, February 1, 1941. This and subsequent quotes from the Parisian press in Bibliothèque de l'Arsénal, "Articles généraux sur le cinéma 1940–1944."

37. Janine Spaak, *Charles Spaak mon mari*, p. 217. The film was made in 1945, directed by Marcel l'Herbier.

38. Roger Régent, *Cinéma de France de "La Fille du Puisatier" aux "Enfants du Paradis,"* p. 69.

39. Spaak, p. 216.

40. This and following information on Vichy censorship from Bertrand Fabre, "Grandeurs et servitudes du cinéma français," p. 19.

41. Several writers have maintained that after the war Pagnol substituted de Gaulle's June 19, 1940, broadcast from London for the Pétain speech, but Jacques Siclier debunks this assertion. The print presently in circulation in the United States contains no reference to Pétain or de Gaulle.

3. German Initiatives, 1940–1941, and Continental Films

1. Elizabeth Dunan, "La Propaganda Abteilung de France," pp. 19–20.

2. Author's interview with Louis-Emile Galey, Paris, October 1, 1979.

3. Dunan, p. 21.

4. The reports from March 5, 1941, to July 3, 1943, are contained in the U.S. National Archives Series T-501, Reels 141 and 142.

5. In 1942, a joint German/Vichy newsreel service called "France-Actualités" was formed, whose films were shown in theaters throughout France.

6. *Le Film*, May 20, 1944. Figures are for the Paris region only.

7. Unfortunately, there are no available statistics which break down receipts by film or country of origin. See chapter 5 for a more extended discussion of the rise in box office receipts in 1942 and 1943.

8. The choice of name was significant. The firm was part of a plan to establish a German-dominated film industry throughout the continent of Europe. See chapter 7 for discussion.

9. Jürgen Spiker, *Film und Kapital: Der Weg der deutschen Filmwirtschaft zum national sozialistischen Einheitskonzern*, p. 193.

10. For an excellent discussion in English of Winkler's and Cautio's activities, see Julian Petley, *Capital and Culture: German Cinema 1933–45*, pp. 64ff.

11. Ploquin in Panigel, "L'Histoire du cinéma francais," and author's interview with Galey.

12. *Dommages*, p. 30. For comparative purposes, the approximate dollar value of the franc during the 1940–44 period was 44 francs to the dollar (1 franc = $.023).

13. *Dommages*, p. 30, and Spiker, p. 194.

14. Carné, *La Vie à Belle Dents*, p. 177.

15. R142/F761; and Carné, p. 189.

16. Author's interview with Galey.

17. Panigel. The speakers are: Georges Lacombe (to //), Christian-Jaque, Marcel Carné, Christian-Jaque, and Carné. Panigel confirms that he saw the contracts and that they specified the above-stated terms. Author's interview with Armand Panigel, New York, April 15, 1980.

18. Carné, pp. 177–180. Carné never made any films for Continental, managing to win release from his contract after his project for *Les Evadés de l'an 4000* fell through. Nonetheless, after the Liberation, Carné was censured for having signed the contract. [see chapter 8.]

19. Some historians of the period have maintained that Continental was not subject to German censorship review either, but this is not true. All films exhibited in France were reviewed by the Filmprüfstelle, including German films and Continental's productions. However, with the exception of some minor cuts (not specified) on Continental's *Ne bougez plus* (R142/F047), all Continental films were admitted for showing without difficulty.

20. Christian-Jaque in Panigel.

21. Unlike American trade journals, which routinely published box office receipts for individual films, this practice was proscribed in France after a successful lawsuit for invasion of privacy was won by a French producer against the prewar trade journal *La Cinématographie Française*. (Information provided by Paul Léglise). The 27 films named in *Le Film* are noted in appendix A.

22. Régent, *Cinema de France*, p. 52.

23. Dréville in Panigel.

24. Along with Grémillon's prewar *Remorques*, with Gabin and Morgan. *Le Film*, March 14, 1942.

25. Raymond Chirat and Claude Beylie, "Le Cinéma des années noires," p. 82. I can find no other source for this assertion, but if true, the fact that only three films were banned attests to the overall innocuousness of Continental's production.

26. *L'Ecran Français*, March 1944. The film was not shown in Germany under any title, although it was released in Czechoslovakia in 1943 (letter to the author from Jirí Levý, April 4, 1980), and may have been shown in other Eastern European countries as well.

27. According to Armand Panigel, in an interview with the author, the courtroom scene was directed by Clouzot, when Decoin refused to work any longer with Raimu. The speech, not in the original Simenon novel, is considered to be an example of Vichyist propaganda by some critics, notably Jean-Pierre Bertin-Maghit in *Le Cinéma français sous Vichy*. As evidence for this position, a portion of Loursat's accusation is cited, which certainly

appears to reflect Vichy's condemnation of decadence and its belief in the wholesome, outdoor life:

"Gentlemen of the jury, can you show me the way to the stadium, the velodrome, the swimming pool. No, don't try, there is no stadium, velodrome or pool. There are 132 cafes and bistros, I counted them, and 4 bordellos—those, I didn't count. My fellow citizens marked the path to them long ago. Gentlemen, when children cannot get drunk on fresh air and activity, they must seek recreation somewhere. They go to the movies and are spellbound by gangsters, when they are not aroused by the legs of the vamp. And one fine night these spectators, these children, become the actors, and they cover themselves with blood. And this mantle of blood—it is you, it is we—who have thrown it over their shoulders."

The confusion over the political import of this speech is reflected by Roger Régent, who calls it "socialist, and perhaps also national" (p. 64).

28. Continental was so pleased with the film, and so unaware of its thinly veiled allusion to De Gaulle and the Free French, that they premiered the film in Belgium before its Paris opening. It was an enormous success in both countries.

29. Joseph Goebbels, Diaries 1942–1943, p. 215. For a long discussion of Goebbels and German film policy, see chapter 7.

30. According to Christian-Jaque in Panigel, he had to shoot the sequence on the day when the music halls and theaters were closed in order to gather the necessary number of instruments.

31. These rumors, specifically that Continental would be sold to a Portugese firm for MGM, were reported in the clandestine paper Opéra, April–May 1944. The paper pointed out that such rumors were ridiculous, since the Free French government in Algiers had specifically forbidden any company formed after June 1940 to be continued.

32. Dommages, p. 17.

4. The Film Industry and the Jews

1. Billon was banned for the anti-German film Deuxième Bureau (1935). He was later cleared and worked throughout the period in the unoccupied zone.

2. Simone Signoret, Nostalgia Isn't What It Used To Be, p. 46.

3. Reprinted in Le Film, November 2, 1940.

4. See, for example, the discussions in Paxton, Vichy France, pp. 173–176, and Philippe Bourdrel, Histoire des juifs de France, pp. 348–362. The definitive study of the issue is by Michael R. Marrus and Robert O. Paxton, Vichy France and the Jews.

5. Maurice Bardèche and Robert Brasillach, Histoire du cinéma (Paris: Les Editions de Noël, 1935), p. 393. This remark was not included in the edition translated and edited by Iris Barry, The History of Motion Pictures (New York: Norton, 1938). The 1943 edition of Bardèche and Brasillach's history was, of course, even more overtly anti-Semitic.

6. Lucien Rebatet [François Vinneuil], Les Tribus du cinéma et du théâtre, pp. 42–43.

7. Gance's Vénus aveugle, begun in November 1940, was initially refused a distribution permit in the occupied zone for this reason.

8. Among the companies mentioned by name (R141/F450) were: Paris Export Film, belonging to Paul Graetz, who had gone to the United States in 1939; International Films Artistiques (Ifa) and Orpa Soll, belonging to Goldmann and Wohl; and Renova Film, owned by a "Jew Levy, who escaped."

9. Bourdrel, p. 365.

10. Marrus and Paxton, p. 153. This number refers to all businesses, not just to film-related concerns.

11. At the Liberation, no sanctions were applied against any individual or groups who took over this seized Jewish property. Nor were they named publicly. I have found only one administrator mentioned by name in print. On Nov. 17, 1945, La Cinématographie Française noted that exhibitor Jacques Haik (who had fled to Algeria during the occupation) was having difficulty reclaiming his property because it had been bankrupted by administrator Paul Boisserand. The only recourse available against these administrators was for the affected parties to institute individual lawsuits.

12. Exposition le Juif et la France, au Palais Berlitz sous l'Egide de l'Institut d'Etude des Questions Juives.

13. One measure of the lack of popularity of these newsreels are two notices published in Le Film. On November 1, 1940, Le Film warned theater owners that "all cinemas in Paris will be closed if audiences continue to hoot at newsreels." Failing to achieve the desired response, the occupier later mandated that "newsreels must obligatorily be shown with the house lights half on" (Le Film, January 15, 1941) so that the troublemakers could be identified.

14. Information on the number of Jews arrested and deported is from Bourdrel, pp. 429–443 passim. The figures are confirmed in Marrus and Paxton, p. 252.

15. Marrus and Paxton, p. 343. The prewar Jewish population of France is estimated at 250,000–300,000.

16. Cited by Gili, "La Vie cinématographique à Nice," p. 188.

17. David Hull, Film in the Third Reich, p. 209.

18. "Sur l'écran blanc des années noires," p. 87.

19. Sacha Guitry, Quatre Ans d'occupations, 2:97.

20. September 27, 1944, cited in Robert Aron, Histoire de l'épuration, Le Monde de la presse, des arts, des lettres, 2:231–233.

21. Author's interview with Galey, Paris, October 1, 1979, confirmed by Pierre Prévert.

22. Jean Wiéner, Allegro appassionato, p. 164. It should be added, as one of the few happy footnotes to the story of the Jews and the French cinema, that as a result of this clandestine meeting, Wiéner fell in love with, and eventually married, the "short woman" in question.

23. Le Chanois in Panigel, "L'Histoire du cinéma français."

24. Roger Richebé, Au-Dela de l'écran, pp. 151–152.

5. "An Industry Made of Gold": Production 1941–1942

1. The sixteen months from June 1941 to September 1942 were the most stable only in comparison with the other 34 months of the occupation. On the whole, French industrial production suffered enormous losses during the occupation. That the film industry prospered, as discussed in this chapter, is another of the many paradoxes of the era.

2. Le Film, June 7, 1941.

3. Richebé, Au-Dela de l'écran, pp. 135–136.

4. Arletty, La Défense, p. 140.

5. Reprinted in *Le Tout Cinéma*, pp. 64–65.

6. Vichy censorship is discussed in chapter 2; German censorship is discussed in chapter 7.

7. *Le Film*, September 27, 1941.

8. Carné, *La Vie à Belle Dents*, pp. 207–208. The scene was later reshot with larger snakes.

9. Average annual production between 1935 and 1938 had been 116 films, or nine to ten films per month. In 1939, only seventy-five films were made in France, slightly more than six per month. *La Cinématographie Française*, December 29, 1945, p. 45.

10. *Le Film*, Sept. 27, 1941.

11. *Le Tout Cinéma*, p. 119. In addition to inflation, other factors which led to the increase in production costs were: the large number of costume dramas made during the period, the necessity of procuring black market supplies at exorbitant prices, and the high cost of insurance necessitated by war-related risks (e.g., bombings).

The inflation in film production costs was, however, not much higher than the overall rate of inflation for the period. According to Paxton (*Vichy France*, p. 375), the cost of living rose by about 300 percent between 1940 and 1945, while average production costs for the same period rose by about 350 percent. See appendix table 5.1 for production cost by year.

12. *Le Film*, February 1, 1941.

13. Centre National de la Cinématographie (CNC). *Bulletin d'Information*, 7:15. Hereinafter referred to as CNC.

14. Pierre Chéret, "Exposé de la situation financière du cinéma français," 7:26.

15. CNC, p. 23, for the number of German and Italian films released in France. See appendix table 5.3 for breakdown of releases by country of origin and year of release. Continental's films are included in the totals of French film production, as they are in all statistical sources consulted.

There is no hard data on the percentage of box office receipts that went to non-French films. Chéret's figure of 20 percent (p. 26) is the highest of any given. See discussion in chapter 3 of the decline in box office receipts when only German productions were available for exhibition during the 1940–41 season.

16. *Dommages*, p. 9.

17. *Le Film*, August 2, 1941.

18. Calculated from chart in *Dommages*, p. 27. The difference between the rise in salary and non-salary costs is even more dramatic between 1938 and 1944: 295 percent increase in personnel costs, 504 percent in non-personnel costs.

19. Author's interview with Galey, Paris, October 1, 1979.

20. Raymond Borde preface in Courtade, *Les Malédictions du cinema français*, p. 11.

21. CNC, pp. 18–19.

22. Twenty-three films from this period were produced in Vichy, some of which are discussed in chapter 2. One film included in the production count, Christian-Jacque's *Carmen*, was produced in Rome.

23. Unlike the films made in the North, films made in Vichy were often set in the "glorious" present of the National Revolution. In occupied France, however, such reminders were nearly always avoided. Among the exceptions: *L'Ange de la nuit*, in which one character is blinded during the war and another returns from a p.o.w. camp; both *La Main du Diable* and *Donne-moi tes yeux* mention the black market; *Le Carrefour des enfants perdus* refers to the 1940 exodus; there is a word about food restrictions in *Bonsoir mesdames, bonsoir*

messieurs; in *Falbalas*, the wealthy protagonists ride the empty streets of Paris on bicycles. In some of these films, the contemporary references are so understated that an unalert viewer could easily miss them.

24. This characterization seems particularly true of the 1941–42 period; some changes occurred later in the occupation and are discussed in chapter 8. As I will argue in chapter 6, there were significant changes, particularly in style, between the "prestige" productions of the two periods. Having seen only a small percentage of the strictly commercial films, I am making this statement based primarily on the description of these films provided by Régent and other contemporary reviewers.

25. Georges Sadoul, *French Film*, pp. 89, 90.

26. The question of whether the films made in occupied France were reflections of Vichy ideology is a complex one, and much debated among French writers. For a further discussion of the issue, see chapter 6. On the attitude of the right wing in the North toward Vichy, one can consult the published criticism of the time. Critics writing for collaborationist papers—such as Roger Régent and Nino Frank in *Les Nouveaux Temps*, François Vinneuil in *Je Suis Partout*—found Vichy's moralism ludicrous. The Filmprüfstelle reported in January 1943 that Parisian reviewers "criticized without mercy" the films originating in Vichy (R142/F1097).

27. For purposes of discussing trends and styles, I will consider Continental's production as French, since the personnel involved were all French.

28. Régent, *Cinéma de France*, p. 51. I am somewhat skeptical of Régent's claim, since there is no mention of the prohibition in any of the sources I've consulted. The film was released less than five months after production began, indicating that if such a ban had been instituted, it was very short-lived.

29. "Sur l'écran blanc des années noires," p. 54.

30. Signoret, *Nostalgia Isn't What It Used To Be*, pp. 52–53.

31. Given Nazi persecution of the Gypsies, it is odd that a film could be made showing Gypsy life in a picturesque manner. However, another such film was made in 1942, *Le Camion blanc*.

32. René Lefèvre, *Le Film de ma vie*, p. 39.

6. A French School of Cinema

1. The standard French histories of the cinema that treat the cinema of the occupation era are: Maurice Bardèche and Robert Brasillach, *Histoire du Cinéma*, vol. 2: *Le Parlant*; René Jeanne and Charles Ford, *Histoire encyclopédique du Cinéma*, vol. 4: *Le Cinéma Parlant* (1929–1945, *sauf* U.S.A.); Jean Mitry, *Histoire du cinéma: Art et industrie*, vol. 5: *Les Années 40*; and the various volumes by Georges Sadoul. I have singled out for discussion those films that are either mentioned in all of these histories, or else those that the various authors have discussed at length.

Two of the most important films of the period are not considered in this chapter, although they adhere to the tendency under discussion. Both *Les Enfants du Paradis* and *Le Corbeau* are discussed in chapter 8.

2. The exact numbers, and titles, of the films released in the United States and Great Britain are difficult to determine, because many films held by distributors were either not released, or released for non-commercial exhibition. Twenty-six of the films of the occupation received an official New York opening, as gathered from *The New York Times Film*

Reviews 1913–1968, 6 vols. (New York: New York Times and Arno Press, 1970). The American release titles of these 26 films are listed in appendix A.

3. Hazel Hackett, "The French Cinema During the Occupation," p. 2. Hackett's criticism is typical of the response of English-speaking critics. See also, Jacques Laurent Bost, "The French Cinema Under the Occupation"; Roy Fowler, *The Film in France*; Lincoln Kirstein, "French Films During the Occupation"; and William Novik, "Four Years in a Bottle."

4. Defining what is meant by "distinctive thirties' style" is no easier than defining that of the occupation. The discussion that follows is necessarily impressionistic. While individual films have been analyzed at length, there has, to date, been little analysis of the period as a whole.

5. The limited amount of capital available for investment in films was a less welcome consequence of this feeble studio structure. Filmmakers did not always find it easy to get financial backing for their films. Renoir, for example, peddled the screenplay for *La Grande Illusion* from producer to producer for three years before finding one willing to finance it, and then only because of Gabin's support of the project (Renoir, *My Life and My Films*, p. 142). On the other hand, once Renoir found a producer there was no interference with the actual filming.

6. On *Quai des brumes*, see Carné, *La Vie à Belle Dents*, pp. 96–99. The producer, Gregor Rabinovitch, bought the film on the strength of Gabin's name. When he found out that the film centered on desertion, incest, and murder, he was aghast and tried, unsuccessfully, to force Carné to tone the story down.

7. The term will be left in French, since the literal English translation as "escapist cinema" has a different connotation. The origin of the term is unknown, but it was applied as early as 1944 by André Bazin: "In an imprisoned nation which refused to exalt its slavery and could not proclaim its desire for liberty, it was natural for a 'cinéma d'évasion' to develop." *Le Cinéma de l'occupation et de la résistance*, (Paris: Union Générale d'Editions, 1975), p. 122 (my translation). The term has since been used by nearly every critic who has written about the period.

8. Literally, a laboratory retort.

9. Pierre Cadars, "Redécouverte du cinéma de Vichy," *Cahiers de la Cinémathèque* (Winter 1973), 8:27.

10. The limitation on the amount of film stock was announced in *Le Film*, May 8, 1943. (*Le Film* had previously informed filmmakers, in its issue of May 9, 1942, that completed films could run no longer than 2,800 meters.) The limitation on shooting time appeared in *Le Film*, July 24, 1943. These restrictions were overcome in some cases, by procuring film on the black market and finding officials willing to "bend" the rules. Nevertheless, all filmmakers suffered from the material shortages and were unlikely to waste time or film stock through inadequate preparation.

11. Carné, pp. 199 and 206.

12. Autant-Lara in Panigel, "L'Histoire du cinéma français."

13. Jean-Pierre Bertin-Maghit established the 16 percent figure based on a viewing of 130 films. "Le Film historique en France de 1940 à 1944," p. 55. My own count supports this figure, revealing 36 historical films (of 219), ranging in period from the 14th century to the Belle Epoque. Of these 36 films, 11 (of 30) can be considered as belonging to the group of "prestige" films.

14. Barthelemy Amengual et al., "Un Etrange Cinéma dans une Drôle d'Epoque,"

p. 8. The ten films were: La Nuit merveilleuse, La Nuit fantastique, Felicie Nanteuil, L'Homme qui vendit son âme, Les Visiteurs du soir, La Main du diable, Le Baron Fantôme, L'Eternel retour, Sortilèges, and La Financée des ténèbres. Some of these titles are also included among the historical films.

15. An often-cited phrase of the time, of unknown origin, blamed the defeat on "paid holidays, André Gide, and Quai des brumes."

16. This often-observed allusion was cited by Raymond Borde (in his introduction to Courtade, Les Malédictions du cinéma français, p. 8) within the following context: "For those who knew the Prévert brothers, truculent Trotskyists, the unbreakable heart of wounded France was rubbish." Pierre Prévert also denies that any allegory was intended, saying that Jacques Prévert was too subtle a writer to have coined such an obvious allusion. (Author's interview with Prévert, Paris, Oct. 16, 1979).

In a forthcoming critical biography of Carné, Edward Baron Turk convincingly argues that Les Visiteurs is indeed an allegory—not of occupied France but of the demoralization that prevailed before the war and that allowed the Devil to wreak his havoc.

17. Although not explicitly stated in any of the standard histories, the view that these films were allegories became so commonly held that François Truffaut felt compelled to deny it in 1975: "Nevertheless, I cannot accept the sometimes espoused patriotic theory that the historical and fantasy films made during this period deliberately delivered a courageous message coded in favor of the Resistance." Preface to Bazin, French Cinema of the Occupation and Resistance, p. 19.

18. Nearly all critics writing about the period since the program on "Le Cinéma de Vichy" at Toulouse in 1972 have argued, from one perspective or another, that this cinema was Vichyist. See, particularly, the articles that accompanied the retrospective in Cahiers de la Cinémathèque (Winter 1973), vol. 8; the minutes of the discussion held there and reprinted in Cahiers de la Cinémathèque (Summer-Autumn 1973), vol. 10–11; the discussion by four critics in Ecran (September–October 1972), vol. 72; and the articles by Stephane Lévy-Klein in Positif (March 1973, April 1975, June 1975). Jean-Pierre Bertin-Maghit is an especially tenacious supporter of this view. His book-length study, Le Cinéma Français sous Vichy, takes this position as its central thesis.

19. Reprinted in Le Tout Cinéma, p. 60.

20. Le Film, September 4, 1943. The amount advanced in earlier years is not available.

21. Léglise, Histoire de la politique, 2:21–23. Léglise's information comes from the archives of the committee charged with deciding on the subsidies. This "comité d'attribution des avances au cinéma" was composed of the head of Vichy's Service du Cinéma, two members of the COIC, and a representative of the Crédit National.

22. Although documentaries and short films are outside the scope of this study, brief mention must be made of these two filmmakers who were lauded after the war for moving the French cinema in the direction of a neorealism that never materialized. Rouquier, whose short film, Le Tonnelier (1943), was highly praised, followed this succès d'estime with a long, Flaherty type of documentary on the lives of a peasant family. Shot immediately after the occupation, Farrebique was released in 1947, and was greeted as a breakthrough for French documentary filmmaking. For an excellent discussion of the film's production and values, see John H. Weiss, "An Innocent Eye? The Career and Documentary Vision of Georges Rouquier up to 1945," Cinema Journal (Spring 1981), 20:38–62.

René Clément's short film about railroad workers, Ceux du rail (1943), served as the basis for the 1945 feature La Bataille du rail, a reconstructed documentary of the Resistance activities of the railroad workers. Clément went on to become a successful commercial filmmaker.

23. J.-P. Jeancolas, "Cinéma de Vichy," p. 4. Francis Courtade agrees that the film is the only one of the period "that can pass for an authentic Resistance film" (p. 209). This view of the film is widely held among writers on the period.

24. Régent, Cinéma de France, p. 94.

25. R142/F1005. The cuts were not specified. Compared with films like Le Destin fabuleux de Desirée Clary or Vénus aveugle, over which the Filmprüfstelle agonized for months, the lack of comment on this film appears significant.

26. Roy Fowler, The Film in France, p. 34. Fowler provides no source for his information, nor does he elaborate.

27. According to Courtade (p. 209), this line was cut when the film was released. The print I viewed was a restored print, distributed in 1946, and certain other sequences may not have appeared in the original release print.

28. Borde introduction to Courtade, p. 14.

29. "Evocation: Louis Daquin," Cinéma 79 (January 1979), pp. 32–33.

30. Jacques Guicharnaud, Modern French Theater from Giraudoux to Genet (New Haven: Yale University Press, 1967), p. viii.

31. In the introduction to the published screenplay of La Duchesse de Langeais, cited in Régent, pp. 56–57.

32. Guicharnaud, p. 121.

33. Interview with Jean Delannoy in André Halimi, Chantons sous l'occupation, p. 243.

34. The degree of Cocteau's responsibility for the film has been debated, but it seems clear that Cocteau's influence extended beyond the screenplay. In his memoirs, Jean Marais maintains that although Cocteau was present every day at the shooting, he did not interfere with Delannoy's direction. Nonetheless, "his presence cast a shadow [over the production] and everything took on another style. Without our being aware of it, our performances became different, Jean Delannoy directed differently, the light itself became different" (Histoires de ma vie, p. 145).

35. Prior to Le Baron Fantôme, Cocteau's association with the cinema had been limited to the experimental Sang d'un poéte (1930), and the screenplay for l'Herbier's La Comédie du bonheur (filmed in 1940 and released during the occupation).

36. Le Film, in its issue of June 3, 1944, announced that production was set for the film to begin. Three days later, the Normandy landings took place and halted all new production until 1945.

37. In addition to the two new superstars, Jean Marais and Madeleine Sologne, many other actors came to prominence during the period, including: Micheline Presle, Maria Casarès, François Perier, Louis Jourdan, Renée Faure, Martine Carole, and Serge Reggiani. Simone Signoret made several appearances in minor roles and the nearly unknown Gérard Philipe made his debut in Les Petites du quai aux fleurs.

38. Régent, p. 163.

39. Georges Sadoul, L'Histoire Générale du Cinéma, 6:54.

40. "Le Corbeau est déplumé," L'Ecran Français (March 1944), p. 3. The article was later revealed to have been written by Georges Adam and Pierre Blanchar.

41. Cited in Stephane Lévy-Klein, "Sur le cinéma français des années 1940–1944," p. 30.

42. Raymond Borde, "Les Limites du temoignage," Cinéma 56, p. 25.

43. Régent, p. 83.

44. Aurenche in Panigel. As is true with the other political films of the period, there are those who would take issue with my reading. Geneviève Sellier, for one, maintains that the film is sympathetic to the aristocrats and that the blame for Douce's death rests with the servants. "The ending would certainly not have displeased the Maréchal." "Review of La France de Pétain et son cinéma," Cinéma 81 (May 1981), p. 113.

45. Tati almost made his debut in the cinema during the occupation as an actor. Carné had considered him for Barrault's role in Les Enfants du Paradis when Barrault's schedule conflicted with the filming, but an arrangement was worked out to accommodate Barrault (Carné, p. 224).

46. Régent, p. 73.

47. Jeanne and Ford, p. 405.

48. Barthélemy Amengual, et al. "Un Etrange Cinéma dans une drôle d'epoque," p. 7; Bardèche and Brasillach (1964), p. 158.

49. Author's interview with Pierre Prévert. He did admit that there were some financial problems which caused production to shut down briefly.

50. Jeune Cinéma (March 1968), vol. 29.

51. Signoret, Nostalgia Isn't What It Used To Be, p. 61.

52. Régent, pp. 36–37.

53. Author's interview with Daquin, Paris, Oct. 3, 1979; confirmed in Filmprüfstelle reports, R142/F254.

54. Jeanne and Ford, p. 407.

55. Citizen Kane was, of course, not known in France at the time. It did not open in Paris until 1946. Nonetheless, a few individuals in the French film community kept up with developments in the American cinema. According to le Boterf, Bardèche, and Brasillach, who were then working on a revision of their film history, heard about new developments in the American cinema from Pierre Autré of the COIC, who got the news from Switzerland. One of these developments was "the revolutionary endeavors of someone named Orson Welles" (La Vie Parisienne, p. 33).

56. Max Tessier, "Marie-Martine," Ecran (September–October 1972), 72:17. Tessier maintains that "no cinema history mentions Marie-Martine while they all discuss that bombastic monument, L'Eternel Retour." Although Sadoul and Bardèche do not mention Marie-Martine, they do discuss the other idiosyncratic films. Jeanne and Ford devote nearly a page to Marie-Martine.

57. François Truffaut, "A Certain Tendency in the French Cinema," originally published in Cahiers du Cinéma (January 1954), vol. 31; reprinted and translated in Bill Nichols, ed., Movies and Methods (Berkeley: University of California Press, 1976), p. 232.

58. Bazin, p. 89.

7. Goebbels and German Film Policy in France

1. André Weil-Curiel, "Le Temps de la honte," cited in André Halimi, Chantons sous l'occupation, p. 29.

2. Author's interview with Daquin, Paris, October 3, 1979.

3. The film was directed by Jean Mamy, a former assistant to Renoir and Grémillon, who was executed after the Liberation for far more serious crimes of collaboration.

Forces occultes was not widely distributed commercially, but was often seen in private showings.

The French made several short fictional and documentary films for the Nazis or
their Vichy supporters in the Milice and the Légion des Volontaires Français including:
Français, vous avez la mémoire courte (an anti-Soviet film) and *Résistance*, against the resistance.

4. René Lefèvre, *Le Film de ma vie 1939–73*, p. 127.

5. Jean Delannoy interview in Halimi, pp. 243 and 245.

6. Among German holdings were control or shares in Kodak-Pathé, C.T.M. labs,
the Paris-Cinéma and Neuilly studio, and the SOGEC chain of theaters (see chapter 3).
Dommages, pp. 28–30.

7. Spiker, *Film und Kapital*, p. 194. Data on profit/loss for other years is not available.

8. Much of the funds for the company were derived from occupation costs paid
by the French, so that the Germans were, in fact, merely replacing what they had taken
from the French in the first place.

9. Hull, *Film in the Third Reich*, pp. 207–208; Sadoul, *Histoire du cinéma mondial*, p.
287.

10. Goebbels, *Diaries 1942–1943*, p. 213.

11. The stars listed in the text were the ones mentioned in *Le Film*, March 28,
1942. The ostensible purpose of the trip had been to publicize the film *Premier Rendez-Vous*,
which was the first "French" film to open in Berlin since September 1939. The trip was
widely publicized, not only in Germany and France, but in Allied countries where newspapers and magazines accused these actors of being traitors (New York Public Library,
Theater Collection). According to the Film Section's reports, another trip was planned in
the summer of 1942, but it never came off (R142/F710).

12. See R142/F336 for Filmprüfstelle reports of those invited. The information on
Blanchar is from R142/F710; on Luguet from Halimi, p. 252.

13. It is known that the purpose of Greven's trip to Berlin in May 1942 was not
simply to be upbraided by Goebbels. The Filmprüfstelle report for the week of May 2–May
9, 1942, says the head of the Film Section (and Greven?) went to Berlin on May 8 "for
discussions on the export of French films and the final liquidation of American films and
film companies in unoccupied France. Discussions were also held about removing old films
from the market, guaranteeing the distribution of German films and such French films as
have been done under the supervision of German personnel" (R142/F638).

Later in the same report, the Berlin meeting is broken down into 26 points which
were covered, including: "Italian film problems," "production schedules 1942/43," "Gaumont's purchase of Marcel Pagnol's production company," "the propaganda visit (to Berlin) of Sacha Guitry" (which never materialized), and many minor matters, including "Junie
Astor's desire to work at Continental Films in addition to her contracts with French companies" (R142/F642–43).

14. *Dommages*, p.9.

15. There was division in Berlin as to what policy should be pursued toward France.
Some high Nazi officials (including Goering and Goebbels) viewed the captured French
territories as little more than a site for plunder. Anything of value to the German war machine would be shipped to Germany; what was unimportant would be cut back or shut
down. (This policy is formulated in a Goering memo of September 1940, cited in Milward,
The New Order and the French Economy, p. 71. After 1942, overall German policy toward France
conformed to this conception.)

The Foreign Ministry and the Military Command in France both opposed such a policy however. "Whatever kept the civil population quiet and made them easier to govern while giving the armed forces a certain limited access to French industry was best" (Milward, p. 56).

16. Milward states that the evidence points to "a future Europe within which France would be included as an industrial power subsidiary to Germany, not simply a member of a peripheral ring of suppliers" (p. 105).

17. The president of the association was an Italian, Count Volpi di Misurata. The other vice-president was a German, Carl Fröhlich. (R141/F858).

18. This is not a direct transcription of Goebbels' remarks, but a paraphase as reported in the Film Section's weekly report (R141/F860).

19. Reprinted in Le Film, August 30, 1941.

20. Author's interview with Pierre Prévert, Paris, October 16, 1979. (Jacques Prévert declined Greven's offer.)

21. Dommages, p. 19. According to Hull (p. 222), German color equipment was also established in Prague at the end of the war, because of the bombing of German studios.

22. German production levels taken from Hull, pp. 151 and 206. German production in 1943 and 1944 exceeded French production. By then, the Germans were no longer interested in promoting French production.

23. R141/F1024. The directive was issued in the report of August 29, 1941, three months before the United States' entry into the war. The Germans' obsessive hatred of American films undoubtedly made them all the more fascinating. Suzanne Bidault recounted in her memoirs that a high Nazi official invited her to a clandestine screening of Casablanca and then begged her not to reveal the secret for fear of his life (Souvenirs, p. 160). Armand Panigel claims that an unnamed friend who was then employed by the Cinémathèque Française was sent on a special mission to Portugal by the Germans to procure a copy of The Great Dictator for Hitler himself (author's interview with Panigel, New York. April 15, 1980).

24. Cahiers Franco-Allemands (May 1942). The quote is from the unsigned introduction to a special issue on film in the new Europe.

25. Le Film, April 25, 1942.

26. Four films (all Continental) were shown in Holland, according to La Cinématographie Française, December 29, 1945. A letter from Jirí Levý, April 24, 1980, informs me that 11 films were released in Czechoslovakia in 1943, all Continental productions. In 1944, 2 films were released, Le Mariage de Chiffon and Fièvres (neither Continental). L'Assassinat du Père Noel was proclaimed a "great hit" in Sweden by Le Film, February 6, 1943. The films shown in Germany are mentioned in Le Film on April 22, 1942, and August 8, 1942.

27. La Cinématographie Française, December 29, 1945.

28. R141/F847. However, more than thirty Italian films were imported into France during the occupation.

29. Un Chapeau de paille d'Italie, R141/F779; Une Vie de chien, R141/F1045; Le Pavillon brûle, R142/F261; Histoire de rire, R142/F290; respectively.

30. Bertrand Fabre, "Grandeurs et servitudes du cinéma français," Paris Cinéma (1944), p. 29. The Filmprüfstelle report (R142/F933) indicates that cuts were required, but does not specify. However, a film by Henri Decoin was released during the period titled L'Homme de Londres (a murder mystery set in le Havre), which would tend to contradict Fabre's point.

31. *Le Film*, Jan. 23, 1943 and April 22, 1944. Among the prewar Gabin films previously cleared for exhibition were *Pépé le Moko*, *La Belle Equipe*, and *le Jour se lève*.

32. Claude Autant-Lara, "La Parole est à Claude Autant-Lara," *Cahiers de la Cinémathèque* (Summer-Autumn 1973) 10–11:65.

33. *Le Film*, March 18, 1944. This order was the only specific injunction ever made public.

34. Author's interview with Galey, Paris, October 1, 1979.

8. The War Without and the War Within

1. Milward, *The New Order*, p. 281.

2. Richebé, *Au-Delà de l'écran*, p. 150. Unmarried women between the ages of 21 and 35 were, however, also subject to the S.T.O.

3. Author's interview with Galey, Paris, October 1, 1979.

4. Régent, *Cinéma de France*, p. 249.

5. *Le Film*, October 9, 1943.

6. *Le Film*, January 8, 1944. The clandestine paper *L'Ecran Français* reported the number dead as 35 (March 1944).

7. *Dommages*, p. 29.

8. *Le Cinéma français* 1945, p. 23.

9. *Le Film*, August 7, 1943.

10. *Le Film*, August 21; June 10, and November 6, 1943.

11. *Le Film*, January 9, 1943. This latter order was later rescinded and days of closing were staggered.

12. L 'Echo de la France, April 15, 1944.

13. Parisian theaters were closed altogether between July 27 and October 13, 1944. Production was halted in early July and did not resume until December 1944.

14. Carné, *La Vie à Belle Dents*, p. 225. Both the film and its production history are well-known and will not be discussed in detail here. Carné provides a colorful account of the production in his memoirs (pp. 217–243); however, his version has been disputed by other participants. A few details which are not widely known or which involve differing interpretations are discussed in the text below.

15. Carné, p. 227; author's interview with Panigel, New York, April 15, 1980.

16. *Le Film*, February 5, 1944; May 20, 1944.

17. In L'*Avant-Scène du Cinéma* (November 1, 1978) 215:34.

18. Frank, *Petit Cinéma sentimental*, p. 180. The film was not made.

19. Spaak, *Charles Spaak*, p. 129. Some French writers have disputed Spaak's account, charging that the arrest was engineered by Spaak himself in order to avoid post-Liberation difficulties.

20. Spaak in Panigel, "L'Histoire." Among the tenants of the Hotel Majestic was the Propaganda Abteilung.

21. This and all following information on the resistance in Nice from Gili, "La Vie Cinématographique," p. 188.

22. Lefèvre, *Le Film de ma Vie*, pp. 65–66.

23. Jean-Louis Barrault, *Souvenirs pour demain*, p. 152.

24. *La Cinématographie Française*, May 1944. This paper, put out by the C.G.T., was named after, but not related to, the prewar trade journal of the same name.

25. Author's interviews with Panigel and Daquin. These and other claims of Resistance activity must be looked at with a certain amount of skepticism. After the Liberation, nearly everyone in France claimed to have aided the Resistance in some way.

26. Ploquin in Panigel; author's interview with Panigel.

27. Léglise, Histoire, pp. 116–117.

28. All information on the three clandestine films from Paul Léglise, "Août 44: La Libération du cinéma français," pp. 35–36.

29. Léglise, "Août 44," p. 34.

30. Léglise, "Août 44," p. 24.

31. Léglise, "Août 44," p. 35.

32. Frank, p. 197.

33. Author's interview with Galey.

34. Author's interview with Daquin.

35. Léglise, "Août 44," p. 33.

36. For a comprehensive discussion of the motives and actions of the various "épuration" committees, see Peter Novick, The Resistance vs. Vichy.

37. Jean Marais, Histoires de ma vie, p. 168.

38. Pierre Fresnay and Possot, Pierre Fresnay, p. 74.

39. Maurice Chevalier, The Man in the Straw Hat, pp. 225–240.

40. For Arletty's account of her "épuration," see her La Défense, pp. 158–177.

41. Interview with André Pousse in Halimi, Chantons, p. 204.

42. Richebé, pp. 167–168.

43. Robert Aron, Histoire de l'épuration, Le Monde de la presse, des arts, des lettres, 2:244.

44. Louis Daquin, Le Cinéma notre métier, p. 112.

45. Sadoul, L'Histoire générale du cinéma, p. 67.

46. Bulletin Municipal Officiel de la Ville de Paris, No. 187, August 13–14, 1945. Hereinafter referred to as B.M.O.

47. B.M.O., August 13–14, 1945.

48. Bardèche and Brasillach, Histoire du Cinéma (1948), p. 498. Bardèche continued to list the name of his executed brother-in-law as co-author. It should be noted as well that Christian-Jaque received no censure for having worked in Mussolini's Italy, collaboration with that country seeming to arouse little antipathy among the "épurateurs."

49. Spaak Charles Spaak, p.133.

50. Frank, p. 221.

51. B.M.O., August 13–14, 1945; August 31, 1945; October 1–2, 1945.

52. B.M.O., August 13–14, 1945. De Limur did not work for Continental and the reason for his penalty is unknown.

53. B.M.O., August 31, 1945.

54. Courtade, Les Malédictions du cinéma français, p. 208. No source given.

55. Mitry, Histoire du cinéma, 5:307; and Genêt [Janet Flanner], "Letter from Paris," The New Yorker, June 2, 1945, p. 69.

56. Author's interview with Daquin.

57. For portions of the attack on the film published in L'Ecran Français, see chapter 6.

58. Author's interview with Galey. Greven responded that he would consider Vichy's request but that the film was presently breaking all box office records in Switzerland.

59. Films français parus pendant l'occupation avec leur analyse morale (Paris: CCR, 1945).

60. Chavance had been an assistant director and editor (for Vigo, among others)

in the thirties, before working on such screenplays as *La Nuit fantastique* and *Le Baron Fantôme* during the occupation.

61. All quotations from the film are taken from *L'Avant-Scène du Cinéma* (April 15, 1977), vol. 186.

62. The announcement of the sub-prefect's transfer is reported in a Paris paper, indicating that the seat of government is in Paris, not Vichy. However, the year of the film's action is never specified.

63. Both cited in Gérard Walter, *Paris under the Occupation*, pp. 110–111.

64. Clouzot in Panigel.

65. Although this scene has often been commented on, observers have failed to mention the globe prominently displayed in the foreground. It may be inferred that Clouzot intended this disquisition on the relativity of good and evil to apply not merely to men's characters but to the political situation as well. On the line of dialogue, "Where is the border of evil?" ("Où est la frontière du mal?"), the globe clearly shows Europe, European Russia, and Africa (i.e., the European theater of war.) As the camera tracks around the desk, the position of the globe changes, but returns to the original position for Vorzet's line, "All moral values are more or less corrupted." His next line, "Vous êtes atteint comme les autres," can mean both to be afflicted or, in a military sense, to be overrun, so that the "vous" could as well refer to France both overrun and afflicted by Nazi corruption, as to Germain himself.

The difficulty in making a definitive case for a political reading of this scene also makes a case for *Le Corbeau* as a quintessential occupation film. It expresses its political viewpoint, vis à vis the Germans, no more directly than do any of the other films of the era.

Conclusion

1. The problem of American domination of the French market was exacerbated by an agreement signed in 1946 (known as the Blum-Byrne agreement) which instituted a quota system under terms highly favorable to the United States.

Bibliography

Included in the bibliography are all primary sources consulted, all articles and books about the French cinema of the occupation, and a select list of books on general topics related to the occupation period as a whole. Omitted from this list are articles and books (except memoirs and personal interviews by the author) that deal only with a particular person or film.

Primary Sources

Contemporary Critical Writings, Memoirs and Interviews by the Author

Arletty. La Défense. Paris: La Table Ronde, 1971.

Aumont, Jean-Pierre. Sun and Shadow. Bruce Benderson, tr. New York: Norton, 1977.

Barrault, Jean-Louis. Souvenirs pour demain. Paris: Le Seuil, 1972.

Bazin, André. French Cinema of the Occupation and Resistance: The Birth of a Critical Esthetic. Stanley Hochman, tr. New York: Frederick Ungar, 1981.

Bibliothèque de l'Arsenal. Clipping Files: "Articles généraux sur le cinéma, 1940–1944."

Bidault, Suzanne. Souvenirs de guerre et d'occupation. Paris: La Table Ronde, 1973.

Carné, Marcel. La Vie à Belle Dents. Paris: J. P. Ollivier, 1975.

Chevalier, Maurice. The Man in the Straw Hat. Caroline Clerk, tr. New York: Crowell, 1949.

Cinémathèque Royale de Belgique. Clipping File: "France 1940–1945."

Daquin, Louis. Le Cinéma notre métier. Paris: Les Editions Français Réunis, 1960.

Daquin, Louis. Interview. Paris, October 3, 1979.

Eisner, Lotte. Interview. Neuilly sur Seine, September 25, 1979.

Fabre, Bertrand. "Grandeurs et servitudes du cinéma français." Paris Cinéma (1944), p. 19.

Feuillère, Edwige. Les Feux de la mémoire. Paris: Albin Michel, 1977.

Frank, Nino. Petit Cinéma sentimental. Paris: La Nouvelle Edition, 1950.

Fresnay, Pierre and Possot. Pierre Fresnay. Paris: La Table Ronde, 1975.

Galey, Louis-Emile. Interview. Paris, October 1, 1979.

Goebbels, Joseph. *Diaries 1942–1943*. Louis Lochner, ed. and tr. Garden City, N.Y.: Doubleday, 1948.

Guitry, Sacha. *Quatre Ans d'occupations*. 2 vols. Cannes: Raoul Solar, 1954.

L'Institut des Hautes Etudes Cinématographiques. Clipping Files (various).

Jeanson, Henri. *70 ans d'adolescence*. Paris, 1971.

Lapierre, Marcel. Papers. Bibliothèque de l'Arsenal.

Leclerc, Ginette. *Ma Vie privée*. Paris: La Table Ronde, 1963.

Lefèvre, René. *Le Film de ma vie 1939–73*. Paris: Editions France-Empire, 1973.

Léglise, Paul. Interview. Paris, September 26, 1979.

L'Herbier, Marcel. *La Tête qui tourne*. Paris: Pierre Belfond, 1979.

Luchaire, Corinne. *Ma Drôle de vie*. Paris: SUN, 1949.

Marais, Jean. *Histoires de ma vie*. Paris: Albin Michel, 1975.

New York Public Library, Theater Collection. Clipping File: "Cinema: France: 1940–1944" and various.

Ozeray, Madeleine. *A Toujours Monsieur Jouvet*. Paris: Buchet/Chastel, 1966.

Panigel, Armand. Interview. New York, April 15, 1980.

Prévert, Pierre. Interview. Paris, October 16, 1979.

Rebatet, Lucien [François Vinneuil]. *Les Tribus du cinéma et du théâtre*. Paris: Nouvelles Editions Françaises, 1941.

Régent, Roger. *Cinéma de France de "La Fille du Puisatier" aux "Enfants du Paradis."* Paris: Editions d'Aujourd'hui, 1948.

Régent, Roger. Interview. Paris, September 15, 1979.

Renoir, Jean. *My Life and My Films*. Norman Denny, tr. New York: Atheneum, 1974.

Richebé, Roger. *Au-Delà de l'écran*. Monte Carlo: Editions Pastorelly, 1977.

Rosay, Françoise. *La Traversée d'une vie*. Paris: Laffont, 1974.

Signoret, Simone. *Nostalgia Isn't What It Used To Be*. New York: Harper & Row, 1976.

Spaak, Janine. *Charles Spaak, mon mari*. Paris, 1977.

Wakhevitch, Georges. *L'Envers des décors*. Paris: Laffont, 1977.

Wiéner, Jean. *Allegro appassionato*. Paris: Belfond, 1978.

**Newspapers, Annuals, Government Reports
and Miscellaneous Sources**

Annuaire Général du Spectacle. Paris, 1943.

Bulletin Municipal Officiel de la Ville de Paris (1945). (BMO)

Cahiers Franco-Allemands. May 1942. (Special cinema issue.)

Centre National de la Cinématographie. *Bulletin d'Information*, January–February 1949. Vol. 7. (CNC).

Chéret, Pierre. "Exposé de la situation financière du cinéma français." *Productions Françaises*, March 1946. Vol. 7.

Ciné-Guide. Bordeaux, 1942.

Ciné-Mondial, 1941–1944.

Cinéma 1943. Paris: Les Publications Techniques, 1943.

Le Cinéma Francais. Paris: Editions de la Cinématographie Francaise, 1945.

La *Cinématographie Française*, 1939–June 1940; 1945.

La *Cinématographie Française*, May 1944. (Published clandestinely by the Confédération Générale du Travail.)

L'*Ecran Français*. 1944. (Published clandestinely with *Les Lettres Françaises*.)

Exposition le Juif et la France au Palais Berlitz sous l'Egide de l'Institut d'Etude des Questions Juives. September 4, 1941. Catalogue.

Le *Film*. 1940–1944.

Films français parus pendant l'occupation avec leur analyse morale. Paris: Centrale Catholique du Cinéma et de la Radio, 1945.

France, Commission Consultative des Dommages et des Reparations. *Dommages subis par la France et l'Union Française du fait de la guerre et de l'occupation ennemie (1939–1945)*. Vol. 8: *Emprise Allemande sur la pensée française*. Paris: Imprimerie Nationale, 1950. (*Dommages*).

France 1941. La Revolution nationale constructive: Un Bilan et un programme. Paris: Alsatia, 1941.

"French Motion Picture Industry Faces Forbidding Obstacles." *Foreign Commerce Weekly* (July 18, 1942), 8:46.

Hoover Institute on War, Revolution, and Peace, Stanford University. *La Vie de la France sous l'occupation (1940–44)*. Paris: Librarie Plon, 1957.

Militärbefehlshaber in Frankreich. Propaganda Abteilung. Referat Film. Reports March 5, 1941–July 1943. U.S. National Archives Series T-501, Rolls 141–142 (cited by roll and frame number). Translated by Liesel and Fritz Ehrlich.

"News from Occupied France." *Sight and Sound* (May 1944), 49:11–12.

La *Nouvelle France Economique*. December 2, 1943. Vol. 25 (Special issue on COIC.)

Opéra. April–May 1944. (Published clandestinely.)

Panigel, Armand. "L'Histoire du cinéma français par ceux qui l'ont fait." Téléfrance, 1975.

Repertoire Général Illustré des Films. 1944. Lyon: Ofda, n.d.

La *Revue de l'Ecran*. Marseille, 1940–41.

Statut Légal du Cinéma en France. Les Droits des préfets et des maires, par les contentieux de l'Office familiale de documentation artistique. Lyon: Ofda, 1943.

Le *Tout Cinéma*. Année 1942. Paris: Editions Guilhamou, 1942.

Secondary Sources

Amaury, Philippe. *De l'information et de la propagande d'état*. Paris: Librairie Générale de Droit et de Jurisprudence, 1969.

Amengual, Barthélemy, Claude Beylie, Jean A. Gili, and Max Tessier. "Un Etrange Cinéma dans une Drôle d'Epoque." L'*Ecran* (September–October 1972), 72:2–17.

Amouroux, Henri. *La Grande Histoire des français sous l'occupation.* 1939–1945. 8 vols. Paris: Robert Lafont, 1976–.

Aron, Robert. *Histoire de l'épuration.* vol. 2: *Le Monde de la presse, des arts, des lettres.* Paris: Fayard, 1975.

Baldizzone, J. "A la recherche de la mythologie des Français de 1940 à 1944." *Image et Son* (November 1972), 215:51–90.

Bardèche, Maurice and Robert Brasillach. *Histoire du cinéma.* Vol. 2: *Le Parlant.* Paris: Les Sept Couleurs, 1964.

Bertin-Maghit, Jean-Pierre. *Le Cinéma français sous Vichy.* Paris: Editions Albatros, 1980.

—— "Le Film historique en France de 1940 à 1944." *Image et Son* (December 1976), 312:55–61.

—— "Propagande sociologique dans le cinéma français de 1940 à 1944." *Image et Son* (June 1978), 329:71–84.

Borde, Raymond. "Les Limites du témoignage." *Cinéma 56* (November 1955), 7:23–27.

Bost, Jacques Laurent. "The French Cinema Under the Occupation." *Tricolor* (January 1945), 2:114–120.

Bourdrel, Philippe. *Histoire des juifs de France.* Paris: Albin Michel, 1974.

Campet, Jacques. "Les Rapports financières entre l'état et l'industrie cinématographique." Ph.D. dissertation, Bordeaux, 1953.

Chirat, Raymond and Claude Beylie. "Le Cinéma des années noires." *L'Avant-Scène du Cinéma* (September–October 1972), 127–128:81–83.

"Cinéma de Vichy." *Les Cahiers de la Cinémathèque.* Special Issue. (Winter 1973), vol. 8.

"Cinéma et histoire." *Les Cahiers de la Cinémathèque.* Special Issue. (Summer/Autumn 1973), vol. 10–11.

Cotta, Michèle. *La Collaboration.* 2d ed. Paris, 1964.

Courtade, Francis. *Les Malédictions du cinéma français.* Paris: Alain Moreau, 1978.

Daniel, Joseph. *Guerre et cinéma.* Cahiers de la Fondation Nationale des Sciences Politiques, no. 180. Paris: Armand Colin, 1972.

Dunan, Elizabeth. "La Propaganda Abteilung de France." *Revue d'Histoire de la Deuxième Guerre mondiale* (October 1951), 4:19–32.

Durand, J. *Le Cinéma et son publique* (Recherches économiques). Paris: Ed. Sirey, 1958.

Ehrmann, Henry W. *Organized Business in France.* Princeton: Princeton University Press, 1957.

"Filmographie des années noires." *Cinéma 71* (June 1971), vol. 157.

Fowler, Roy. *The Film in France.* London: Pendulum, 1946.

Gili, Jean-A. "La Vie cinématographique à Nice de 1939 à 1945." *Aspects de Nice du XVIII⁰ au XX⁰ siècle. Annales de la Faculté des Lettres et Sciences Humaines de Nice.* (1973), 19:173–196.

Hackett, Hazel. "The French Cinema During the Occupation." *Sight and Sound* (Spring 1946), 15:1–3.

Halimi, André. *Chantons sous l'occupation.* Paris: Olivier Orban, 1976.

Hull, David Stewart. *Film in the Third Reich.* Berkeley: University of California Press, 1969.

Jeancolas, Jean-Pierre. "Cinéma de Vichy." *Jeune Cinéma* (September–October 1972), 65:1–9; 66:37–45.

——— *15 ans d'années trente.* Paris: Stock, 1983.

Jeancolas, J.-P. and Daniel-Jean Jay. "Cinéma d'un monde en guerre 1939/45." *La Documentation Photographique* (August 1976), no. 6024.

Jeanne, René and Charles Ford. *Histoire encyclopédique du cinéma.* Vol. 4: *Le Cinéma parlant* (1929–1945, *sauf aux* U.S.A.). Paris: S.E.D.E., 1958.

Kirstein, Lincoln. "French Films During the Occupation." *Museum of Modern Art Bulletin* (January 1945), pp. 16–20.

Le Boterf, Hervé. *La Vie Parisienne sous l'occupation.* 2 vols. Paris: France-Empire, 1975.

Léglise, Paul. "Aôut 44: La Libération du cinéma français." *Ecran 74* (October 1974) 29:33–37.

——— *Histoire de la politique du cinéma français.* Vol. 2: *Entre deux républiques 1940–1946.* Paris: Filmeditions, 1977.

Lévy-Klein, Stephane. "Sur le cinéma français des années 1940–1944." *Positif* (April–June 1975), nos. 168–170.

——— "France 1940–44: le cinéma de Vichy." *Positif* (March 1973), no. 148.

Marcabru, Pierre. *Allons au cinéma.* Paris: Gallimard, 1964.

Marion, Denis. "Le Cinéma français sous l'occupation." *L'Arche* (August 1945), 8:119–127.

Marrus, Michael R. and Robert O. Paxton. *Vichy France and the Jews.* New York: Basic Books, 1981.

Maze, Lucien. "Le Cinéma français de septembre 1939 à février 1949." *Cahiers du Travail* (March 15, 1949), pp. 1–8.

Milward, Alan S. *The New Order and the French Economy.* New York: Oxford University Press, 1970.

Mitry, Jean. *Histoire du cinéma: Art et industrie.* Vol. 5: *Les Années 40.* Paris: Jean-Pierre Delarge, 1980.

Noell, René. "Histoire du spectacle cinématographique à Perpignan." *Cahiers de la Cinémathèque* (Winter 1973), 8:3–19.

Novick, Peter. *The Resistance vs. Vichy.* New York: Columbia University Press, 1968.

Novik, William. "Four Years in a Bottle." *Penguin Film Review* (1947), 2:45–53.

Paxton, Robert O. *Vichy France: Old Guard and New Order, 1940–1944.* New York: Knopf, 1972; reprint, New York: Norton, 1975.

Petley, Julian. *Capital and Culture: German Cinema 1933–45.* London: British Film Institute, 1979.

Pevsner, M. "Les Actualités cinématographiques de 1940 à 1944." *Revue d'Histoire de la Deuxième Guerre Mondiale* (October 1966), vol. 64.

Prédal, René. *La Societé française* (1914–45) *à travers le cinéma.* Paris, 1972.

Pryce-Jones, David. *Paris in the Third Reich.* New York: Holt, Rinehart and Winston, 1981.

Sadoul, Georges. *French Film.* London: Falcon Press, 1953.

—— *Histoire du cinéma mondial.* Paris: Flammarion, 1949.

—— *L'Histoire générale du cinéma.* Vol. 6: *Le Cinéma pendant la guerre 1939–1945.* Paris: de Noël, 1954.

Saint-Jours, Frédéric. "Chronique du cinéma: Aspects d'un cinéma occupé (1940–44)." *Ecrits de Paris* (November 1974), 342:106–112.

Siclier, Jacques. *La France de Pétain et son cinéma.* Paris: Henri Veyrier, 1981.

Spiker, Jürgen. *Film und Kapital: Der Weg der deutschen Filmwirtschaft zum national sozialistischen Einheitskonzern.* Berlin: Volker Spiess, 1975.

Strebel, Elizabeth Grottle. "French Cinema, 1940–1944, and Its Socio-Psychological Significance: A Preliminary Probe." *Historical Journal of Film, Radio and Television* (1981), 1:33–46.

"Sur l'écran blanc des années noires." *Les Dossiers du Clan* (May 1967), vol. 2.

Vaughn, Olwen. "The French Cinema under the German Occupation." *Theatre* (Winter 1945–46), 2:28–31.

Walter, Gérard. *Paris Under the Occupation.* Tony White, tr. New York: Orion, 1960.

Werth, Alexander. *France 1940–1955.* Rev. ed. Boston: Beacon Press, 1966.

Index

Printed in the USA
CPSIA information can be obtained
at www.ICGtesting.com
JSHW021321221024
72173JS00011B/1626

9 780231 059268